The Lion and the Honeycomb

by R. P. Blackmur

THE LION AND THE HONEYCOMB

LANGUAGE AS GESTURE

THE EXPENSE OF GREATNESS

THE DOUBLE AGENT

THE GOOD EUROPEAN, *and other poems*

THE SECOND WORLD

FROM JORDAN'S DELIGHT

R. P. BLACKMUR

THE LION AND THE HONEYCOMB

Essays in Solicitude and Critique

A Harvest Book

HARCOURT, BRACE & WORLD, INC.

New York

Thanks are due the editors of the following magazines for permission to reprint some of the hitherto uncollected essays in this volume: *Accent, Art News, Hudson Review, Kenyon Review, Sewanee Review,* and *Southern Review.* "The American Literary Expatriate" is reprinted by permission from *Foreign Influences in American Life,* David Frederick Bowers, ed., copyright, 1944, by Princeton University Press.

LIBRARY OF CONGRESS CATALOG CARD NUMBER: 55-5638

PRINTED IN THE UNITED STATES OF AMERICA

M. S. e S. R.
della vera città almen la torre

Contents

The Lion and the Honeycomb

1

Toward a Modus Vivendi

Henry Adams used to argue that the great question was whether the American mind could catch up with American energy. He doubted it, but thought a good jump might do it. Adams also worried whether the enormous Russian momentum—race-inertia—could be converted into intellect at all. Since as he saw it in 1904 (and as we now see it) the world was to be divided between American energy and Russian momentum, the questions are important.

Looking at America from abroad the answer is: she is nowhere near catching up and had better start serious jumping. As for Russia, she seems more bent on converting her momentum into energy than on finding intellect in the Western sense valid at all.

Adams's third notion—based on a piety much older than either America or Russia—that perhaps, some day, in the contest between the two powers the nature of true empire might be found, now becomes a notion of the greatest possible urgency to apply.

How do we go about converting energy and momentum into intellect? I take it that the power of the intellect is at work when the whole mind is engaged in the whole field of its interests.

This has nothing to do with intellectualism: where the intellectual arrogates the mere interests of his class as they clash with others.

It has nothing to do with that intellectual power which converts itself into pure energy, sometimes called ambition or the struggle for personal power.

It has a great deal to do with the idea of a modus vivendi as the first and continuing and ever-necessary act of the mind. A modus vivendi brings out agreement and disagreement. It encourages discernment of the consequences of our own action and should determine whether or not we undertake it. Only under a modus vivendi do we see the cost of action, because it is only in the condition of a modus vivendi that we feel the actual clash of adverse wills. It is only then that the rule of universal love becomes intelligible policy: on the probability that God loves our enemies as much as ourselves, and sometimes more.

It is precisely because of the fundamental imperfection of any given intellect—whether individual, national, or cultural—that the steadily attended conception of a modus vivendi is necessary. The intellect was never intended and ought never to be expected to be a free agent. Its only freedom is in the necessity of its action; that the action is always provisional, problematic, and contingent only ensures the freedom. The more necessary an action, the more certainly it leads to further and other actions. Even the same action differs when repeated.

If we look at the modus vivendi (which like orthodoxy always exists whether we know it or not: there is a modus vivendi between god and the devil) as the immediate and permanent field of the intellect, it seems to me we are in the frame of mind to see what is likely to happen. Then we either attempt to secure it at the least friction and cost, or if it is contrary to our vital purpose, we try to avert or modify it. In the modus vivendi spring the values of the intellect—what happens when we use it—like poppies in the Italian wheatfield or anemones in the Lebanon. The experience of modus vivendi may lead us to revise our notion of our vital purpose: even to revive it by reconceiving its effective nature.

It is under these high considerations that I venture to present a few of my reactions to peoples and politics in thirteen months of brief visits to England, France, Germany, Austria, Switzerland, Italy, Egypt, the Lebanon, and Turkey. If there is a bias or an intent in my presentation it is toward re-creating or even creating *de novo* at the cultural and intellectual level the sense of a modus vivendi. I do not say I know how this can be done as a whole, but I believe I can see some of the problematic and alternative steps that can be taken along the way. Most of these steps are second nature to five thousand years of the mind's feet. But some of the old steps must be taken over new terrain: the terrain of the new physical energies available and, more important in these notes, the new terrain of approximate universal literacy. The new physical energies sweep us along at a rate and with consequences beyond our intellectual power to grasp. The new literacy degrades the verbal aspects of our culture into a new illiteracy almost wholly indifferent to the fund of intellectual power.

I suggest that the two problems are inextricably related. The new physical energies will remain beyond control—external and indifferent to our vital purpose—so long as the new illiteracy gathers unimpeded sway and becomes if not the seat at least the source of political power. The present American hysteria in the conduct of world affairs exemplifies this: we are governed half by the energies that push upon us, half by our fear of the energies that push our postulated enemies. It is our own illiteracy that cuts our chance to control our energies, and it is the geometrically progressing new illiteracy of the rest of the world that, as it frightens us in thought and action, gives us our new talent for hysteria. I do not know how much of an exaggeration it is, but I know it is a forcible truth to say that the world is on the way to moral suicide—a stoicism of utter and hysterical stupidity—for the lack of a continuing and vital sense of the Word: through which only, so far in either Western or Eastern history, has been found a sufficient means to create a modus vivendi. There may be a new form of culture in the offing which will not require the intellect to join its issues and express its purposes in words—or in the various other languages of the mind. But it is only in the offing. For at least half a century to come we can neither determine nor judge our actions except in verbal language; and our need is for a higher not a lesser grade of literacy. Universal literacy, not in theory but as we so far see it in action, only multiplies ignorance by confusion. The product is half idiocy, half fanaticism; and what arises from it in political and cultural experience is dissension, distrust, and dismay: in short, hysteria, when you act in excess and disproportion of the legitimately understood impulse. In private love we can perhaps afford this, not in long-term public affairs; we know love is blind; political power must strain its vision fifty years ahead.

II

To put the whole matter another way: No amount of reflection has deflected me from the conclusion that the special problem of the humanities in our generation—I mean of course the official or institutional humanities, not the agitations and deracinations of individuals—is to struggle against the growth of what I have called the new illiteracy and the new intellectual proletariat together with the curious side consequence of these, the new and increasing distrust of the audience by public and quasi-public institutions. All three of these are results of the appearance, in combination, of mass societies and universal education. All three occur, in different stages and with different emphases, throughout the world. Everywhere chronic, they are likely to produce critical explosions from time to time and place to place. The crises cannot be touched; the chronic form may be treated. The patient is human intelligence: we deal not with ignorance but with deformities of knowledge, not with natural monsters but with maimed spirit.

My terms will perhaps clarify in loose definition (for too much definition would let the problem escape into another form or turn into mere methodology). *The New Illiteracy.* The old illiteracy was inability to read; as the old literacy involved the habit of reading. The new illiteracy represents those who have been given the tool of reading (something less than the old primary-school education) without being given either the means or skill to read well or the material that ought to be read. The habit of reading in the new illiteracy is not limited to, but is everywhere supplied by, a press almost as illiterate as itself. It is in this way that opinion, instead of knowledge, has come to determine action: the inflammable opinion of the new illiterate is mistaken for the will of the people, so that arson becomes a chief political instrument. Senator McCarthy is a local master of this kind of arson in a society with perhaps the highest level of literacy in the world except New Zealand; the majority of his readers and listeners have not the skill or familiarity to distinguish the relation of his words to facts or purpose. Neither does the Senator: he is illiterate with regard to his own ideas and his own purposes: he will disappear. In Iran, Dr. Mossadegh was not illiterate, but used the techniques that belong to illiteracy; and in the new illiteracy of Iranian society he had to be destroyed by the same means he had himself used. In Egypt General Naguib and Colonel Nasser defeat their own intelligence by the necessary resort to the methods of the new illiteracy which their constituency alone understands. Their success, with themselves unchanged, will be a calamity for Egypt. These are simple and conspicuous matters: they show at once that we all—all countries—need a larger truly literate class: educated to the needs and purposes of the society—and beyond, since there may well be needs and purposes not now recognized. A larger truly literate class is a euphemism for the concept of an elite.

The concept of an elite is out of favor. One of the reasons for this is that serious literacy is out of favor in the world of higher education. It is precisely in the world of higher education that the new illiteracy is spreading the greatest damage to the available fund of general intelligence adequate to the conditions that confront us. Thus we get the Franklin Press going to the Arab world with the products of our own illiteracy. Thus we get the Salzburg Seminars in American Studies in effect deliberately reducing the quality of their work to freshman level in a freshwater college. Thus we find the USIS in Tel Aviv competing against Russia with the Tarzan books as indicator of the American way of life and all its superiority to the Russians who came bringing Tolstoy. It should seem clear that if you deliberately sink yourself to the level of the new illiteracy you will lose confidence in what remains of your own literacy: you have given up, and have only a nonce respect for what brought your mind into existence in the first place. If the salt hath lost its savor, wherewith shall it be salted? True literacy is the salt of the intelligence. The grease of the new illiteracy is the nausea of intransigent stupidity. How salt grease?

This brings us to the *new intellectual proletariat:* all those in all parts of the world who as a result of their own initial talents (not necessarily great) and the better routines of higher education find themselves in a society where they are alienated because there is nothing serious for them to do with their training. A proletariat is that class uprooted, usually by social action, from the soil of its culture. (This is perhaps why the dictatorship of the more or less urban proletariat in Russia has been cruel in revenge upon its origins. Let us pray the intellectuals never achieve a dictatorship!) A proletarian has no capital interest in his society; he works for day wages only. In America the intellectual, as such, is now the only proletarian. Call it what you like, the double apparition of mass society and universal education is producing a larger and larger class of intellectually trained men and women the world over who cannot make a living in terms of their training and who cannot, because of their training, make a living otherwise with any satisfaction. The American distrust of the intellect, and the painful shrinkage of the confidence of the intellect in itself turns out to be a natural phenomenon of mass society and universal education. Even in Egypt, the Lebanon and Turkey the intellectual has no collectable claims on society. I think the cause is in the dilution of literacy, and the intrusion of the new illiteracy into higher education; so that it is only an effect, and wrongly understood, when we say, as Italy and France and Germany have to say, and as America will say in the next depression, that we have too many college graduates or too many Ph.D.s or too many what-nots. It struck me as much in Cairo or Ankara as in Bologna or Munich or Princeton or Harvard that our distrust of the intellectual, as he becomes a massive phenomenon, is a result of the inadequacy of his preparation and the following failure of the independence of his mind. We think we can make the intellectual with the tools of the new illiteracy. All we do is uproot an increasing number of individuals from any vital relation either to society or to themselves. We create out of our possible intellectuals a proletariat. We grease the salt.

As if we were not content with that, we proceed to develop a habit of mind in which we think we "believe" (we do nothing of the sort; we opine) that we must *distrust the ability of the audience* to respond adequately to any expression of purpose or choice. That is to say, we deliberately take the quality out of our thought precisely when it is most valuable: when we wish to persuade others of the truth or desirability of what we believe. In the end, it is only the quality of thought that commands attention; for the quality of expressed thought is the effect it takes on from the conviction of the thinker, the impregnation of the cliché with life blood, the restoration of doggerel to poetry, the redemption of slogan to insight. Instead of telling our audience what we believe, we tell it what we suppose in our own more futile moments they already believe; tell them with a little more outward noise and considerably less inward intensity than we ourselves feel. We believe our audience is not up to what we really have to say, and so we end up inferior to the potential response of the audience, and there is no more good in our talking at all. If we win, we are playing a game with the stakes left out; if we lose, our very best instincts are distrusted in return.

In either case we have degraded both our audience and ourselves: we have in each case induced one more step into the general new illiteracy, and got further and further from the project of understanding (the hoped-for concert of conflicts that lie between us) with which we take up our effort of thought and set about building on common interests. Our distrust of the audience is a result of our distrust of our own reason and our own imagination, of our own sinking into the sloth of hope, of our fearful unwillingness to rise into that energy of hope which has something to do with faith; all this we throw away because we have come on a skill which has nothing to do with thought but which we fancy can substitute for thought in securing the purposes of thought. Sometimes we call this skill psychology, or psychological warfare, sometimes we call it advertising or aiming at the target. As it comes from, it can only touch, except with horror, the baser parts of both audience and ourselves: the parts where we act willy-nilly, having given up. At worst, we buy the refrigerator we don't want; at best, we murder the manufacturer; in the middle, we subscribe to the Book of the Month Club or *Time* magazine. We forget that thought in action (and nobody can tell for sure when thought is going to take to action) is the most intense of human energies and cannot be dealt with by any energy less intense, except with degradation and incalculable uncontrol. This is indeed the "uncontrollable mystery on the bestial floor." Force is better: thought best.

III

Illustrations. As I write I hear on the radio of the *New York Times* that a Congressman says we are in desperate danger of a Russian hydrogen bomb. Therefore he calls for an increase of many billions of dollars in the budget. The *Times* selected this statement to headline its news. When Mr. Toynbee returned to England from America not long ago he announced a new slogan for Great Britain: "No annihilation without representation."

Again, in Italy, under the same arcade, on neighboring walls or pillars, you will daily see pasted up full copies of *Unitá,* the Communist newspaper, and such a paper as the "independent" conservative *Corriere della Sera.* (It is always *Unitá;* but the center is represented in different cities by different journals.) The headlined news usually rises from the same facts, but the headlines tell contradictory stories, with *Unitá* as a rule contrary to *any* rational interpretation of the facts. The point is, that the Italians, with both papers immediately confronting them, read only the paper which expresses their allegiance. Yet the Italians are of the "illiterate" peoples the most highly "literate." What does "literate" mean?

Still again, in Egypt the Arabic language press frequently threatens to drive the British out, while the English and French language press merely wishes Egypt could. It is the same in the Lebanon. Italy has a mild and mostly hidden censorship, except what is imposed by the parties for immediate purposes. Egypt has a police censorship obedient to the regime. The Arab world is working explosively toward literacy and has so far produced small but magnificent examples of the new illiteracy. Etc. Etc.

To be "literate" sometimes opens new avenues of corruption: That is what has happened throughout the Western world: *Corruptio optimi pessima.* The current of the new illiteracy has followed the course of universal education and has there run a general course eastward, beginning in America in the Jacksonian era, striking England about 1900 (with France and Germany), proceeding along the shores of the Mediterranean with increasing prospective virulence until now it has struck the Middle East and Turkey; where it seems likely to become a vastly debilitating disease, of wide incidence and incalculable effect of uncontrol, precisely where it is meant to give promise of redemption and wise control of the forces which actually move society.

In the West, until recently, there has been the background security of a proportionally large reading class, fortified and maintained not only by the university system but by the bourgeois family. Even with the great increase of population, that class remained till after the First World War an important fraction in every important social institution. We are now, in the West, developing the characteristic problems of universal education in late forms; and these are our problems—to which these notes will return—of the academic and intellectual proletariats in conflict with the technical and largely anti-intellectual elites; these together with the further problems that go with the emergence into power of classes indifferent both to the intellectual proletariat and the technical elite except as they may be of immediate use to immediate objects. (Examples: The active lowering of standards in state universities; the constant difficulty of maintaining the integrity of the Bureau of Standards or the Bureau of Labor Statistics; and the preservation of our forests and oil lands. In England, the folly of the Labour land policy.)

What is happening in the Middle East and in Turkey only repeats the earlier experience of the West with increased violence. In these countries the reading class was never more than a minor fraction. In Cairo and Istanbul street signs, except in the foreign quarters, are missing; they are only reforms that have not yet been carried out: very few would be able to read them. The population of Egypt multiplied by five, from four to twenty millions, under British rule and American medicine. The reading class increased absolutely by only a few thousand and has lost in relative power. The technical elite is only now being forced into existence by the pressure of huge populations without external resources. Egypt today is a country which can be exploited, even by its own government, and no matter how benign that government, only as one exploits poverty: that is to say, along the lines of Swift's *Modest Proposal,* one form or another of commercial cannibalism. Under such conditions it is natural that neither the reading class nor the technical class can exert political power in any effective way. Egypt shows no greater truth than this to her present masters (or to those recently deposed): it is no more expensive to extract energy out of mass poverty than it is, by ordinary means, out of coal, which is about 15 per cent efficient. Thus literacy will be improved only to the degree that gives the optimum malleability to poverty, and the technical elite will be created only to the extent necessary to the survival of huge populations, or perhaps for the augmentation of surplus energy for the aggrandizement of further and still lower grade energy of poverty, say in the Sudan.

Here is the secret message to the sons of morning. The generals, colonels, majors, and policemen who are the present masters of Egypt are in the early revolutionary state where they themselves believe in their own ideals. They are engaged in an enormous project of universal education, which with any kind of luck will be successful at a low level. They do not realize the dross they would become if faced with any quantity of active mind. So far, in the history of the Western world, active mind has had the two functions, mutually destructive, of saving society from, and giving the tools to, adventurers like Nasser and Naguib (whom all Italian papers see clearly as little Mussolinis and to whom *Time* and Mr. Dulles give their partial blessings together with a revolver). Therefore these masters of Egypt seem likely to me to accept any program aimed at raising the standards of education: that is, the creation of a sufficient educated class, humanistic *and* technical, actually to manage Egyptian society. There is much to be done at relatively little cost to help to train and stimulate active mind, not only in Egypt, but throughout the Middle East, and also in Turkey and Greece. The governments of these countries—all police states of various and shifting degrees of severity, but not, or not yet, totalitarian states—have done and are continuing to do the initial work in their programs of universal education.

In this they are compulsively imitating the West: they are teaching the beginnings of literacy because no modern society can operate without it. But they are teaching it, so to speak, without being themselves literate in a serious sense. (I saw a school in a Turkish village of 2,000 some twenty miles in the mountains south of Ankara where the stock of books was locked in a box of two cubic feet, and where the two enthusiastic teachers had something approximate to a high school education—and nothing behind it in the home or social life—in America. A mountain Moslem school in the Lebanon and a village school in the Nile Delta were much the same.) Therefore what they are producing or preparing in these countries is a series of explosions into a new illiteracy. In the U. S. and in Great Britain universal education produced, between 1880 and 1900, the yellow press, and later, the mass-circulation magazines, all the other mass-circulation items on the newsstands, and the comic books. We have our own troubles as a result of these productions. But think what these troubles would have been like if higher education had not kept proportional pace with universal education. And how much worse still would these troubles have been had there not also been a continuing habit of reading in the considerable fraction of society called the educated upper middle class. In the countries of the Middle East there is neither a proportional increase of higher education nor a surviving historical reading class of any appreciable size. But there is already a relatively enormous circulation of American comic books and picture magazines, along with grade B and C American movies; and each country has produced, under censorship, its own form of the yellow press. A police state is interested in producing, besides the low-grade literacy needed for daily life in an increasingly mechanized society, the largest possible audience capable of listening to the radio and talkies, and able to read the pretty much official line in the papers. Ten years of universal education will probably, and twenty will certainly, produce an overwhelmingly dependable new illiteracy in these countries which will by then have institutions requiring high and serious literacy to maintain a modus vivendi either at home or abroad. I do not see how a more precarious society could be more deliberately produced: only demagogy and hysteria will be able to manage it, and in worse forms than we know at home.

But there is, in each of these countries, a small educated class, surviving from the old regimes, which at present inhabits the universities, publishing houses, and smaller public office—with a few in more powerful positions of trust and administration. This class is larger and better of health in the Labanon and Turkey; smaller in the rest of the Arab world; but larger and smaller will mean little in ten years. Most of its members already lead individually precarious lives because the class itself is not being recruited fast enough to take in its own washing or to exert pressure upon the state for a sufficient subsidy for its own purposes. The population that is growing is not *their* population and those whom government recruits into their class will instinctively overthrow or destroy it: their education will prompt them to obliterate those functions of their new class of which they have never been taught the quality and of which, therefore, they distrust the old functions.

Yet this remnant of the old elite, wherever found and however it may be genuinely recruited, is the only class whose cause can be promoted with any hope of tempering, reducing, and perhaps obviating the dangers of the new illiteracy which flows from universal education. This elite remains, by reason of history and snobbery, an attractive force in society. What should be done is to provide this elite with the means of exerting its attractive force, both to gather fresh members to itself and so invigorate its own work, and also to infiltrate or modify the new illiteracy of other classes. All the Middle East governments believe in their own version of the liberal arts as a matter of history and tradition. But in their triple new experience of population growth, universal education, and the new more or less increasingly technically managed society, all of them, even Turkey since the death of Kemal, need an initiative push from outside before they can see reason to support the form—whatever it is—that liberal arts must take under the new conditions. Never having consciously had the experience of the results of universal education (and the rest) they cannot be expected to have a clear view of the dangers. They have had no great writers since Mohammed and no philosophers since Averroes, Avicenna, and Ib'n Khaldun; the Arabian Nights are at least five hundred years old. And so on. All this is their contemporaneity. So they have from five hundred to a thousand years of Western history to traverse in two decades—including the history of literacy. Thus, so far as we are aware of our history, and feel the urgency of its repetition, it is for us to provide the initiative: it is they themselves who must go on.

What is the present situation at its best? There is no proper intellectual-literary journal in Cairo, which is the cultural and publishing capital, not only of 20 millions of inhabitants of Egypt, but of the whole Arab world—even of the whole Moslem world. This is not from lack of interest and probably not from lack of talent. It is partly from lack of money and partly from lack of freedom. It seems evident that in Egypt journals are more sensitive to censorship than books. Book publishing of new books, with few exceptions, is carried on by booksellers under subvention from the author; of translations with subventions by foreign governments and foundations; of classics with subventions by the Egyptian government and the universities. Circulation is very small. A thousand copies is an excellent circulation. (This does not apply to the publication of textbooks, or does so to a lesser extent.)

In Beirut the situation is much the same except that there exists there, in this second capital of the Arab world, a literary and intellectual magazine called *El Adib* (Man of Letters) which spreads its circulation of 3,000 among ten or a dozen countries, a considerable fraction of this number being paid for by the governments of the various countries. Here again the editor survives under a watchful and touchy censorship; survives with caution—like the U. S. Information service.

In Turkey the situation is in part ameliorated, and, from my point of view, in part aggravated. There is or was a poetry journal and there is or was (both were in precarious financial and political condition) a literary-intellectual journal circulating from two to three thousand copies. There is one ambitious high-minded public-spirited publisher in Istanbul and in Ankara an able and ambitious editor, presently rewarded by a fourth tour of duty in the army at the frontiers. The publisher supports his affairs by a somewhat glorified and altogether pirated "Readers' Digest" taken from European as well as American sources: the digest sells the enormous number of 20,000 copies an issue, the largest more or less serious circulation in the whole region. The Ankara editor supports his ventures by the sale of freshly bottled orange juice; and has no expectation whatever that his magazines could pay for themselves. And so on.

Yet at the same time there is a rapidly developing and profitable business in each of these countries—especially in Turkey—of mass-circulation journals on the model of *Life, Click, Pick,* and *Look,* necessarily at a lower level of literacy because of the lower literacy which they must exploit. Also—especially again in Turkey—there is an increasing business in comic strips for the magazines and newspapers and in comic books which only waits to make fortunes on the successive waves of what we would call grammar school pupils which are needed for exploitation. It is in this way and against this situation that the new literacy—necessary but only at a low degree to operate even a limited modern technical society—is turned rapidly into a new illiteracy. There is a special danger to the mind's fabric here which could not threaten a wholy illiterate country and which, *so far,* it has been possible to alleviate, but not obviate, in countries where higher literacy serves as an anchor in the higher bourgeois and professional classes.

There should be nothing surprising in either the emergence or the severity of this danger. Ignorance is a permanently urgent problem in any society. The new illiteracy is merely the form ignorance takes in societies subject to universal education. Literacy—education—improves itself and spreads only so long as the society concerned still believes, at a level above pi-jaw and eyewash, that the dignity of man is in his intelligence, his reason, and the intuitions that come to him through these.

Without his dignity man dies. How then can the necessary elite be recruited? Dignity is a part of action, not education; education can only point to action, or at best can only bring back to mind the incentives to action. Education is a lever, not an evangelist; may destroy work already done, or may economize work yet to do.

Education may not only economize but may also create work yet to do. Perhaps it does so best by pointing to possibilities. The possibility of a respectable newspaper *in Egypt* does not appear to have occurred to the Egyptians: it is a characteristic symptom of the new illiteracy that people themselves still literate distrust the ability and the potential ability of the newly educated. The audience is expected to be incapable of pleasures not meretricious merely because the pleasure of the meretricious is universal, and where not actual is the substance of temptation. Again, the possibility that children might read "good" books in a newly literate society, such as fragments of Egypt, tends to be dismissed in favor of books deliberately written below the threshold of known intelligence: as if children's books should be pacifiers sweeter than the more instinctive forms of masturbation. The Egyptians, with the aid of American foundations and Information libraries, are greedy to translate books aimed at children from five to eight, from eight to twelve, teen-age books for girls and teen-age books for boys: the greed is to puerilize children who have no vested interest in puerility at all. And so with history: the books that are translated (and some that are written in the Eastern languages) are written at that level of popularity which makes for facility of reading but which never commands attention. The grasping force of an idea is ignored; hence the possibility that ideas may be degraded out of their own semblance is somehow obscured in the belief that if ideas are to be spread they must be watered. One would suppose there was a clear possibility of spreading at least a tenth as many good books whether for children or in history, as those of the puerile and commercial kind. What is commercial by definition takes care of itself; what is cultural cannot. But this is so only because commerce has money as an immediate object, whereas "culture" seldom finds expression in any form of monetary exchange which is taxable for the cost of production or transmission or circulation. Yet culture is the mind's money and everybody not forbidden wants a little of it in his pocket, if only to rattle. Culture is the cash and carry of human action: the one form of currency we ought not to debase, or inflate, but must enrich.

The Egyptians, Lebanese, and Turks—so far as I met them—know all this very well; but they all give the effect of living under a culture (the *form* their behavior takes) which prevents them from true literacy or "great" culture or freedom of intellectual action. This is true only so far as the police reign supreme in their various countries and only so far as positive talent does not emerge. They could not otherwise have a point of view from which to complain, with wit and passion, as they all do, of Hollywood and the American *kitsch* culture which they see coming in faster than the fastest American automobiles. They think they live in submission to resistless forces and at the same time think themselves helpless before a resistless national or political fate in which they do not share except as victims, or, at best, in jobberies. Malish (which means: never mind), hashish, and baksheesh: this phrase for what is wrong with Egypt is not only wit, it is a nightmare dream of escape. But because they have these thoughts and use this phrase they have the chance of internal and spreading liberation; and the chance depends on seeing it as the possible matrix of action. We—the West—ought not to drown them in the flood of our puerilities, at least as a matter of policy, any more than we should drown them in our plumbing. We ought not to pretend, for it is not yet true, that the enterprise of our society has collapsed into the business of the state; we ought not to admit, for the admission is moral suicide, that we have lost our individuality in favor of a mass culture. We ought rather, on the contrary, to insist that, in so far as we have vitality and the power to affect other societies, our government is our balance not our momentum, our servant not our master, and that it is *we* as individuals that redeem *us* as mass. We should say how well we know, whenever we take breath, that only reaction to present anarchy enlivens order; so that we will save our anarchy at all costs. Every Mediterranean mind from Gibraltar to Suez or the Bosporus would understand this in the pulse of his own syllables and the scope of his own ambition; and if we said it often enough we might remind ourselves of its plangent truth striking against ourselves.

IV

Why do we not, then, take courage from its only source, our own hearts: our own hearts which have never benefited for more than a night's sleep from any palliative whatever; why do we not say truly: Look, you are performing, in your own way and your own time, the terrible experiment of universal education which we ourselves, with more defenses than you, now labor with. It is because our own defenses are running out that we see your risks. You are creating a mass society without mass resources (or, if you like it better so phrased, without an effective continuing tradition of a leading class not only at the top but running down into a learned middle class) and are therefore sacking, in advance, the possibility of willed purpose as the governing element of response to the experience of your own motion. You are—so we might continue—an early object lesson to our own probable forthcoming experience of an overwhelming helpless energy: the uncontrollable conturbations of the Lonely Crowd, of which only adventurers can take advantage. This is another way of saying (so we might still continue) that we are creating different forms of highly precarious society where the peril—the failure of balance—lies in the progressive development of energy without a corresponding development of intelligence. We surrender ahead of time to a momentum whose direction we do not understand; hence we depend for our ordinary daily safety on an increasing series of incalculables. The old safety—the immortal hard straw pillow—of undifferentiated ignorance in the masses is being replaced (as we see everywhere in the world at different velocities and intensities) by the differentiated and energized ignorance which results from low level universal education. Security, as the old playwright, John Webster, says—"Security some men call the suburbs of hell, only a dead wall between"; and he wrote better than he knew: the intellect is in the suburbs, and commutes, entering the city only in deliberate disguises of the scarecrow and the prophet: the two roles to which the modern city has reduced the unwelcome intrusion of active mind.

Scarecrow and prophet let us be; we are still nevertheless *lares et penates:* household gods at work in the closets and attics and cellars—where they exist—of the best housing projects that Cairo, Robert Moses, or the London County Council can think up: they couldn't think without us. It is no new thing, as readers of the Arabian Nights will remember, for the intellect to become the Djinn in the privy: 'Tis catch as catch can still, and it is our lower and open parts the intellect catches best hold of—when who squeals last is the innocent and everlasting soul, brooked at stool.

Scarecrow and prophet the intellect must be. And why so? The industrial, technical, mass-society world lives in and is committed to history. History is a new thing in the older story, Christians think it is Christian; think Christ Jesus entered history, with a rape of fertilization and compassion and a kind of vast loneliness of free action and all the harshness of love in action. Those not now Christians think merely that history suddenly imposed itself, sometime in the eighteenth century, upon a suddenly fertile mankind. History came with food; and the food has outrun the capacity of our peoples to endure history. We have the multiplication of peoples in the Middle East and the multiplication of food (the grain lying in the fields of the Canadian Northwest, the mountains of dyed potatoes in eastern Maine) in the West, and we have the sweet-acrid odor of babies everywhere: all in a direct analogy with the explosions of universal education.

It was a strange dream of the early nineteenth century that by the industrial revolution, we obviated politics and had escaped history. History jerks us every second. It always has, but it did not matter until there were too many of us. We cannot any of us be Swiss except the Swiss: whom we have thrown off as a sport, the one possible collection of people impervious to history. But the Swiss have no Djinns in their privies; their faces never wince.

The Egyptians, and all the Arab world, wince at the suddenness with which they have been thrust into a late stage of Western history, and they are perhaps more precarious in that history than we feel we ourselves are. They have not inherited the protective strengths of our past, and it may be that the casual strength of their own past will not suffice for safety in the new conditions. There is a magnificent remark in the *Table Talk* of Coleridge. England, said he, had had three silent revolutions: "When the professions fell off from the Church; when literature fell off from the professions; and when the press fell off from literature." Under the unrestrained, that is, low grade, impact of universal education, all three revolutions are happening at once in the Arab world. Hence the urgency to see that these revolutions happen in a relatively high phase of literacy rather than in an absolutely low phase. In the Middle East the problem is acute; with us it is only chronic and will remain so as long as we maintain and improve our vast educational institutions and our expressive cultural institutions.

Looking at the acute urgency in Egypt perhaps makes it easier to see the nature of the urgency in America. In the *New York Times* (31 October 1953) Mrs. Anne O'Hare McCormick, in her column "Abroad," was much worried by the sentiment in Western Europe which believes a modus vivendi with Russia possible: she thought this sentiment is the cause of the distrust and fear with which so many Europeans regard American military policy. But she went on: "This hope springs eternal in the European breast. It survives every disappointment. While it lives, while talk of meetings and faith in negotiations persist, there will never be all-out popular support for defense programs. A lot of confused people cannot believe that the leaders of the world could not make peace if they tried."

The last sentence is a barbarous example of the new illiteracy. Mrs. McCormick wrote (I exaggerate deliberately) in the spirit of the Albigensian crusade, which was one of the foulest blots on human history. The "confused people" in her sentence are the leaders of Europe and the only leader missing is the United States. Many Europeans (and I should suppose all Russian officials) reading her sentence would regard it as an effect of a deliberately aggressive American military policy in which the sense of the nature of peace has become submerged in a sense of the nature of war.

I submit that Mrs. McCormick's sentence is evidence that America has suffered from the new illiteracy more than Western Europe has so far suffered. No wonder we are regarded as an imperialist power. Unfortunately there is a sense in which Mrs. McCormick is right: on the tacit fact about the nature of American (and perhaps Russian) leadership.

Perhaps we may have a maxim here. It is the new illiteracy that prevents a modus vivendi; it cannot admit either the vitality or the desirability of the concept. The highest forms of professional advertising are the highest form of the new illiteracy. President Eisenhower's television show of himself and his cabinet only carried one step further Senator Kefauver's crime show; Senator McCarthy's Army show only improved on the klieg-light techniques of his colleagues' hearings. The new illiteracy prevents a modus vivendi.

Taking Egypt and America as extremes, let us examine lightly some of the problems which result from universal education in a mass society in some European countries. The fundamental problem is everywhere the same, but its accidental forms will vary. The swollen populations of Western Europe are both imitating and importing the work of their elder American brothers (elder in the world-wide spread of the new illiteracy) in the characteristic mass media of mass entertainment in the newsstands and along one wall of the bookshops. The American "*gialli*" glow everywhere in sunny Italy: so that if one did not *stop* to think, one *would* think the American soul deeply jaundiced if not bilious. It is only that the Americans got there first with mass production in this particular form of entertainment; the Italians are catching up with their own versions. It would seem that a swelling population requires universal education for spouse, and that the combination fructifies according to kind. The difference between Europe and the Middle East (and also between Europe and America) is that in Europe there is a more powerful, persistent, and prevalent tradition of higher literacy—the literacy which was anterior to universal education. In all Egypt there are perhaps fifty bookstores selling respectable literature; in the Lebanon perhaps twelve; in Turkey another dozen: representing a clientele of at least fifty million. In Italy's provincial city of Bologna, with a population of 350,000, there are thirty-two bookstores (some twenty of quality and size) selling new books and nearly a hundred selling second-hand books. Bologna is rather like Boston, Massachusetts, of thirty-five years ago: Boston is now much more like Cairo or Istanbul; and a city like Trenton or Worcester is now almost as barren as Ankara and much less fertile than Beirut. When I was a boy Boston had a hundred bookstores. I do not say that Bologna will follow Boston; but that is certainly the result that seems likely to follow from the increasing impact of universal education. Even the Italian character will change under the application of sufficient uncontrollable force. The question is whether control is not possible. And since the force is, initially and historically, American, so is the question.

In the *Saturday Review of Literature* (31 October 53) there is an interview with T. H. White, the foreign correspondent, of which the last sentences he is quoted as speaking bear on this problem. "What I want to say is that America is so much the energizing center of the whole world today that the whole frame of foreign correspondence has changed. The place to cover the world now is from America." Mr. White knows better than this, as many of the pages of his *Fire in the Ashes* show. But, in the interview, he sank into the bog of uninterpreted fact. My point is that we, having the primary energy at this moment of history, must needs find the quality and phase of that energy. None of us, Beirut, Bologna, or Boston, can afford the mere bog of fact.

It is a curious thing that the cushion of tradition against the blow of education on the old intellect of Europe, has allowed not only the survival but the gross multiplication of the intellectual class without providing the new recruits with the means of life. In this sense Western Europe is ahead of America in time, but not for long. The present experience of Europe shows us (what we had a sample of in the great depression) our probable future general experience; to contemplate it raises an aspect of our general problem only less urgent than that which shows now in the Middle East. This is the problem of the intellectual, academic, and professional proletariat: a kind of frothy or elite *fellaheen* thrown off by the coupling of mass and mechanized society with universal education. This is the other side of the triumph of the new illiteracy.

The Byzantine empire showed early examples of such a proletariat in the fifth and sixth centuries, as may be seen in Burckhardt and Cochrane. The earliest modern experience is perhaps in Russia in the sixties and seventies of the last century when the increasing flood of graduates from the Russian universities and other new intellectuals were exported to Siberia at the rate of a thousand a month. In the nineteen-twenties, Julien Benda wrote a book called *The Treason of the Intellectuals,* in which he complained that the class most fitted to direct and understand society was refusing to take any part of it. What Benda failed to recognize was that the society would have none of the intellectuals, who were becoming an unwanted proletariat. Treason had become the only possible occupation of the intellectual class in its major fraction; treason, obloquy or frustration—and of these only treason furnished a livelihood. Benda understood neither the economic nor political necessities, short of either heroism or great talent; hence his complaints shriek. In Italy, Switzerland, Germany, France, and England there are many who make a more accurate diagnosis. They recognize an epidemic which is sweeping from country to country so soon as each country is ripe—is *matura* or *robusta* enough, if I may borrow for a moment the Italian forms of two of our regular words. The academic class, being within living memory tolerably secure, is somewhat more acutely aware of its impending experience as a class, than either the intellectuals or the professionals. In Italy some 3,000 presumptively qualified young men and women take every year the post-doctoral examination for the licentiate to teach in the schools and universities of the state. The waiting list of those who have already passed similar exams is so large that only influence, or personal claims of some other variety, can possibly find jobs for any of the successful candidates. In Germany, France, and England the question was frequently asked in so many words whether America yet had an academic proletariat. Proletariat is the name given to a class of persons who have no fixed and vital position in society. It is an equivocal and problematic fact that modern Western society is training, for many years and at great expense, an important fraction of its best talent to the end of membership in an intellectual proletariat.

It should be self-evident that no corruption of that training, no treason to the needs of the society which trained them, no deliberate resort to the institutions of the new illiteracy, will be too great or too repulsive for the great majority of this group. It is only *as* intellectuals that they become members of the proletariat: that is, in the very last role in which it would have been expected of them. The human cost might not be too great to pay if it ensured a superlative academy. It does not do so, either in Europe or America; the new society does not require a superlative academy, and will neither pay it an ample salary nor maintain standards of selection competent to secure it. The new society wants something less than mediocrity, since its ends are considerably less than mediocrity. This is clearer in Europe than in America because in Europe the 'professor' still maintains his social and even his political prestige (which he does not do in America: where he is expected to do something else besides if he is to have any general prestige at all) at the same time he has lost several degrees in economic status.

In other words, society, as it gathers into itself the forces of universal education, puts a smaller and smaller value upon the forms of intellect from which it derived its power. It makes the mistake of believing that intellect is self-created and that gifts are to be had for the asking. No society will pay for what it does not value, nor will it pay more than a courtesy sum for what it thinks ought to be free or its own by nature. The craft of intellect ought never to have disclosed its secrets of hard work and human difference if it had hoped to survive: for it has unwittingly, by so disclosing its secrets, created the illusion that machines will do the hard work and obviate the human difference. These tasks the machines will do at every level except that of the intellect and in every phase of life except that of the emotions, the senses, and human relations. The crisis of our culture rises from the false belief that our society requires only enough mind to create and tend the machines together with enough of the new illiteracy for other machines—those of our mass media—to exploit. This is perhaps the form of society most expensive and wasteful in human talent mankind has yet thrown off.

The existing surplus of talent in the academic proletariat in Western Europe is only an advance form of the surplus which will appear in 1970, at latest, in America and earlier if there is a major depression. This seems inescapable, not only in humane studies, but also in the social and physical sciences. Possibly the psychiatrists and the inventors of sedative and stimulating drugs will show still the present geometric progression. The graduate schools will neither be able to shrink their number of students nor to richen and generalize their standards of study. Or at least they will not be able to do so without the shock of new will on old purpose; and any such shock will have initially to come from outside the universities and aside from the state. It seems unlikely any such shocking force will appear.

V

And it seems all the less likely to appear when we consider the European and American situation of writers and artists in relation to *any* existing economy. These classes have merely added a new dimension of disestablishment, unreality, and insecurity to their prewar situation: they are further and further outside the economy which they express in its human consequences. The new economy—at any rate all existing economies—has no means of supporting its writers and artists as a serious class, but has increasing means of supporting them—or some of them—at a degraded level. To a great extent this has always been so, but it has not mattered much since the fourteenth century till our own time. That is, so long as there existed wealth which was also committed to literacy at a high level, whether in the church, aristocracy, Crown, or, later, in the *haute bourgeoisie,* it was possible to support a reasonable number of writers and artists; and indeed, many, perhaps the bulk of them, came from such economic and social classes. Lately there has been reduction of all the leisured forms of wealth, and the new forms of wealth are committed *against* high literacy: since it has nothing to do with the sources from which they sprung, and in their view has only a frilly relation to their lasting power.

Yet, at the same time, such is the vestigial strength of the old committed society, and such is the attractive force of an artistic career to all humans, there has been a vast increase in the number of persons who find their theoretic primary career in the arts and letters. Only taxes and inflation can put them under cover: nothing can kill them; they live, in increasing numbers, with the hope only of total frustration for all but a small and probably accidental minority. Here we strike on a startling feature of our new society in its present stage: it insists on attracting and partly training great numbers of writers and artists not only whom it cannot use but whom it holds in contempt. Contempt, which is allied to fear, is the basis of many forms of lip-service, eyewash, and pi-jaw.

Even this state of affairs might be acceptable if only it produced talent to correspond remotely to the number of persons. Unfortunately, to be held in contempt tends to arouse martyrdom without belief; contumacy without devotion; and these are the characters that seem to be predominant in the new artistic and literary proletariat. We get the buffoonery of the half-created soul: futility masquerading as fanaticism. Dostoevski saw it long ago in his "Notes from Underground," in an insight which covers a part of all of us. Shakespeare had it cold, in *Love's Labour's Lost:* the figure of Berowne. Today we have them all round us: we have them as a proletariat: that is, too many of them; and it is neither an insight nor a satire, but a heavy fact.

Another form of the heavy fact is this. The paying audience has, under present conditions of publication, exhibition, and performance, nowhere grown in relation either to population or to performance, and has sometimes shrunk. It is not the state that is withering in the modern social revolution. As the relative literate audience withers we create the waste of new proletariats; and, as Empson's poem says, "the waste remains, the waste remains, and kills."

The waste will kill us yet if we do not find a means of absorbing and transforming and taking care of the best of it; not all of it, only the best of it. Out of the great waste come the prophets and the masters, as well as the monsters and the pretenders. If we can find methods of supporting the first pair we can afford the second. But we shall have to get off the long diminuendo in which our concept of mediocrity slides lower and lower. We shall have to stop all that we mean by polling opinion and selling policy and turn once more to creating opinion and finding policy.

For all these are matters of politics: the adjustment and administration of existing forces with a view to survival: the constant re-establishment and care of a modus vivendi. In the matters in hand no one is much against intelligence except by indifference and contempt. When asked, everybody is for it. Only we all distrust ourselves even more than we distrust the masses of people we work on. Our only true enemies are our defaulting selves; for we default most when we have to do an old job under new circumstances. St. Paul would call us Laodiceans.

What are the facts with which the politics has to contend in the literary world? One is that an increasing number of persons want to be writers and half of them call themselves so, in the face of a diminishing rather than an increasing means of subsistence by writing. Another is, that despite the growth of population and education the audience for serious literary magazines or general journals has remained, not absolutely but relatively, the same. Three thousand copies an issue for the literary journals and up to a hundred thousand for the general seem to remain the absolute maximum. Neither figure represents self-support, and neither commands the form of endowment called advertising. These figures are not only American; they are also European. England, France, Germany, Switzerland, and Italy all furnish the same figures, with all but Switzerland having about three-eighths to a quarter the American population.

The figures for serious books which have not become reprints are comparable. The German-language Swiss publishers have, for serious books which have not struck fashion, a safe sale of 3,000. If the work was German to begin with it can pay for itself in the gross; if it is a translation, and of any quality, it is a present to the German-reading peoples. Texts, technical, and "popular" books and magazines are expected to pay for the serious in both kinds. But in all countries an increasing amount of serious publication requires subsidy from outside the publishing business; not so much from unwillingness as from inability of the publishers to subsidize themselves. The great, and even the small, continental publishers continue to subsidize their own serious publications. The English and Americans are, with exceptions, doing less and less. The difference perhaps reflects the present incidence of universal education. If so, the German and Italian near future resembles the English and American present. It is the audience that must be improved as well as the publishing system.

The problem of audience belongs to education, both within and outside the educational systems—and what is usually meant by "adult" education has little to do with it: "adult" education is *kitsch,* an expansion, with illusions of power, of the new illiteracy; the problem belongs to education in two fields, both dedicated to conceiving and negotiating a modus vivendi, whether national or international: a means of getting along without loss of vital purpose in a concert of conflicts, not a unison, not a solo, not a harmony, but a concert of the conflicts with which we necessarily find out our problematic relations with others, nations, jobs, or friends.

One field of education has to do with training superior individuals to regard themselves as at least as useful under the new conceptions of leisure as they ever were as members of the historic privileged classes: useful, that is, to society in general without reference to their direct means of livelihood. Much of the best English poetry was written by men to whom literature was at most a secondary occupation, and in no way a profession. The professions of culture we must have; we must have them small, say no more than fifty times the number actually needed to ensure and cushion and take up the slack of positive talent. When Dryden said, "Cousin Swift, you will never be a poet," it was, although perhaps judicious, certainly a gratuitous remark. Today there are too many thousand common chimney swifts trying to fly like poets. For the first time in modern history (to forget the Byzantine and the ancient Egyptian) professionalism has created a proletariat of poets merely because the career seems attractive, just as it has attracted a superfluity of Ph.D. graduate students and far too few candidates for teaching in the secondary schools, too many engineers and architects and too few mechanics and carpenters (but also, curiously, too many bricklayers and too few masons). Professionalism and trades-unionism (of which it is another form) are, in these undesirable senses, one of the chief problems rising from unattended universal education. Professionalism is a form of illiteracy.

There is even, I think (and this brings in our second field of education), a kind of undiscriminated professionalism of the older, and as we like to think natural form of the proletariat of the masses. And this too is a product of universal education; or at any rate we had never to fear their dictatorship (their management by the elite of the new illiteracy) until they had been infused with the narcotic and dismaying jag of low grade universal education. Here we go back to the cradle of culture where we began, the Middle East, but we go back only for emphasis—in another place—on what we have in front of us here at home. It is easy to see that the education in the Middle Eastern countries is inadequate to the intelligent declaration of their vital purposes: we knew that the elections of November 1953 in the Sudan could not express the will of the Sudanese since the Sudanese have no way to crystallize their will; we know instead that the people of the Sudan, being illiterate, could merely choose between brands of packaged goods offered to them. So it will be in the next election in the Lebanon—theoretically 60 per cent literate, quite the highest theoretic literacy in the whole Middle East; with the further impediment that the polls are based on a census, false even then, of a generation ago, taken by the French with their own purposes in mind. Without adequate literacy, and in the face of gerrymandered polls, the people cannot express their will through popular elections.

Here we know what to do: the populace must be educated to the level required for the honest and informed discovery of their will; and saying that we shudder, for we know what calamities may occur if the degree of literacy is not quite conformable to the necessities. The literacy must grow a little faster than the movement of history in order to overcome the force of the most corrupt and purchaseable (since that most immature of all forms of human behavior, the emotional, is for sale) of all proletariats, that created by the new illiteracy. If we shudder at what may happen in the Middle East, we ought positively to quake at what may happen in Italy or France if the special, and extremely professional, communist forms of the new illiteracy should grow unimpeded. And if we quake at the possibilities in Italy and France, we must needs be frighted out of fear at the much higher, more professional, and more hysterical forms of illiteracy in America which we misinterpret as national policy and world leadership when they are actually native evangelism and a tendency to immolating adventure. The degree of true literacy required—and reversely the tolerable degree of the new illiteracy—is determined by the amount and intensity of the energy to be controlled, deflected, and joined with other energies in the hope of a true modus vivendi: a livable world.

At this point, with all the exaggerations and ejaculations in the above paragraphs cut down to size, it begins to emerge that literacy (the aim of education) is itself an energy comparable in intensity, delicacy, and mass to the energies we locate in the natural sciences. What is more important, imperfect literacy, degraded literacy, or what has been called the new illiteracy, though it has lost its capacity to control other energies, has not only not lost but has gained in uncontrollable and unpredictable energy of its own: much like the physical energies themselves when, once released, they are let alone. What is needed, from Cairo and Ankara to Paris and New York, is an energy of mind equal to both the new physical energies and their natural concomitant the new illiteracy. Institutional education alone, like institutional religion in the Christian past, is not enough: though these may persuade what is necessary into being: the multiplication and heightening of individual intelligence. Some people call the mode of this intelligence in action criticism. It had better be called the charity of compassionate understanding. Its aim is no less than a modus vivendi for those who must live together; no more, in the end, than true empire: *della vera città almen la torre.*

1954

2

The Politics of Human Power

Part of the pleasure of seeing Mr. Trilling's essays [1] brought together surely consists in finding what he has been up to all along. As they came out in periodicals, or as one heard them from platforms, it always seemed that their author wrote from a solid, though developing, point of view, from some vantage, not precisely that of the audience, but which the audience was under the natural expectation to share, like the weather, or even like the momentum of society. The words seemed to have a source and a purpose, an origin and a destination. It was rather like Reinhold Niebuhr's iteration that in Christianity, and in Christianity alone, history is meaningful—but the meaning is not yet. Now reading the essays all together, although we see that the meaning is still not revealed, we see better by what means, and against what difficulties, the author goes about the business of cultivating his long hope.

We see that he cultivates a mind never entirely his own, a mind always deliberately to some extent what he understands to be the mind of society, and also a mind always deliberately to some extent the mind of the old European society taken as corrective and as prophecy. He is always aware, to use one of his phrases, of the *cost* of civilization. He knows the price of glory and the price of equity; that the price of one may be the expense of the other; that the two are incompatible; and that both prices must be paid. He knows; or at any rate he knows that he does not know. I suppose

[1] THE LIBERAL IMAGINATION: Essays on Literature and Society (Viking, 1950).

that if he accepted this language at all, he would allow that this knowledge represents the Human price; and he might go on that this is why he has cut down on tykish impulses and wild insights, why he insists on using a mind never entirely his own.

He has always wanted a pattern, whether a set or a current, a pattern of relevant ideas as a vantage from which to take care of his occasional commitments. When he can find the current he will swim in it, when he cannot he will accept the set; in either case they will be the ideas which seem to be the furniture of the American liberal imagination; and in either case he tries to make these ideas the tools of positive reaction and response. He does not ask the question in so many words, but his book asks it: What on earth else is the American mind to do in the effort to control the understanding of that new thing in history, the mass urban society? What else can be done in a society committed to universal education which yet at every level distrusts the intellect?

One of the alternatives is to call Mr. Trilling's habit of mind, as R. W. B. Lewis has done, the New Stoicism, and that is the alternative I would rather expect to be popular among the heirs to nineteenth-century humanism whether in its liberal form or not. Stoicism is a confession of failure and in our society the confession of failure is a howling success. But Mr. Trilling does not confess failure; it is one of the freakish qualities of his mind that he does not make any confessions at all. More formally, I do not believe that Mr. Trilling makes virtue the highest good in any practicable sense; nor does he concentrate on ethics and the control of passions; nor is he indifferent to pleasure and pain; nor does he blot himself out in favor of self-control. He wants only to control what is there; he finds special forms of reality in the quarrel of pleasure and pain; he finds passion a source of thought and the overestimation of virtue a tragic impulse. These are very different matters, and whatever they may be called they ought not to be called stoicism. Nor does he grin and bear it in the Boy Scout adulteration of stoicism. His fortitude, which he shares with the stoic, and most other forms of surviving life, is of a very different order; his fortitude may cut his gains along with his losses out of obstinacy in particulars or weakness in sensibility, but so does any fortitude that rests on choice. He has the fortitude, in his essays, to act by choice as a public (res publica) mind. It is his business to take a position, to react and to respond, between incommensurable forces. He is an administrator of the affairs of the mind. He is everywhere against the passive as he is against escape into the long view or aggression into the moral view. (He quotes approvingly Niebuhr on Kant that the Radical Evil is "man's inclination to corrupt the imperatives of morality so that they may become a screen for the expression of self-love.") There is a world of difference between the kind of acceptance which is a surrender of the insurrectionary and initiatory powers of mind and the kind of acceptance which is an insistence (even when it does not share them) on the conditions of effort and which derives from that insistence the necessity for insurrection and initiative. It is the difference between saying that the job cannot be done and saying that the job must be done over again at the cost of any insurrection and any initiative. It may be that to hold such notions and be without the power of anything but critical action is to be a stoic in fact. To Mr. Trilling it is an aspect of what he calls moral realism; it is a very different thing from the stoicism which Henry Adams used to call moral suicide. Put another way, Mr. Trilling requires the development not the attrition of values in the conflict between morals and experience; and his chief complaint is against the attrition of value after value, often mistaken for the hardening, and sometimes for the prophecy, of value in the contemporary American mind.

It is true that he makes these distinctions chiefly in discussing novelists, but I do not see any radical distinction between the novelist's mind and other minds. He gives us Faulkner and Hemingway as exceptions to the very stoicism which Mr. Lewis fastens upon him; he presents them as writers in whom ideas flourish and the mind has power. The mind in question would seem to be the mind of primitive terror and childhood piety, almost a nightmare piety, and it would seem to me Mr. Trilling gives this mind more credit than it deserves, for it reaches full action in the "moral realism" of the reader, not its own.

But let us take an example of what Mr. Trilling actually does in an essay which raises these questions in a substantively remote form, though it no doubt reached Mr. Trilling as a piece of occasional writing, that is, as a book review. This is the short essay on a new printing of the Annals of Tacitus. The commitment of course was to find a living value in a classic, a classic which perhaps Mr. Trilling had never previously read. A living value is what the liberal imagination is supposed to find in a classic, especially in one newly read or re-read. Well, Tacitus is an historian, and the relevant pattern of ideas with which to think about an historian has to do with the special relation of the individual to history, to *historismus* as it trespasses into literature, and to the philosophy of history as it corrects the other two relations. In the Annals, there is the staring fact that the Rome Tacitus described is such a sink of human degradation that it ought not to have survived but did survive. Tacitus left out all the history which to most modern historians has to do with survival; he contented himself or exacerbated himself by giving a close account of what did actually survive. Tacitus had nothing of that long view of the modern historians of the Empire which abstracts the survival from those who lived. His own "long view" was republican and ancestral and his ancestors were dead: alive only as standards of perception and indications for judgment; and under those standards he made a work of art. It is one of the possibilities of history, taken as an art, to remind us in images of permanent horror and permanent glory, that although we live because of the long view, because of some leap or at least some overlap of minds, the conditions of life are anterior and posterior to any long view whatsoever. Seeing that, Froissart and Bede are better historians than we think when we do not see that. The conditions of life are immitigable; its significance always to be created, again.

This is of course not Trilling's language, and he might take affront at these mutilations of his ideas. Yet something of this sort of translation of what he actually wrote is the only way I know to make a response to it; my part of the general mind is not exactly his; and to translate his remarks on Tacitus, surely the most occasional piece in the volume, seemed on reflection to give the best illumination of the general working of his mind. Think of Tacitus, think of literature, think of society in between. It is because in his thinking none of these terms can be ignored that Mr. Trilling is primarily a literary critic, and neither an historical critic nor a social critic except secondarily; and it is because all three terms are continuously present (no one can be used to get rid of either of the others) that he is, in intention, finally the critic plain, without distinction. It is only in his excesses, or lapses, that he teeters into the social or the historical; the balance for that would be a teeter into either the purely literary or the purely speculative, the wild or the tykish; but that balance his decorum does not contain. His is a public mind.

No doubt his special form of public mind—more valuable than anything except a special form of the individual mind—is the result of his modification and development, his *correction,* of his two masters, Arnold and Freud. If, remembering this, the remarks on Tacitus are re-examined, we see at once that Mr. Trilling is providing us with a double example of the rational mind at work to control the irrational mind in the name of wholeness, virtue, and humanity. There is the example of Tacitus and the example of Mr. Trilling himself. Because of Freud, the contingency of incentive and dread is clearer than in Arnold; because of Arnold, the intellectuality and sanity of art are clearer than in Freud. For Mr. Trilling—who says that it is elementary "that whenever we put two emotions into juxtaposition we have what we can properly call an idea"—for Mr. Trilling, Freud and Arnold are two emotions which, in the concert of conflict, generate the dominant ideas of his criticism; and it is thinking of this conflict and this concert that we see that Mr. Trilling is praising his own hopes when he says of the novelist: "His inconsistency of intellectual judgment is biological wisdom." Neither Arnold nor Freud would have said exactly this. It is precisely what of Arnold and Freud remain in conflict in one mind, that gives Mr. Trilling a sense of incentive in this characterization of the novelist. As he is primarily a literary critic, Mr. Trilling is also fundamentally a novelist; and for the same reason that he is in intention finally the critic plain, so, finally, as a novelist, he would deal "in his co-existent hatred and love" not with the individual as a literary, or historical, or social object, but with the individual *in* literature, *in* history, *in* society, the individual, where as Eliot says he can alone exist, *in* a community. In short, let us say that Mr. Trilling takes for himself the vantage of the humanist who is also the critic and the novelist. It is not the only role appropriate to the writer, but it is in any society a dignified and necessary role.

The reader will perhaps come nearer to accepting this short view of Mr. Trilling's vantage as accurate if he will run lightly through the essays in *The Liberal Imagination,* and count as he runs how often the word *human* turns up, how often what is human is found or is disastrously missing in the novel, and how often the human is linked with three powers of mind: the power of story (as for Thomas Mann, the focus of the novel is in the anecdote, and Mann, too, is a liberal humanist in hard straits, a creature of Goethe and Freud); the power of meaningfully presenting the conditions of daily life; and the power, the generalizing, abstracting power, of the systematic intellect. The repetition is sometimes harsh, sometimes forced, and has sometimes the strident tone that goes with things never let alone: quite as if the discourse had the urgency of scholarship, or religion, or politics. Indeed, for Mr. Trilling, his discourse has this urgency. His subtitle is *Essays on Literature and Society*. There is a sense in which his subject is the politics of human power, with his platform that of the independent liberal imagination so far as it survives in him and us.

The essay on Tacitus is perhaps not the best example of this aspect of Mr. Trilling's mind. The essay on the Kinsey Report, with an emphasis on the indignation with which he wrote it, will at least serve. If anger, as Aristotle thought and Dante agreed, is the emotion most kin to reason, then the liberal imagination, as Mr. Trilling observes, finds its natural relief in moral indignation. Though the indignation may falsify, it is better than a half truth, and is often the only admirable response a mind can make. If you see your great subject as the politics of human power and are confronted by a world which sees its subject as power simply, a world which is fearful of politics and distrustful of the human, you have your maximum right to moral indignation. And if you see your colleagues in the liberal imagination going along with that world, you will say, as Mr. Trilling says, that the loss amounts to the loss of the prevailing sense of human politics, the loss of piety, of history, and purpose. It is precisely like the absence of Alma Venus in the Kinsey Report: the loss is unnoticed because it is total. In dealing with Dr. Kinsey, Mr. Trilling reaches his peak of indignation: his sense of the enormous indignity of a work on sexual behavior which pays no tribute to the goddess of love and no attention to love either as a personal or as a social relation. There used to be a question which troubled Henry Adams, whether the force of sex had not degenerated in America into a sentiment. The Kinsey Report, as Mr. Trilling sees it, suggests the question whether the sentiment has not become a kind of idiosyncratic appetite, satisfied at evacuation: a mere unimplicated puny act of individual power, of which, as Mr. Trilling says the Report concludes, the "more the merrier." And he ends: "In short, the Report by its primitive conception of the nature of fact quite negates the importance and even the existence of sexuality as a social fact. That is why, although it is possible to say of the Report that it brings light, it is necessary to say of it that it spreads confusion." No novel could be written on the experience handled in the Report; it is behavior without its politics and without its humanity, but with a kind of power conceived to be in charge which in any other field would be called brutal, murderous, and arbitrary, without memory, purpose, or horror. Mr. Trilling would have said this better; and I wish he could have added his version to his present concluding sentence, for it would have raised, at a very apt point, the whole question of the politics of human power. However, he does not; his book goes on into the next essay, on Scott Fitzgerald, with a remark of Racine's Orestes: "So be it! I die content and my destiny is fulfilled." Mr. Trilling is quoting from Gide on the glory of the exemplary role as envisaged by Racine and rehearsed by Goethe; he then proceeds to praise Fitzgerald by affixing to his intention, if not to his achievement, the sense of this role. I should myself say that Fitzgerald was more representative than exemplary; but I am in the minority of those who do not feel the greatness of Fitzgerald; to me even the horror of his career is of the accidental kind which lurks in any corner. But, assuming that Mr. Trilling is right in the sense that we have no better exemplar available of the role of greatness, is not that, too, in a way other and deeper than that represented by the Kinsey Report, an example of the failure of the politics of human power? In asking that, I am not certain whether it is American culture or Mr. Trilling who has failed along with the politics. I would myself say that Mr. Trilling's essay gives an excellent account of a man who had fallen into Kant's Radical Evil: Fitzgerald made of his morality a screen for his self-love. If the novelist in Mr. Trilling had only got the upper hand, I must believe that on the basis of his own facts he would have seen this for himself. It would not have made Fitzgerald less readable, but it would have made more certain what was read, which is a human and political gain.

But this is only a disagreement in judgment, the one part of an argument least likely to stand. I would say that Fitzgerald would do very well to represent, not the calling of greatness, but what had happened to the idea of greatness in the America of the 'twenties and 'thirties. Mr. Trilling took the long view; if he had taken the direct view, with only the standard of perception in mind of some longer view, he would have altered only the tone of what he said about Fitzgerald. With that alteration it would have been in consonance with the tone of what he says about Wolfe and Anderson and O'Neill; not the same thing but in consonance with the tone. Then the essay would have stood appropriately between those on Henry James and Mark Twain. What a correction of Gatsby would be involved by the pressure, on either side of him, of Hyacinth and Huck! As Mr. Trilling notes that Huck said, the conscience is bigger than the self—which is I suppose why one's conscience is better than one's morals, which are so much smaller than most selves. This is what Mark Twain and Henry James understood, and what, like the nostalgia for the unknown, merely tortured Fitzgerald.

The question raised by the Fitzgerald essay, the one I mention and others which I do not, make a very good and not at all excessive road to Mr. Trilling's own final questions: those he asks about the failure of the liberal imagination (a phrase which the more I repeat it the less am I willing to use on my own account) to provide an even relatively great literature. Mr. Trilling ties his questions in—it is a matter of counting his frequencies of reference again, just as if we were Kinseys—to the terms which have to do with intellectual power *and* emotion or feeling or passion or sensibility. To him great literature has to do with great ideas, and ideas have to do, not with "thought," which is a subject for history, but with thinking, which is a matter of experience, and which is to be apprehended as emotion. Here are two passages from "The Meaning of a Literary Idea" which express his conviction most sharply. Say what we will, he says, "we as readers know that we demand of our literature some of the virtues which define a successful work of systematic thought. We want it to have—at least when it is appropriate for it to have, which is by no means infrequently—the authority, the cogency, the completeness, the brilliance, the *hardness* of systematic thought." That is one; here is the other. "Those poets of our time who make the greatest impress upon us are those who are most aware of rhetoric, which is to say, of the intellectual content of their work. Nor is the intellectual content of their work simply the inevitable effect produced by good intelligence turned to poetry; many of these poets—Yeats and Eliot himself come most immediately to mind—have been at great pains to develop consistent intellectual positions along with, and consonant with, their work in poetry."

I cannot imagine a society, I cannot imagine any form of public mind, though I know and do not have to imagine many individuals of our own time, to whom these texts would not seem either the expression of an ideal or a noble lie for the sake of an ideal not yet revealed. But I do not know of a time when a body of such literature flourished, or when a body of literature animated, as it thought, by such an ideal, was great literature. There is the Athenian literature, which Plato attacked; and there is the literature of the Enlightenment, to which we are still in reaction. There is also Dante, but Dante is singular. It is with these reservations, and only when I am exercising the public part of my mind in the public interest, that I would assent to Mr. Trilling's use of language in the passages quoted. I like the intention, but I deplore the record of those who wrote or wanted others to write on a similar declared intention. In short, the intention is only good if kept at an impassable remove from the practical work of the mind. For my own evangelism, I much prefer the intellectual inconsistency which is biological wisdom, the "holy stupidity" of the novelist, and the "negative capability" of the poet, all of which Mr. Trilling praises on one page of the essay called "Art and Fortune." I prefer them because they seem in better support than the texts quoted of the very power of the mind, its *hardness,* brilliance, system, and all, which Mr. Trilling wants; and not only that but also better suited to promote the restoration, in the broadest possible sense, of the politics of human power, which has a *harder* seriousness than any system.

In saying all this, I believe I am on Mr. Trilling's side, only further over into the tory anarchy which is just the other side of liberalism, but I say it not to express an irritating sort of agreement but in order to explain my repudiation of his question of why it is, of the ideas which have been generated by liberal democracy, that they "have not infused with force and cogency the literature that embodies them." I don't mind the question so much as I do the attributes he gives it. "This question is the most important, the most fully challenging question in culture that at this moment we can ask."

This is the trouble with a feeling for systems; it makes such questions possible and makes them seem legitimate. The law I know says that liberal democracy, like Stalin's communism, the despotism of the seventeenth century, or the omnicompetent state of Dante's Italy, is an incentive to literature only in the sense that it is a barrier to it. The politics of existing states is always too simple for literature; it is good only to *aggravate* literature. The politics of the state is the politics of what Lord Acton meant by power, and it is only when it is "out of power" that it can construe life, as literature needs, in terms of the politics of human power.

This is half the objection to Mr. Trilling's question; and the second half is like this first. The true business of literature, as of all intellect, critical or creative, is to remind the powers that be, simple and corrupt as they are, of the turbulence they have to control. There is a disorder vital to the individual which is fatal to society. And the other way round is also true. The reader who thinks Mr. Trilling does not know this when he is not thinking about it has only to consult the remarks about Kipling and Nationalism. The trouble is that his masters, Arnold and Freud, both extremists in thought, occasionally overpower him: they make him think too much. The remedy is Tacitus; the enemy Kinsey; for all of us. But as Mr. Trilling says, thinking of the great image of the politics of human power, "We are all ill."

1950

3

The Artist as Hero: A Disconsolate Chimera

The place where morals hit hardest on the arts is in the center, where the hero is; or at least it seems to me we may think so when we remember how often we identify the work of art with its chief character or with the role which that character plays. It is the hero who becomes the symbol for all the reality which has been made actual in the work of art, and if there is no hero as such we give the hero's role to some feeling or emotion or theme that runs through the work and find in it the symbolic form of all we value. Morals is how we estimate the relation to life of what we value; not how we find the value or change the value but how we estimate it. It is a secondary labor that must follow, and cannot precede, understanding and apprehension. With this in mind as an approach it should be an observation of commanding interest that the hero of some of the most ambitious art of our time should have become the artist himself and that in a vast amount of other work the theme of the role of art should have become dominant in value. Since this has never happened before, it will take a little fresh moralizing to make good morals out of our estimation of it; and that fresh moralizing, which I hope will halt short of stridency, is the task this paper is meant to take hold of.

The subject is easier for me to handle in literature than in the other arts, but as I see it there is nothing I can say about it in literature that does not have its parallel in painting, sculpture, dancing, and music, and for all I know architecture as well; for all of these arts have had half a century's relation to the frame of mind and the habit of value called expressionism in the widest sense of that term. It is with the expressionistic hero that we have to do. But let us take the hero first, and see how far he has come, before we look at what expressionism has now done to his features.

There is no sense starting with the Greeks and Romans, lest we should merely find ourselves repeating them. But there is good sense starting in the Middle Ages, which is as far away from ourselves as we can get. In the literature of the Middle Ages the characteristic hero was the prince or the soldier, someone in high station, represented as a type by a poet nearly anonymous. The prince or the soldier was the conscience and the motive of the action. By the Renaissance both the artist and the hero had become somewhat more individualized, the motive and the conscience somewhat obscured. By the eighteenth century the artist was rooted for his inspiration in a relatively fixed national society; his heroes were descendants of the earlier breeds and had fallen in social position—they were the same heroes but were celebrated at a less heroic level. Motive and conscience had become easy. Here is the crisis in this sequence. With the romantic period, when the historical sense came in, a new decision was taken: the artist himself might be a hero, as Byron, Goethe, Hugo were themselves heroes greater than any of the heroes in their works; motive and conscience had got outside the works. But the day of this hero was short, though it has never been forgotten. Except for the virtuosi who did very well, the artist became the hero *manqué,* the *poète maudit,* and celebrated himself or prototypes of himself in his works. Then with the rise of symbolism and art for art's sake the heroes of a considerable body of work began to be portrayed as artists. The subject of the artist and the special sensibility of the artist began to be the heroic subject and the heroic sensibility which best expressed society itself. The hero was expression, without need either of motive or conscience.

I do not know how this long sequence came about, but it seems natural when looked at, especially its latter end. Arnold was making his claims that poetry might save the world by taking on the jobs of all the other functions of the mind. And Tolstoy was making the congruous claim that art could help Christian fundamentalism save the world—or it could if only it got rid of almost everything it ever had been. Between the two, art was to replace both motive and conscience.

Now this happened at the time of the great burst of population, the great expansion of education, and the profound (as it seems, final) division of the fields of knowledge. Man, as he became so many, seemed incompatible with his selves, and he entered upon the era of competition for theoretic supremacy among his isolated and opposed selves. Of these selves the most sympathetic to the artist was of course the artistic self; at once the most isolated and the most opposed, and in an excellent position, because of his work, that he was the higher example of and the only escape from the common predicament: as if somehow all the world had become professional and with nobody left to practice on. Hence it is that the problem of the artist became a version of the problem of man and that the proper human heroism was the heroism of the artist.

This sort of belief is a part of the behavior—it is as deep as that—of a major fraction of the thousands of fresh artists our system throws up every year into fuller isolation and with a more certain end in failure than ever before. But this belief has also been expressed articulately, with a kind of reason and critical power. I think of Delmore Schwartz's article (*Partisan Review,* Spring 1945) called "T. S. Eliot as the International Hero." The ultimate value of this article is apart from the argument about the hero—in the shrewd and illuminating remarks about the depth of the perceptions in Eliot's poetry; but it is with the argument that I am here concerned. The argument runs to the effect that the poetic method—an aesthetic knowledge—alone makes us aware of the nature of our own times by being alone capable of uniting them to themselves and to their history. This, Schwartz says, is a heroic method. It is at this point that I begin to suffer from the word hero; it has begun to mean too much other than itself; but I think Schwartz let a sound instinct guide him to the use of this term; for many will understand it in the isolation of their own natures and in the depths of their own behavior—which is where men if they do not understand each other at least imitate each other. Hero is the high name we give to those to whom we turn for strength in the effort to find ourselves a motive, or in the worse effort to create in ourselves a conscience. What Schwartz is arguing is that the role of poetry is the heroic role for our time: in which is expressed the heroism of the non-heroic: the defeated, the rejected, the impotent, the loveless.

Does it not appear on a mere moment's meditation that the role of this hero is expressionistic and that the one unanimity that this heroic act can reach is the residual unanimity, almost the accidental unanimity, under the babble of differences?

I do not share this view of the world; I regard it with terrified sympathy, like the horror of being about to fall; for this may be what people are getting to be like. It is the terror and the horror of contemplating the individual who, being without the strength of society, finds himself, in full motive and all conscience, committing gradual suicide. It is the predicament in which we turn to the radio or to the whole of literature each hour on the hour to see what has happened.

There is another view which I want to interpose for a moment before we return to the heroes of expressionism. My friend Robert Fitzgerald said recently in a seminar that Oedipus' answer to the Sphinx riddle was a silly answer and that the Sphinx must have died by falling over backward from a kind of shame at his impertinence. What is it that at first walks on four legs, then on two, and at last on three? When Oedipus said Man, he only proposed another riddle, as is clear if you read Sophocles' plays about him. What I propose, to represent a view not expressionistic, is that Oedipus might have answered the riddle thus: That animal which dares to become a man, and dares long enough, will end crippled. This is not to solve the riddle, but to rehearse it in the terms of another heroism than that of Oedipus or the expressionists.

So much for my intervention. What is this word *expression* when it takes on an extra syllable and becomes a mode of the mind? I rest on the dictionary which like faith is the substance of things hoped for. Here is what Webster has to say:

expressionism. 1. The theory or practice of freely expressing one's inner, or subjective, emotions and sensations; a sense originally developed in painting. 2. In 20th-century literature and drama, such interpretation of life in stylized and distorted scenes and characters, symbolic of reality, usually presented so as to reflect the subjective state of the chief character.

3. Belief in, or advocacy or practice of, the free expression of one's individuality, especially as a means toward the acquirement of individual culture.

The order of these notions is interesting; number 2 includes and deforms number 1; number 3 includes and deforms numbers 1 and 2 so there is very nearly nothing left of either the individual or his culture. (Culture, if Eliot is right, is the incarnation of religion whether in the individual or his society: the motive at work in relation to the conscience.) These do not disappear, but are deformed. One thing all three have in common is the resolute avoidance of taking second thought or second sight except on matters of executive form or manners. There is no query and no scrutiny, of the inspiration: upon which we have been more often fooled than upon any other important matter.

Yet there is something wonderfully warm and tempting and heroic about these notions. Like every resort to the primitive they seem to recreate the innocent and to make one at home with the savage; the effect of destroying the burden of the individual while perfecting his freedom. They represent the incentive in a phrase of Maritain: "Art bitten by Poetry longs to be freed from Reason."

It is at this point—in this longing, in these *longueurs*—that all we mean by expressionism shows its warrant for being and the nature of its justification by works. If we think of these longings and how their release may be passionate, with a passion that may seem of universal scope, then I think we can see how great-spirited men have made great works by heroizing the longing to be freed from reason. The whole human world shares and expresses itself in this longing. Not only is the artist isolated and the hero of all his knowledge, but he finds that he has upon his hands the task of the deliberate creation of conscience in a conscienceless society. Especially has this been true in literature. Stephen Dedalus, in the *Portrait of the Artist As a Young Man,* goes forth to forge in the smithy of his soul the uncreated conscience of his race; and H. C. Earwicker in *Finnegans Wake* is, in his dream of the great soul of the world, the very smithy where, to the best of his ability, Joyce forged that conscience: in the ground, the soil, the chthonic home of behavior. Joyce is one of the peaks reached by the artist as hero; in him, at the end, all the nostalgias have come home again in the great spreading stain of general expression from which he started.

In Henry James the motion is the same but he neither went so far nor started, consciously, so far back. I think the argument of his whole work is that art gives you all you have of conscience before official morals come in, and his tales of the artist—whether writer or painter—put up the artist as the characteristic impersonal hero of that enterprise: a scapegoat paying with life for art. That is what I mean by the creation of conscience in a conscienceless world. James himself put the matter best at the practical level. The theme of the artist remained interesting, he said, only so long as the artist was a failure, that is, so long as he remained a person. For if the artist succeeded, he went on, he disappeared into his work, and there was no person left. If there is something thin and meager about all James's fables of the artist's failure and success, there is also something haunting and demonic: all that fades in an embrace, and is yet there, all that is heroic in the artist who has disappeared into the hero.

If in James it is his impersonality that makes the artist the heroic form of conscience, in André Gide it is the other way round. In *The Counterfeiters* the personality contains almost everything that is at stake; the book is indeed an effort to create a personality for the author himself at the expense of anything that used to be called the individual, and it is a personality so frail and precarious that it is at the point of extinction and needs the food of some fresh adventure either in life, or in the classics expressionistically conceived, to keep it alive at all. You will remember that this book contains the journal of the novelist Edouard in which he both writes about the other characters with relation to another novel and also engorges them for his own sustenance: he eats what he expresses, he expresses what he eats, and he does both conscientiously. It only adds to the involvement in personality to remember that Gide also kept and published the journal of his own experience in writing *The Counterfeiters*—the journal of what it was like to express himself in the guise of Edouard. The conscience has become merely personal, and the motive an appetite. The final value is in the success of the artist, by the success of his art, in the struggle against the world: an expressionistic struggle toward individual culture, as the dictionary says, in which the old-style individual is sacrificed and demolished. This is the excruciating triumph of moralism which has lost its religion or the substance of its religion. It is also, I think, the characteristic triumph of expressionism. We have climbed the tower of Babel; we hear each voice make invocation of a private Pentecost; and we see what is merely possible masquerading as opaque prophecy.

Let me suggest that this comes about, because of what Gide did with Dostoevski's notion of fundamental caprice—the goat-like act of our underground natures—as animating so much of our behavior. Gide turned caprice into the free act—the *acte gratuit*—in which we create our natures and derive our behavior. If the word were in fashion I would say that Gide's form of expressionism operated on a diabolic aesthetic, but I should have to add that it is a protestant devil, withal scrupulous and deeply adventurous.

Gide's sensibility may or may not be diabolic; Thomas Mann's *Doctor Faustus* is avowedly an essay in humanistic diabolism. Its hero, Adrian Leverkühn, becomes a great composer by selling the humanity of his life to the devil; which was neither a capricious nor a free act, but historic, compulsive, fatal, done to raise the expressive irresponsibility of the artist to the breaking point of absolute responsibility: which is to say total, because unimplicated, response. Adrian Leverkühn's music is the naked human voice of the actual world and collapses at the apocalypse of the world to come.

Because that voice is given precise and independent form in the art of music it is so far separated from the world that it can act as the naked and intolerable conscience: the expressive judgment of the chaos of the German 'twenties and the horrible order of the German 'thirties and 'forties. Because that voice is still the human voice, Leverkühn's music in the very act of formalizing it discerns its motive. Conscience and motive together, in this case, lead to damnation. So much for the tragic role of the art of music as hero: it could be carried no further in accounting for the journey of the war, in which Dante tells us we are all engaged. What of the other war, the war of the pity, which must engage our contemplation? What of the hero Leverkühn who composed the heroic music?

Craving personality as much as any character of Gide, ambitious as any in Joyce, quite as willing as any in James to surrender himself to his art, his own adventure is carried, I think, a step further than any of these. He is not impersonal, he does not disappear into his work; he is cut off even from that; he is depersonalized humanity, depersonalized to the point where he becomes the anguished expressive parody of that very humanity of which his music created the conscience and revealed the motive. His first large work was the opera *Love's Labour's Lost,* which being interpreted here means, he could not do love's labors; without love, he had to live without faith and without reason. He knew only what they expressed: but he himself could only express it as parody, however heroic. I should like to think that *Dr. Faustus* is the last novel in which the artist as such is the hero. The hero of expressionism could go no further, in magnitude or depth.

1951

4

The Economy of the American Writer

PRELIMINARY NOTES

Something like a century ago Alexis de Tocqueville in the second volume of his great work, *La Démocratie en Amérique,* made the following observations on The Trade of Literature:

> Democracy not only infuses a taste for letters among the trading classes, but introduces a trading spirit into literature.
>
> In aristocracies, readers are fastidious and few in number; in democracies, they are far more numerous and far less difficult to please. The consequence is, that among aristocratic nations no one can hope to succeed without immense exertions and that these exertions may bestow a great deal of fame, but can never earn much money; while among democratic nations, a writer may flatter himself that he will obtain at a cheap rate a meager reputation and a large fortune. For this purpose he need not be admired, it is enough that he is liked.
>
> The ever-increasing crowd of readers, and their continual craving for something new, insures the sale of books which nobody much esteems.
>
> In democratic periods the public frequently treat authors as kings do their courtiers; they enrich and they despise them. What more is needed by the venal souls which are born in courts, or which are worthy to live there?
>
> Democratic literature is always infested with a tribe of writers who look upon letters as a mere trade; and for some great authors who adorn it, you may reckon thousands of idea-mongers.

De Tocqueville was addressing himself to this country; but he used general terms, and I think they apply pretty generally elsewhere, if not in his time, at least in ours. The trade of writing is the chief positive obstacle, in our world, to the preservation and creation of the art of literature, and it is an obstacle all the harder to overcome because there is a greater and negative obstacle, which goes with it, in the absence, through all our societies, of any social, public, or quasi-public institution which consistently and continuously encourages the serious writer to do his best work. This is again, I think, the general situation and has to one degree or another always been so. It is only that to us who live in it, the situation seems worse today than it seems to have been in the past. The serious writer has had always to overcome the obstacle of the audience who wanted something less than he could provide and the obstacle of institutions which wanted commitments of him he could not make and which rejected the commitments he did make. What makes the serious writer think he is worse off today in both respects, is that his readers if he has any, and his institutions if he can find any, both seem to judge him by the standards of the market and neither by the standards of literature nor by those of the whole society. He has therefore rather less to fight either for or against than at previous times.

The causes for this unwelcome and I think morbidly disintegrative situation can be laid down in terms of this country's experience. Some of the causes are common to Western Europe, and to these I shall return. But let us begin with those which seem peculiar to this continent. Whether they are true causes is immaterial; they make up some part of the predispositions with which the American writer has gone to work in the past, and which still work harm—and occasionally strength—in the minds of young men and women at work today.

First, there is the fact that there has never been a dominant class in our society which has set a high value on the aesthetic mode of understanding or expressing human life. There have always been individuals and often coteries or groups, but never a dominant class, nor, until possibly our own day, any dominant institutions.

This fact has had two consequences. One is that without such a dominant class there was no existing prestige the power of which the new writer or new artist of any kind could borrow in order to attract an audience. He had either to make his own prestige by personal means—as an entertainer, like Mark Twain; or to do without prestige if he stopped being an entertainer, which is what happened to Herman Melville when he quit writing South Sea Romances and published *Moby Dick*. Besides the lack of a continuing fund of prestige, the absence of a dominant class with aesthetic values had a direct consequence upon the personality of the artist. He became, like the individuals, coteries, or groups who alone took an interest in him, full of snobbery or preciousness with relation to his society and a victim to subjective, even introspective standards with relation to his work. This applies largely of course to writers whose names and works have disappeared, but it applies also, and with much greater damage, to the work of Hawthorne and Melville and Whitman even, for the great dross in Whitman, it seems to me, is far more due to a kind of inverted snobbery and subjectivism than it is to defect of inspiration.

Perhaps the absence of a dominant class that understood aesthetic value itself had causes in our nineteenth-century history, among which at least two worked directly upon the role of the artist. One is the fact that the United States was during that century a society expanding physically at a rate hitherto unknown. The other is the fact that while there was no cultural capital, no economic capital, and indeed for the most part no political capital in the country, the country did have a kind of *engineering* capital which had no fixed locus but which rather moved to that place or places where things most needed to get done.

The breaking of a continental wilderness and the explosion of population from five to a hundred millions within a century built up over what it used an enormous dispersed, unorganized reserve of human energy—intellectual and artistic as well as mechanical and economical. It did not begin to concentrate the intellectual energy till about 1900 and has not yet effectively concentrated the artistic energy; and until energy is concentrated—or organized in some way—it can have only a low degree of availability. Thus intellect and art in the United States tended to operate on a kind of average or low level of potential though in relatively great quantity. That is, the mass was great but the intensity was almost non-existent. Thus our society has been administered more by the forward drive of its inertia in the mass, which happened to be accelerating and therefore kept ahead of its problems, than it was administered by direct intelligence and imagination. Nineteenth-century Russia had a similar experience, except that its movement of mass did not accelerate.

It was natural in such a society to do without a cultural capital, and even more natural that the society should either ignore or indifferently reject attempts to provide it with one. Thus the efforts of Presidents Jefferson and J. Q. Adams to create a National Observatory and a National University failed. The intelligence trained by a common education was thought not only to be enough but also to be the most practicable and the only useful version of the ideal. Even the private universities and colleges—except insofar as they trained the clergy—operated at very low standards until 1875 at the earliest and have not yet, as a general rule, overcome the obstacle of the tradition of the all-sufficing average intelligence. There was, to repeat, no way to concentrate, organize, and make available for its best work the original talent that existed in the literary and artistic realms. The bigger movements of mass either obliterated or drove out the smaller movements of intensity.

That is, I think, why on the one hand the country has always been full of eager young talents forming into abortive and sterile groups, and why so many of those who, on the other hand, succeeded in keeping their talent alive into middle age either reduced their standards, fell silent, became eccentric, or went abroad. Their work had neither a center where it could gain strength and by concentration penetrate the mass, nor was it congruous to any purpose of which the mass was conscious.

Gradually, as a result of increasing economic wealth and power, the number of men and women grew who felt personally, if only partially, committed to a life in which aesthetic values ruled, or in which, rather, it was felt that they ought to rule. Mass education and relative mass-prosperity gave them opportunity and time to multiply until, in the Census of 1940,[1] some 11,806 persons reported

[1] The Professions volume of the 1950 census makes a different breakdown; but it is plain that the authors have increased numerically faster than the population.

themselves as professional authors, and some 44,000 additional reported as editors and reporters. These figures, of course, take no account of the thousands upon thousands who at one time or another would have liked to be authors, nor of the thousands more who write on the side or as a subordinate function of their profession—as scholars and scientists and military men and autobiographers; but say there might well be something over a hundred thousand in all who spend a major fraction of their effort in writing for publication. It is a small per cent of the population, but still, a hundred thousand writing persons make up something like an inert mass of their own in a society of a hundred and thirty millions, and of these the 11,806 may be thought of as the relatively intense concentration. They would not so long ago have been thought of as a small army, impossible to manage except by low and rigid standards, moving no more rapidly than the slowest man could march.

How slow that is may be roughly estimated as a generous average by dividing the total receipts of book publishers, or $130,000,000, by ten to reach $13,000,000 or the royalty paid the 11,000 professional authors. This gives an average income to the authors from the sale of books as about $1,181 a year. But this is too large, because the authors of non-literary works and autobiographies are necessarily included and would bulk large in the totals. The account may be clarified a little by particular examples. One of the most distinguished poets of my acquaintance, well and favorably known here and abroad, who devotes his entire time to writing, has never in thirty-odd years of writing earned more than three thousand in a year, and has averaged about five hundred. One of the most distinguished novelists in this country, who has sold widely in England, and has been translated into French, German, and Russian—and who has not, I should add, any extravagant tastes or heavy burdens—was nevertheless only able to live a year or so ago with the aid of a $2,000 Guggenheim Fellowship, and subsequently applied for a job teaching freshman composition at Harvard. Of the three most distinguished painters I know, one has private means but has never sold more than enough to pay his overhead as a painter, one lived—or starved—on about six dollars a week, and the third told me that he had not paid an income tax for six years even though his children were grown and he could no longer claim a dependency for them.

What I want to point out as a result of these figures is, first, that the theory of a cultural market does not work. I do not know that a cultural capital is possible in our time—unless it be on the lines of Hollywood; we may not have the kind of culture which it is possible to capitalize; but I do know that the market system of open competition does not work at all from the point of view of our presumed over-all social aim: the fostering and evaluation of the serious arts and the discouragement and devaluation of, not the frivolous, but the plain bad arts. It may work well enough for the secondary or popular entertainment arts, but only at the expense of engulfing the serious arts in the new illiteracy of the nineteenth and twentieth centuries which has more than kept pace with the new literacy of the common schools.

The market system as it affects writers is very much like the market system as it affects society as a whole; it dissolves all but the lowest values and preserves only the cheapest values: those which can be satisfactorily translated into money; for it is only the cheapest sort of life, of thought, of art that can throw its values into the competition of the open market as the market developed in the nineteenth and early twentieth century without loss of the values themselves. In the market system the automatic adjustment of economic value under free competition is supposed to take care of all the human values which make economic value significant, and it is supposed to do so by natural law. As an illustration of what actually happens instead I suggest consideration of the transformation of the policy of *The Saturday Evening Post* from an editorial to an economic policy. That magazine no longer tries either to create or to buttress opinion or a special form of entertainment; it no longer attempts to get the best material within its standards on subjects which its editors believe important; instead, it runs a sort of Gallup Poll among its readers, and commissions contributions according to its findings.

But *The Saturday Evening Post* is only going one further step towards accepting the standards of the new illiteracy, than has been the general tendency of magazines ever since automatic universal education and the automatic free market began their double growth.

Year	1872	1904	1921	1926	1934	1939	1944	1954
U. S. population in millions	38	75	105	113	122	131	131	150
North American Review (Q)	2,000	30,000 *	22,000					
Harper's Monthly	130,000	150,000	85,000	69,000	100,000	101,000	105,000	154,000
Scribner's Monthly	55,000	175,000	97,000	71,000				
Atlantic Monthly	35,000	25,000 (1910)	107,000	119,000	99,000	107,000	109,000	201,000
Nation	6,000 (1880)		28,000	30,000	37,000	38,000	33,000	31,000
New Republic				30,000	25,000	27,000	29,000	30,000
Dial			7,000	10,000				
Poetry					about 3,000 throughout			
Foreign Affairs				11,000			14,000	15,000
Fortune					75,000	138,000	177,000	219,000
Time					544,000	766,000	1,000,000	1,747,000
Life (160,000: Harper's Weekly)						1,891,000	3,745,000	5,400,000
Mercury					33,000	61,000	62,000	100,000
Saturday Review of Literature							23,000	127,000
Saturday Evening Post							3,393,000	4,559,000
Esquire							691,000	772,000
New Yorker							205,000	377,000
Virginia Quarterly							regularly about 3,000	
The American Scholar							regularly about 5,000	
Journal History Ideas							700	
Comic Weeklies aggregate of three-fourths reporting							23,000,000	59,000,000

* Monthly.

The table printed on p. 57 presents circulation figures extracted from one or another of the directories of newspapers and periodicals. Those from 1904 to 1954 are taken from Ayer; earlier figures come from different but similar directories. Unfortunately figures are lacking on many of the most interesting magazines, either because they carried no advertising or because the publishers were unwilling to release figures or because the management of the directories overlooked them.

It will be observed that under the year is inserted the population of the United States in millions from the nearest census. This is to make possible more nearly actual comparisons between different circulations of the same or comparable magazines. Thus, to take the only magazine for which figures are supplied for the whole period from 1872 to 1944, *Harper's Monthly* had in 1872 a circulation of 130,000 against a population of 38,000,000, and a circulation of 105,276 in 1944 against 131,000,000 population. Would not this represent a reduction by three-fourths of potential circulation? The question becomes sharper if the figures for *Harper's Weekly* in 1872, or 160,000, are compared with that of its counterpart in 1944, *Life,* with a circulation of 3,750,000. The ratio seems about right to suggest that the old *Harper's Monthly* readers now read *Life,* and that *Life* also got the additional stock of literates. If the figures for *Fortune, Time, Esquire* are added to those of *Life* it seems certain that the new Literacy is of a very different quality from that of the old.

On a somewhat higher editorial level, note that *The Atlantic Monthly* was held to 25,000 through the editorship of Bliss Perry, but that when it reduced its standards to those of *Harper's Monthly,* it began to approach *Harper's* circulation. So, in more recent times *The American Mercury* under Hazlitt was unable to reach the circulation it had in tabloid form, under Eugene Lyons. Perhaps more striking is the 3,000 maximum paid circulation for a literary quarterly, 10,000 for a monthly, and 23,000 for a weekly. Against this is the relative high success of *Foreign Affairs* with a maximum circulation (1944) of 14,796 which on a comparative basis is half again as large as the 2,000 circulation in 1872 of *The North American Re-*

view, a journal of much wider scope and greater influence—perhaps even in foreign affairs.

But the number of comparisons that can be set up is endless, and most of them are self-evident. *Life* and *Fortune* and *Esquire* have apparently taken over art as well as literature. What the comic weeklies have taken over is not certain.

Worse than that, these figures suggest that De Tocqueville was exactly right in the first sentence in the passage quoted above. I repeat it. "Democracy not only infuses a taste for letters among the trading classes, but introduces a trading spirit into literature." Even in a society so populous as ours, there cannot possibly be, unless the creative ability of man should profoundly change, 11,806 professional authors, and if there were they could not possibly be read. A few hundred good authors of all kinds—a half-dozen great authors of any kind—would be the greatest stroke of luck plausible. Yet the few hundred—and the half-dozen, if they existed—must under present conditions compete in open market for a limited possibility of paid publication. It follows that most of them must, like the society which they express, lower their standards; or as an alternative earn their livings otherwise and devote only their spare time to their arts.

The alternative is clearly the desirable course, when it exists and can be seen, and when the writer can bring himself to accept it. For only the great and rare genius can accept the conditions of the trade of writing and yet make great literature out of them. It has never seemed possible to educate either oneself or others of lesser talent to do so. It is the writers who have reacted to their failure to do so who have so far felt themselves no part of their culture as to write the poems no one can read and the novels in which nobody exists and the plays in which no one can bring himself to action. Their reaction was false, but natural; almost the only possible reaction without great will and great ability and extraordinary luck.

I do not know how far these remarks may apply to the British Commonwealth or to the countries of Western Europe; I should expect that some fairly close parallel would apply. Certainly both the general production of literature and the general complaints of authors the world over suggest as much. But I am at least certain of this, that with the possible exception of Soviet Russia, and I am very doubtful there, there is no country in the world in which there is at this time, or likely to be in the future, either a dominant class or dominant institutions which assert a high aesthetic value against either the market system or its evident successor, the monopoly system. This is contrary to the most part of history—at least in those times when the arts greatly flourished.

I do not know that there is a cure, or if it is even the kind of an evil that can be cured; but I do know that it is an evil. I can only ask a few questions. Can contemporary artists deliberately ally themselves with existing institutions which show potential aesthetic bias—the universities and foundations? or (put the other way) can contemporary artists in any probable society permit themselves the pride, or the waste, as the case may be, of the total role of artist? Must not all serious artists rather grasp, both for their livelihood and for anchorage for their art, at any institutions, no matter how otherwise unlikely, that remove their values from the market? In this country writers and artists have for some years been penetrating the universities; but it is too soon to tell with what results. The risk in the experiment is that the universities are themselves increasingly becoming social and technical service stations—are increasingly, that is, attracted into the orbit of the market system. The hope in the experiment is that it is being tried, as every experiment in value must be tried, against the economy that makes it possible. Not good in itself, and with the clear possibility that it will help mostly only the middling good, the experiment might yet redeem in a few instances the paradox of a flourishing literary trade that has found no means to pay for its source in literary art. But the universities will need the courage as well as the judgment to see how vitally implicated are their own standards in the experiment. All's Alexandrian else.

1945

5

The American Literary Expatriate

Of all the terms used to argue the peculiar relation of the American to his Europe there is none that argues on more confused premises than the term "expatriate." There is none, either, that has been so used to judge by default or in ignorance of the issues. It is only today—in 1944[1]—that we can understand our ignorance and can distinguish some of the forces we had felt as confused. We know now that the expatriate is not a monster overseas, for he is with us, here at home, in the only sense that he was ever actually elsewhere, whether in Paris or London or Rome. The expatriate is the man or woman who chooses to live in a country not his own because he cannot do his serious work as well in his own country as he can in another. His reasons may be good—as were the reasons of the scholars who settled at the medieval universities; or they may be dubious—as were the reasons of some of the Americans who went to Paris to die but who lived to languish on the Riviera; or they may be bad—as were the reasons of the young Russians who went for culture to the German spas in the 'seventies. But in few cases was the expatriate a monster, or more than usually depraved, either for what he sought, for what he took with him, or for what he found in his exile. The expatriate is orthodox as a human type, classic in the nature of his struggle, romantic only in the ordinary sense of being strange in appearance or nostalgic in some of his attitudes.

We see all that now. We have in the cities and university towns

[1] Only more so in 1954.

of America large numbers of distinguished men and women from the countries overrun by the war or by the manias of the years preceding the war, and a few Englishmen besides. We call these men and women refugees, exiles, men in flight and condemned. Their own countries may in later years call some of them expatriates, precisely to the extent that they will seem to have *chosen* America as their place of exile—chosen America rather than Australia or South Africa or the Argentine, in any of which they could equally well have made a mere living, and where, perhaps, they would have been more warmly welcomed as examples of economic man. They came to America—these distinguished scientists, artists, scholars, professional men—because America exerted attractive forces upon them which were not merely economic or even merely political, but which were cultural. Thus many of them plan never to return, for they see that it is in America they can best use—or sell—their special talents.

For us the situation is unusual. We know the half-truth that money breeds money, and we know that America has been the economic capital of the world since at least 1917. There is another half-truth, in the expression of which we are not so skilled, that culture breeds culture, and it has taken the renewal and intensification of war since 1939 to show—whether in actuality or in hope—that the only immediately possible capital of the world's mind is also in America. It is our refugees, our new host of exiles, who declare the possibility. We should be grateful to them less because they will enrich our culture than because of the reasons implicit in their coming itself. A century and a half ago America showed the first plasticity of youth, which was political; today we show a second plasticity, which has to do with the arts in all their versions. But we show it less in ourselves than in the European expatriates among us who hasten to block themselves from subsequent return to Europe by the process of naturalization. We had better see if they are not right, and if they are, act accordingly, responding fully and consciously to the stimuli which our visitors feel, not so much in ourselves as in our situation. The chance may not be single but certainly it is not frequent.

It is a chance to reverse our historic role, to co-operate with history in playing fully the role she seems to have cast for us. But we shall reverse nothing but the perspective or our snobbery unless we understand better the cultural roles we have played in the past. For seventy or eighty years before the war—back to 1860 or 1870—it was customary for America to expatriate annually good numbers of its blessed or its damned to one or another European capital. Men went away more or less permanently because they couldn't stand themselves in America—though some of them thought it was America that was intolerable. They starved, they shriveled, they yearned; they cultivated a positive avarice of exile; also they fled where no man pursued, out of inner guilt, themselves pursuing the chimera of a European salvation. Others thought they heard the sirens sing in their own ears. Others—the rarest of the lot—heard the sirens sing in Europe, and of these a few actually not only heard, but wooed and won the muses in London or Paris or Rome. What is striking is that all of these men behaved reasonably enough in the circumstances as they saw them.

Their fathers or grandfathers behaved reasonably, too, but differently. During the first seventy years of American national life—that is, roughly up to the Civil War—men had gone abroad with the clear purpose of returning with one or another thing that America needed, or, in some cases, with the even clearer purpose of playing America's part abroad—for safety, for growth, for doctrine, or for money. In the thirty years divided at 1800, America was far more integrally—and consciously—a part of the European political and commercial system than she was in the thirty years that divided at 1900, when the system had become in fact, if not in consciousness, an intercontinental system. Where in 1800 the capitals of economic, political, and cultural power were the same, sometime between 1900 and 1920 they had become different. London, New York, and Paris made a division of human roles—of human powers or subjection to powers—that has seemed in its present consequence very near fatal to human intelligence. The peculiar chimera of the American cultural expatriate developed by metamorphosis during the interim till he became portentous. Looking at the chimera solemnly, made us think that there was either to be no culture in America or that the new American culture would differ in essential quality from the

European culture which had preceded it, and in any case it seemed to many that the cultured man or woman who was cultured in the European sense could not find himself at home in America. Often, besides, it seemed that the man who aimed at culture in purely American terms—Mark Twain or Hawthorne—found himself even more homeless than the other fellow, who aimed, however wildly, at the old European bull's-eye. It seemed to those who did this thinking that as America aimed at democratic content, so it ought to produce contented great men.

There would seem to be two main lines of argument by which the chimera can be successfully exorcised. One is the argument attached to the fact that the cultural centers of the Western World were not to be found in America at any time between 1870 and 1930. The second has to do with the peculiar relations between the artist and the social institutions of the modern world. The second argument is more significant than the first, but it gains its full significance only if the first argument is understood to begin with.

By 1870 a good deal of money had concentrated in America in such a way as to release the energies of those who possessed it. Of these many had social ambitions which could not be gratified at home, and of these some also had artistic ambitions. Henry James has given us the records of this group in his novels and tales of the International Scene, and in his life of Story; and in a famous paragraph of his life of Hawthorne, he summarized the snobbish form of the forces that drew them abroad. The snobbery comes from the terms in which the values of these forces were felt and has nothing to do with either the values or the forces. The whole passage is worth examining, not only for its application to the American generation of 1840-1875, but because it throws light on the bias of the chief American expatriate artist, James himself. He was making apologia, as he never ceased doing, for his own action.

James has been describing the early entries in Hawthorne's journals, and has begun by quoting a sentence from Hawthorne's preface to his novel *The Marble Faun:* "No author, without a trial, can conceive the difficulty of writing a romance about a country where there is no shadow, no antiquity, no mystery, no picturesque and gloomy wrong, nor anything but a commonplace prosperity, in broad and simple daylight, as is happily the case with my dear native land." James then proceeds in commentary upon Hawthorne's text:

For myself, as I turn the pages of his journals, I seem to see the image of the crude and simple society in which he lived. I used these epithets, of course, not invidiously, but descriptively; if one desires to enter as closely as possible into Hawthorne's situation, one must endeavour to reproduce his circumstances. We are struck with the large number of elements which were absent from them, and the coldness, the thinness, the blankness, to repeat my epithet, present themselves so vividly that our foremost feeling is that of compassion for a romancer looking for subjects in such a field. It takes so many things, as Hawthorne must have felt later in life, when he made the acquaintance of the denser, richer, warmer European spectacle—it takes such an accumulation of history and custom, such a complexity of manners and types, to form a fund of suggestion for a novelist. If Hawthorne had been a young Englishman, or a young Frenchman of the same degree of genius, the same cast of mind, the same habits, his consciousness of the world around him would have been a very different affair; however obscure, however reserved, his own personal life, his sense of the life of his fellow-mortals would have been almost infinitely more various. The negative side of the spectacle on which Hawthorne looked out, in his contemplative saunterings and reveries, might, indeed, with a little ingenuity, be made almost ludicrous; one might enumerate the items of high civilization as it exists in other countries, which are absent from the texture of American life, until it should become a wonder to know what was left. No State, in the European sense of the word, and indeed barely a specific national name. No sovereign, no court, no personal loyalty, no aristocracy, no church, no clergy, no army, no diplomatic service, no country gentlemen, no palaces, no castles, nor manors, nor old country-houses, nor parsonages, nor thatched cottages, nor ivied ruins; no cathedrals, nor abbeys, nor little Norman churches; no great Universities nor public schools—no Oxford, nor Eton, nor Harrow; no literature, no novels, no museums, no pictures, no political society, no sporting class—no Epsom nor Ascot! Some such list as that might be drawn up of the absent things in American life—especially in the American life of forty years ago, the effect of which, upon an English or a French imagination, would probably, as a general thing, be appalling. The natural remark, in the almost lurid light of such an indictment, would be that if these things are left out, everything is left out. The American knows that a good deal remains; what it is that remains—that is his secret, his joke, as one may say. It would be cruel, in this terrible denudation, to deny him the consolation of his natural gift, that "American humor" of which of late years we have heard so much.

The catalogue, and the bitterness of its iteration, are exhaustive. James has simply expanded for his own generation what Hawthorne saw with a greater intensity and a more passionate sense of lack. He goes on to argue that what the American kept in reserve—his "joke"—does not appear anywhere in Hawthorne's journals, but he does not argue that the joke did not exist; he was to spend the greater part of his artistic life in the effort to dramatize images which should express his ineradicable, but intellectually ineluctable, conviction that he knew what the secret joke was. What it was, it may be said in passing, shows clearest in the sacred rage for goodness and charity, fine feeling and candor in human relationships, that inhabits all his works like the atmosphere of a house; and it shows most precisely as he discovered that the English also had their joke—their reserved being—quite aside from their symbolized and catalogued possessions.

But at the time James wrote, perhaps even more than at Hawthorne's time, what a certain number of cultivated Americans wanted could only be expressed in the values and symbolized by the social and institutional features which England and the Continent had and which America did not have: an available formula in which a man's mind could be taken up, standards by which corruption could be understood as well as virtues judged. For men weak in will and ability the symbol was equivalent to the substance, and the formula—because easier to handle—was better than the form. Symbol and formula represented the overwhelming desire of the weakness of free men to be absorbed into an institution. For men of great will, desperate to capture ability, the symbols could be personally enacted and the forms could be made to enclose whatever the men could compass of the substance of experience. Thus the desire of strong men was, if anything, greater than that of the weak for the release of imaginative energy, otherwise merely personal, through objective institutions. Through institutions a career seemed possible.

If, in the pursuit of a career, the American discovered that the English or the French or the Italians turned out frauds or fools, brutes or pirates, it was because they had failed of possibilities which London and Paris and Rome still presented to those able to take them up and which America did not present at all. London, Paris, and Rome—and in their special way the university towns of Germany—remained the magnetic capitals of civilization. London was politics and society, Paris was art and light, Rome was the corrupt face upon the purest or at any rate the most ancient vein of the European tradition. It was not only Americans who felt the magnetic attraction; the rest of Europe was drawn to the same centers, more to Paris than to Rome, more to Rome than to London. Only the American was drawn culturally to London because of his special ancestral craving for the Old Home. The British themselves were drawn like the Russians and the Spanish and the Scandinavians to Paris and Rome and the international resorts.

This account is of course a simplification; it is accurate only of tendencies along which social patterns shifted, and these tendencies may be thought of as directed by the double rise of economic and "scientific" power without a corresponding rise in political and cultural powers. At any rate the cultural and political intelligence of man seemed unequal to controlling or understanding the actual changes which great access of economic and physical power had brought about in society. But society reacts to the forces which shape it whether consciously or not, and it makes symbolic gestures to affirm its reaction. We may risk saying then that society began to make the experiment of setting up cultural capitals separate from political and economic capitals. America was rich enough and energetic enough to help the experiment along with certain of its chosen or prodigal sons whom in giving it tended to cast off. In doing so, America only ratified the general heresy of the late nineteenth and twentieth century that the arts and learning can be divorced from the power and the resources of society without danger to both.

The danger involved is social impotence. When the divorce reaches its greatest extent—it is never complete—the economic power distrusts first the cultural power and second the political power; the political power tends to submit to the economic because it has no cultural assurance to confirm its policy; and the cultural power either refuses contact with both politics and economics or whores after both in the dark. The relation between what was meant by the symbols of New York, London, and Paris during the 1920's and 1930's makes a paradigm of the disintegrations which followed the divorce. More important, the relation during the fifty years from 1870 to 1920 within the American experience, taken separately, between the businessman, the statesman or politician, and the artist or scholar, suggests that, *at least on the conscious level,* the same disintegrative disease was prevalent within the unit of society. What was happening unconsciously, what was really happening, is another matter; the unity of culture is not killed by attitudes and relations, but it is made impotent, and it is the impotence with which we are concerned. The expatriate as a class was the extreme or hysterical symptom of the general disorder; he was held in contempt by the businessman, ignored by the statesman or politician, and regarded with either hatred or envy by the artistic or scholarly man who had to stay at home.

In each case the attitude toward the expatriate was justified. He *was* contemptible, ignominious, and treasonable from every nationalistic point of view; he was in fact an anti-nationalistic phenomenon in the supreme age of economic nationalism. That he was also a product of the same economic nationalism made only the more excuse to mistreat and misunderstand him—especially if he came or stayed at home and practiced ingrown expatriation like Melville or Ryder or Dickinson or Adams, who by silence, remoteness, moral isolation, or enriched irony reacted to the scene from which the others fled. The only form of artist or scholar the economic nationalist could tolerate was the dilettante or freak who had the sanction of conspicuous waste. There were exceptions: Whitman had the advantage of scandal and Mark Twain had the prestige of the clown, but each was treated, not as an artist or a great man (let alone with tolerance or indifference), but with the fickle alternation of privilege and obloquy usually afforded to commercial entertainers, to the dilettanti of low life. America was, as Van Wyck Brooks observed, not mature enough for poetry.

But the expatriate was justified also. One of the reasons that he went abroad was because of his delusion that the American view that culture *belonged* abroad and could be *brought* from abroad was right; and another reason was in his corresponding illusion that the symbols of full social unity—and those listed by James will do—were actually sustained by an existing and developing tradition. Sometimes the two reasons impelled the same individual—perhaps William Wetmore Story was an example, with his sculpture and living poetry in Rome; but generally speaking there were, in the period between the Civil War and the First World War, distinct classes of expatriates who based their flight either on one reason or the other. In the one class were the refined "men of the world" who sought neither to discover living culture nor (James's phrase) "to re-ascend the stream of time," but who sought to be exiled, to be strangers in a far land, and sweetly to do nothing; that is to say, they wanted to be men of the world divorced from the world. Since they needed a situation where privileged waste could be exchanged for money with no loss but a gain in the sense of occupation, they were drawn to Europe and became the living representatives of all that is dead in the general idea of culture. The later version of this class may be seen in the coveys of zombies who hustled back to the United States from France and Italy in 1939 and 1940 and settled in the neighborhood of the Ritz, the Modern Museum, and the proper, sheltered shores of Long Island.

The other class, which banked on the existence of "Europe," if not less numerous was less conspicuous: they went abroad for ideas, for growth, for work, and went as men have always done where the chance of those riches was propitious, where the conditions were tolerable, and where acceptance at potential value seemed possible. If most of them did not succeed abroad, neither would most of them have escaped failure had they stayed at home. The best of them knew that success in the great affairs of the mind was providential, but they knew also that they had to help themselves as far as possible into the general situation where on the evidence providence was most likely to strike. They made a gamble where if they won they had an exile in honor and if they lost an exile in defeat, but in any case an exile in the end. Your serious expatriates are like the Swiss a kind of nation of exiles who cannot exist without Paris or Rome, or like the Jews who have a culture in many lands but no nation of their own so that they swarm by second choice to the cultural capitals of the world as if, always, it might be the everlasting home they seek—as indeed some day, if the human race is to succeed, it must be.[2]

In short, the American expatriate through the First World War was either a waste product thrown off like a rash on the face of the economic system or he was a serious and significant phenomenon—and the more so when he failed—of the disintegration consequent upon the division of function in the social system of the Western world. If he idled, he idled with less need of apology in Europe; if he worked, like as not he worked in Europe because he felt that elsewhere he could not work at all. In point of fact, both most of the idlers and most of the workers returned to their native country and served to transmit and circulate ideas—either the "European" idea or the idea gained through revulsive reaction to "Europe," or some combination of the two. Perhaps we may say that in the American experience of this period the expatriate as a type—whether he returned or not—almost uniquely served a major social function; almost alone as a class he made it possible for America to see the disorder and the confusion and the rich possibilities of the world of which America was a continuing and emergent part. And he had, too, the subtler function of re-establishing that pattern of thought which had been lost since the time of Jackson and buried since the death of Emerson, that recognizes that culture, that politics, that economics even, cannot exist and grow in one place alone.

But in a later manifestation the American expatriate had still another function, rising from still another difficulty. During the twelve years between the First World War and the world depression, the increasing numbers of young Americans who sold dollars at high prices in francs, lire, pesos, and marks—and at a smaller profit in pounds—had, it seems to me, as their clearest function to show that nowhere in the world was there a society that believed either in the enterprise of culture or in the adequacy of human

[2] The nation of Israel does not seem to me to serve this purpose—or not yet; its vitality, like its nationalism, depends on too many remote contingencies.

intelligence to cope with human life. That is, he pointed to the consequence of the division of political and economic and artistic powers in Western society by living a life and producing an art as far as possible without meaning to a wide audience and as far as possible without resort to the intelligence. I do not refer to the great exceptions nor to the great masses, but to the run of the mill *valuta* expatriates of the arts and the bars who joined movements and lived lives which were deliberately forced to a maximum unavailability to the society which produced them. They were an accidental result of the dysfunction of society known as *valuta:* speculation on an unstable, unrelated, and inflationary exchange depending on a European political situation which alternated between violence and the apathy of dissolution. It was not the men so much as the arts themselves that had become expatriated. Extreme examples may be found in the American group which attached itself to The Black Sun Press of Harry Crosby, whose relation to society was expressed in black magic and the Black Mass, or in the group which inhabited the later pages of the magazine *transition,* for in that journal was found the Revolution of the Word, which deprived words as far as possible of their history and their idiom and aimed at a free polymorphism of spontaneous expression. *Valuta* was counterfeit.

With the New York crash of 1929 the supply of bad currency dried up and a great many of the expatriates had to return, I will not say to sound money, but to a kind of severely reactionary Marxist currency at first, and later, with the war, either to a blinkered nationalism or to a distrustful, self-persecuted moral isolation. But through these shifts there persisted, whether in the same men and women or in others who followed them, all that the expatriates of the 'twenties had so sharply symbolized: the inability to believe either in the dignity of the cultural enterprise or in the power of human intelligence. In fact, the depression and the war have only made clearer the significance of the true inward expatriation of the larger figures—the men who make the study and the clarification of coteries and their snobberies and agonies either possible or desirable. The cult of expatriation, and a cult is what it had become, may be said to represent the worst difficulty the modern artist has in his relation to society.

This brings us to our second argument. The first argument, to repeat, is that what we call expatriation is a natural consequence of living in a country which does not have a great cultural capital and in a world where the cultural, political, and economic capitals are not the same. The second argument represents the inevitable difficulties of the artist in making and maintaining his attachments to the institutions of such a world. It is along the lines of this argument, with the presence of the first argument for external aids and props, that the inward expatriation of such figures as Hawthorne, James, Whistler, and Eliot can be made plain.

But to begin with, let us get rid of the demon of external expatriation. Hawthorne, of course, never remained abroad, and his attempt to live in the Old Home was a failure, as, in a sense, his attempt to live anywhere was a failure. He makes thus a good archetype of the kind of man who becomes an expatriate in the external sense without showing any of the accidental or secondary features. His society did not feed him either because of an unwillingness, an inability, or a disability within himself; and he had therefore to create a society in his imagination, which instead of enriching the values he found, asserted the values he could not find; but his creative powers being limited—except in *The Scarlet Letter* and a handful of tales—he was left in both his life and letters short-rationed. It was not that he repudiated anything American that he would not have repudiated in Europe, but that he could not find in America the values that he needed for his art. Neither, in the main, could Byron and Shelley find the values they needed in their England, nor Turgenev, for most of his life, in his Russia. All of these figures felt the absence of a cultural capital, the absence of the institutions of a cultural capital in absolute operation; but all succeeded, soon or late, in overcoming that absence to one degree or another. They had the quality, lacking in Hawthorne, which enabled them to create a capital within themselves corresponding somehow to the society outside themselves, or at any rate responding to it. So did Flaubert, with his hatred of the bourgeois whom he made his subjects; so did Dostoevski, with his inability on the practical level to accept any society at all; so did Baudelaire, even, with his positive sense of sin. Poor Hawthorne's luck was perhaps not bad enough to compel in him a positive reaction as it was not good enough to permit a positive assent. His unwillingness or disability remained all his life. Let us say then that his failure was the failure of human weakness in the individual rather than a failure of the artist in relation to society.

It is a very different matter when we come to Whistler and James and Eliot. Reaction in them was positive, and for each of them reaction meant a cumulative act of personal expatriation against which each of them struggled. In Whistler the struggle was not long and he came to an obvious conclusion: Art, he said, was international, and since he was all artist, where he was not all butterfly, he was himself, like one of his paintings, a kind of international arrangement, a modus vivendi, a persuasive pastiche good through the accident of its lasting. That true internationalism was something deeper than that, and depended on the fundamental unity rather than the superficial sameness of the arts, depended on the source rather than the execution, Whistler never suspected. He was safe in the aesthetics of the 'eighties, where men much smaller than he have been safe ever since, in the unconscious exile of art for art's sake. Of his essential attitude, Ezra Pound is a modern example, and, in the doctrine of his life rather than of his art, the James Joyce who wrote *Ulysses* is another only less complete example. Pound in Rapallo lost himself in one adventitious international "movement" after another, primarily because he did not have the ability to play the single role of Whistler, and was thus far more completely divorced from his audience as a poet and his society as a man. If Whistler was the expatriate as butterfly, Pound was the will-o'-the-wisp: the illusion is desperate only to those who follow, intelligible only to those who do not.

The positive reaction of Whistler and Pound, then, can be put as envelopment in illusion and the transformation of the illusion into a cult, almost a religion. James and Eliot made their positive reactions in different directions. Each attempted to seize, to understand, and to use the institutions of English society, the parallels to which they found tragically wanting in American society. Instead of adopting illusions wholesale, they struggled without end—Eliot is still struggling—to achieve them piecemeal. That they found, in Hopkins's phrase, piecemeal peace but poor peace, in short that the struggle can never end between society and the class of artist of which each is an illustrious example, is what made James, and seems likely to make Eliot, the permanent symbol of genuine expatriation. This is, to repeat once more, the expatriation which an artist—or any man—experiences to the degree that he feels the fundamental failure of coherence between the cultural, political, and economic energies of contemporary society, whether in his homeland or in the whole Western world.

This is to contend that the symbolic value of James and Eliot would most likely have been the same if they had stayed at home, and that their going abroad—their physical expatriation—only furnishes external drama, for themselves and for us, to bring out the value of their experience. The psychological reality of expatriation is not, then, American: Americans have no mortgage on the insights concerned; and we could as well have made our points in terms of the careers of Thomas Mann, Marcel Proust, André Gide, and James Joyce as James and Eliot. For the values of psychological expatriation have two main features, which are perhaps fundamental to all the arts at certain stages of their over-all relations to whole cultures, and it is these values—found alike but variously—in all the writers named, with which we are concerned.

There is the value connected with the relationship between the outsider and the insider, the unique and the representative, as groups and individuals feel it, which may be expressed, when it is an imbalance, in the outward act of expatriation. This is the case with both James and Eliot.

There is also the parallel value connected with the balance or imbalance between anarchy and order, the rebellion against or the reliance upon imposed external forms, whether cultural, political, or economic, in terms of which groups and individuals frame their response to society, and which again, when the imbalance is severe, may be expressed dramatically in expatriation. Both James and Eliot seem in the terms of their respective expatriations to symbolize such imbalances.

Throughout the work of both men the protagonists have tended to be cast as artists or saints or seers or men of an intelligence so high as to be generally unavailable; and in each case these figures have been presented both as outsiders to the world in which they lived and as desperately engaged in the effort to capture the sense of that world. Similarly, both men went abroad in a combination of rebellion against the institutions at home and in predisposed submission to the institutions they expected to find in Europe and particularly in England. And in the careers of both men a part of the drama is the gradual revelation of the corruptness and inadequacy of the institutions in which they hoped to find strength. James came to see through "society" and was compelled to retreat for an imaginative moral order upon a concept of the candor of the American soul which apparently rejected social institutions altogether so far as the individual was concerned; yet when the First World War came, he found himself plunged to the full back into the authoritative mystery of British institutions. With Eliot, the case seems to me little different. He too went abroad for British institutions, but judging by his journalism, he has had to a considerable degree to make them over for himself in order to make them tolerable, and has found himself arguing for Scottish nationalism and the disestablishment of the Church of England, for which, it once seemed, he had quite settled.

This is to say that the imbalance between the insider and the outsider, between anarchy and order, which both men felt in their lives, was never settled, but was left, rather, always teetering on the little fulcrum of the soul's balance, always precariously perched on the branch of consciousness just beyond reach but fascinating full attention. The struggle for balance, not balance but the struggle for it, preoccupied both, and became the major theme in the work of each as they dramatized it, hopefully or desperately, in expiation or in pride. The expatriation was almost exile. Perhaps we should think of Dante exiled from Florence, Villon with his murderous luck, and the deep-riven swindling chasm between perfection of life and perfection of work and the stresses between these in a society which, for whatever reason, leaves the soul exiled in its only home.

There is luckily a tale of Henry James and a play of T. S. Eliot which combine to produce a single image upon which our sense of the maximum drama possible to the struggle with expatriation, with exile, may be left to rest. In James's "The Jolly Corner" we have dramatized the homecoming of Spencer Brydon, an exile from New York—from economic America—who has been spending a rich life in the great world of Europe. It was his business affairs that brought him back, and once back he becomes obsessed by the possibility of what he might have become had he never gone away. The house in which he was born and in which he grew up—which the family called the Jolly Corner—is empty and about to be torn down to make room for the growth of the New York monster. With the image of the Jolly Corner always in mind, Brydon works up his obsession of what he might have been and begins to prowl from room to room of the house after midnight, stalking the big and dangerous game of his unrealized self. After a few nights he begins to feel that it is his unrealized self that is haunting, hunting, ambushing him. Finally he finds himself actually ambushed and forces himself to meet, at dawn, in the vestibule, his beast of prey. Its hands are raised over its face, and from one of the hands two fingers have been shot away. When the hands drop there is revealed the face of a stranger: evil, odious, blatant, vulgar, and mutilated; the figure overwhelms him and he collapses. Though he recovers, later, and his other self has been exorcised, we have to remember, for the significance and the drama of it, that the other self has been in him, unrealized, all his life long, and that he could never assent to it except as intolerable, which is no assent at all. Yet it was part of the whole man, made monstrous only, it is possible to think, by the imbalance of the society which he represented. The monster had lived, so to speak, in the Jolly Corner of Brydon's happy childhood all his life long.

Eliot's play, *The Family Reunion,* deals, as its title indicates, with the return of a man to his family after a long absence. Unlike James's tale, however, it is not an American who returns to his home and makes an exorcism by the power of imagination; it is an English nobleman who returns to his mother's country house—the deserted temple of dead institutions—to find himself driven out and on by the Furies—the Eumenides—whom he had brought with him. The play could have as well been called The Family Destroyed, for when the protagonist, Harry, Lord Monchensey, departs to renew his inexplicable mission of expiation in exile, it is the family, the whole institution of British society, that has collapsed, though it has not, as in James's tale, been exorcised: it is perhaps one of the Furies pursuing Harry.

But there is in the first part of the play one speech in which James's and Eliot's versions of the theme of spiritual expatriation become united. It is Harry's Aunt Agatha who speaks out of her special knowledge. Wishwood, with its Dantesque overtone, is the name of the country house in which the family reunites and collapses. Agatha and Harry's mother have been arguing as to whether Harry will find anything changed, and for Agatha it is everything that will be changed even though and because everything will be the same.

Yes. I mean that at Wishwood he will find another Harry.
The man who returns will have to meet
The boy who left. Round by the stables,
In the coach-house, in the orchard,
In the plantation, down the corridor
That led to the nursery, round the corner
Of the new wing, he will have to face him—
And it will not be a very *jolly* corner.
When the loop in time comes—and it does not come for everybody—
The hidden is revealed, and the spectres show themselves.

F. O. Matthiessen, in his *American Renaissance* [3] supplies two lines from Eliot's manuscript which should be read just after the phrase "*jolly* corner."

> I am sorry, Gerald, for making an allusion
> To an author whom you never heard of.

In the context, Matthiessen has been demonstrating the connections between Hawthorne and James. "Certainly there is no question of any specific debts to Hawthorne at this point, but of a fundamental reassertion of kinship in moral values, which defied for both writers any merely realistic presentation." [4] The reader is referred to the whole chapter on Hawthorne and James for material which, from

[3] Page 295 n.
[4] *Ibid.*, p. 294.

another point of view, illustrates the strength and continuity of the themes which rise from spiritual expatriation or exile through the work of the two novelists into the poetry of Eliot.

The search, the struggle, which James and Eliot pursued in England for the strength and solace and the comfortable words of old and living institutions, came, if this account is correct, to no more than the outward and personal dramatization of their inward and inevitable experience which they made objective and permanently symbolic in their art. If we exclude from consideration what seems the physical accident of alien citizenship, I think we can see clearly that their lives and their works were neither eccentric nor escapist, but orthodox and direct in their seizure of a theme which has been both fundamental and inevitable, as well as tragic, in the European and American world since 1860 or 1870. It was merely the newness of the country, the doubtfulness of its experiment, and the relative absence in it of formalized institutions, that made the American experience of cultural, political, and economic imbalance more consciously anguished. That this same Western world is now pressing upon us the opportunity to make a society where these forces reach a balance and to which artists cannot help giving assent as a whole, will never prevent individual artists returning to the theme of inward dissent and dismay, for that theme will always represent one aspect, if he can be but persuaded to see it, of every individual's actual experience.

1944

6

The Expense of Greatness

THREE EMPHASES ON HENRY ADAMS

Where your small man is a knoll to be smoothed away, Henry Adams is a mountain to be mined on all flanks for pure samples of human imagination without loss of size or value. That is the double test of greatness, that it show an attractive force, massive and inexhaustible, and a disseminative force which is the inexhaustible spring or constant declaration of value. As we elucidate our reaction to the two forces we measure the greatness.

In Adams the attractive force is in the immediate relevance that his life and works have for our own. The problems he posed of human energy and human society are felt at once to be special and emphatic articulations of our own problems. The disseminative, central force, which we find objectified in his works, may be felt and seen as the incandescence of the open, enquiring, sensitive, and skeptical intelligence, restless but attentive, saltatory but serial, provisional in every position yet fixed upon a theme: the theme of thought or imagination conceived as the form of human energy. We feel the incandescence in the human values and aspirations that were fused by it, from time to time, in persuasive form; and the cumulus of his life and works makes a focus, different as differently felt, whereby the particular values actually rendered shine concentrated as it were in their own best light. We make the man focus upon himself, make him achieve—as he never could for himself in the flux and flexion of life—his own most persuasive form. To make such a focus is the labor and the use of critical appreciation.

The approaches to such a labor are varied and must be constantly renewed and often revised. No single approach is omniscient or even sufficient. Here, in this essay, I want to take Henry Adams in a single perspective and submit it to three related emphases. I want to regard him as he often chose to regard himself, as a representative example of education: but education pushed to the point of failure as contrasted with ordinary education which stops at the formula of success.

The perspective is worth a preliminary emphasis of its own. It was as failure both in perspective and lesson by lesson that Adams himself saw his education. Success is not the propitious term for education unless the lesson wanted is futile. Education has no term and if arrested at all is only arrested by impassable failure. Surely the dominant emotion of an education, when its inherent possibilities are compared with those it achieved, must strike the honest heart as the emotion of failure. The failure is not of knowledge or of feeling. It is the failure of the ability to react correctly or even intelligently to more than an abbreviated version of knowledge and feeling: failure in the radical sense that we cannot consciously react to more than a minor fraction of the life we yet deeply know and endure and die. It is the failure the mind comes to ultimately and all along when it is compelled to measure its knowledge in terms of its ignorance.

Most failures we have the tact to ignore or give a kinder name. That is because we know by instinct at what a heavy discount to put most proffered examples of failure. There was no effort of imagination in them and only private agony, where for great failure we want the utmost unrelenting imagination and the impersonal agony of knowledge searching the haven of objective form. Most failures come too easily, take too little stock of the life and forces around them: like the ordinary failure in marriage, or business, or dying; and so too much resemble the ordinary success—too solemn and scant and zestless for realization. A genuine failure comes hard and slow, and, as in a tragedy, is only fully realized at the end. A man's success is in society, precarious and fatal; his failure is both in spite and because of society—as he witnesses its radical imperfection and is himself produced by it, its ultimate expression. Thus in a great man we often find inextricably combined the success which was his alone, though posthumously recognized, with the failure which as we feel it is also our own in prospect.

Let us take for our first emphasis Adams as a failure in society. If we assume that an education means the acquisition of skills and the mastery of tools designed for intelligent reaction in a given context, it will appear that Adams's failure in American political society after the Civil War was a failure in education. Society was bound for quick success and cared only for enough intelligence to go on with. It cared nothing for political mastery, and commonly refused to admit it had a purpose beyond the aggregation of force in the form of wealth. The effect on Adams as a young man was immediate but took time to recognize. If *vis inertiae* was enough for society, any education was too much; and an Adams—with the finest education of his times—was clearly useless. The question was perhaps not initially of Adams's failure but of society's inability to make use of him: its inability to furnish a free field for intelligent political action. Washington was full of wasted talent—of able young men desperately anxious to be of use—as it is now; but no one knows what talent might accomplish, then or now, because talent has never been given a chance without being at the same moment brutally hamstrung.

The discovery—that he was to be wasted whether he was any good or not—was all the bitterer to Henry Adams because he had three generations of conspicuous ability and conspicuous failure behind him. Every Adams had ended as a failure after a lifetime of effort—marked by occasional and transitory success—to handle political power intelligently. Their intelligence they had kept; none had ever succumbed to the criminal satisfaction of power on its lowest terms—whether power for interest, or, worst of all, power for its own sake: the absolute corruption, as it seems to a scrupulous mind, of giving in; but all equally had failed at the height of their abilities. If times had changed for Henry it was for the worse. Where his ancestors found in a combination of scruple and temper an effective termination of useful public careers, Henry found his scruple alone enough to preclude a public career altogether. Scruple is sometimes only a name for snobbery, stiffness, or even an inner coldness—all, forms of disability; but in an Adams scruple was the mark of ability itself, and its limit, as it made intelligence acute, responsible, and infinitely resourceful, but a little purblind to the advantage of indirection. An Adams could meet an issue, accept facts, and demonstrate a policy, but he could never gamble with a public matter. Jefferson's epitaph for John applied to them all: as disinterested as his maker. If the odds grew heavy against an Adams he resorted to an access of will—or, if you choose to call it, a wall of stubbornness, which is merely will grown hysterical. But acts of will or stubbornness are merely the last resorts of minds compelled to act scrupulously against the unintelligent or the unintelligible.

Thus it is that many great men, if seen as examples of intellectual biography, seem either sports or parasites upon the society that produced them. They were compelled to act against or outside it; and our sense of radical connection and expressive identity is only reestablished in the examples of their works aside from their lives. Certainly something of the sort is true, with different emphases, of Whitman, Mark Twain, Henry James, Melville, and in our own day of Hart Crane and George Santayana. They stand out too much from their native society: all outsiders from the life they expressed and upon which they fed. If all knew the ignominy of applause, applause from the wrong people, for the wrong thing, or for something not performed at all, it only accented their own sense of eccentricity and loneliness. That is how Adams stood out, but without much applause ignominious or otherwise, eccentric and lonely; but within him, as within the others in their degrees, was an intelligence whose actions were direct, naked, and at their best terrifyingly sane.

If, as I think, it was the scruple of his mind that made Adams an outsider and that at the same time gave precise value to his eccentricity, then the scruple should be defined both for itself and in terms of Adams. It is what I have been deviously leading up to: as it represents the single heroic and admirable quality of the modern and skeptical mind as such; and a quality not called for by the occasion but crowning it, even when disastrously.

Scruple, generally speaking, is the agent of integrity, what keeps action honest on the level of affairs, or on the level of imagination when actuality or truth is the object. The etymology of the word refreshes the meaning I emphasize, where we have the Latin *scrupulus,* a small sharp stone, a stone in one's shoe, an uneasiness, difficulty, small trouble, or doubt. Scruples differ with the type of mind and education. Most men either get rid of them or show pride in their calluses. In either case the process of thought is made easy and reaction insensitive; you give in, you are practically carried along, but you get nowhere except where you are taken, and you know nothing at all of what you have been through, or of its meaning.

Specifically, with Henry Adams, scruple of thinking and thence of action was the whole point of his education for public life. Men without scruples either victimized power or succumbed to it; and if you had the wrong scruples you succumbed, like Grant, without knowing it. Political education was meant to supply the right scruples at the start, to teach sensitiveness to new ones as they came up, and to ingrain a habit of feeling for them if not apparent. It is scruples that compel attention to detail and subordinate the detail to an end. When excess, whether of scruples or the lack of them, atrophies the mind, it is because either an impossible end or no end was in view. In science the adjudication of scruples is called method and taken for granted; but the whole test of the democratic process is whether or not the seat of power attracts the scrupulous intelligence and gives it rein. Here we may conceive Henry Adams as a provisional focus for that test.

In a sense no test is possible. Adams never held office. He only made himself embarrassingly available in the near background of Grant's Washington. Power was what he wanted, but on his own terms: the terms of his training. Perhaps he offered too much; perhaps his offers seemed too much like demands; at any rate he got nothing. But if we take him as a type—whether of 1868 or 1932—we can see that he was in the predicament of all young men whose abilities seem to lie in public life but who refuse waste motion. Society has no use for them as they are, and the concessions it requires are fatal to self-respect and taste, and lead either to futility, the treason of submission, or an aching combination of the two.

Both Adams and society saw politics was a game, but the difference in their angles of vision made their views irreconcilable. Adams saw the game as played impersonally with, as ultimate stake, the responsible control of social energy. Since ultimate value was never sure, every move ought to be made with the maximum intelligence and subject to every criticism your experience provided. If you stuck scrupulously to your intelligence you had the chance to come out right in the end under any scruples, democratic or not. You had a chance to put your society in control of itself at the center of its being. That was Adams's idea of the game, the idea of any honest young man.

Society played differently. The stake was immediate power, the values were those of personal interest. Thus the actual stake—control of social energy—was left for the ventures of interests irresponsible to the government meant to control them. Society in its political aspect cared more for chaos than unity; and the democratic process was an unconfessed failure, obliviously committing itself to social anarchy. Yet the failure remained unconfessed; the society lived and gathered energy; it was omnivorous, rash, and stupid; it threatened to become uncontrollably leviathan; it seemed occasionally on the point of committing suicide in the full flush of life. Always it had been saved, so far, by its vitality, its prodigious capacity for successive ruination, or by the discovery of a new and available source of power.

There was the young man's predicament. Should he assume that society was no field for intelligence and that its own momentum was sufficient to its needs? Should he rather enter the field, outwardly playing society's version of the game, while inwardly playing his own as best he could? Or should he work on society from the outside, accepting his final defeat at the start, and express the society rather than attempt to control it?

The first choice is the hardest; taken mostly by weak minds, it resembles more the dullness of indifference than disconsolate impartiality. Most men of ability, fortunately, make the second choice; it is they that make the administration of society possible and intermittently tolerable. Individually, most of them disappear, either lose office or succumb to it; but the class is constantly replenished from the bottom. A few survive the struggle in their own identity, and these are the ideals the young men hope to cap. J. Q. Adams was one of these, Gallatin and Schurz are clearly two more, as Senators Walsh and Norris make two examples for our own day. Men like Cleveland and Theodore Roosevelt are partial survivals. Adams thought his friend John Hay not only survived but succeeded in establishing a sound foreign policy; history is a harsher judge than friendship. As a general thing promise in politics not only dies early but is resurrected in the corruption of party or unwitting interest, which is what happened to Adams's friend Lodge. For the most part Adams's reiterated sentiment remains apt: "A friend in power is a friend lost." Small men might pass unnoticed to honorable graves but the great were lost.

Henry Adams lacked the dimensions suitable to a small man in public life and lacked the coarseness of will and ability to dissimulate to seize the larger opportunity, had it offered. Hence he made gradually the third choice, and brought the pressure of all the education he could muster upon society from the outside. It took him seven to ten years to make the choice complete. The first form of pressure he exerted was that of practical political journalism, of which the principal remaining results are the essays on "The New York Gold Conspiracy," "The Session, 1869-1870," and the essay on American financial policy called "The Legal-Tender Act." The second form of pressure was also practical, and combined the teaching of history at Harvard with the editorship of *The North American Review*. Already, however, the emphasis of his mind was becoming imaginative and speculative. Seven years in Cambridge taught him the impossibility of affecting society to any practical extent through the quarterly press, or through any press at all. Two of his essays were made campaign documents by the Democrats—their import reduced to the level of vituperative rhetoric—and then forgotten; so that by the test of the widest publication possible their practical effect was nil. There remained a third form of pressure not so much indirect as remote, and that was pressure by the imaginative expression, through history and fiction and philosophy, of social character and direction; and the aim was to seize the meaning of human energy by defining its forms and to achieve, thus, if it was possible, a sense of unity both for oneself and one's society.

Expression is a form of education, and the form that was to occupy the rest of Adams's life, the subject of our second emphasis. Put another way, society had failed to attract Adams to its center, and Adams undertook to see whether or not he could express a center for it. Unity or chaos became the alternative lesson of every effort. Here we have gone over or climbed up to a second level of failure, which is the failure of the human mind, pushed to one of its limits, to solve the problem of the meaning, the use, or the value of its own energy: in short the failure to find God or unity. What differentiates Adams's mind from other minds engaged in the same effort is his own intense and progressive recognition of his failure; and that recognition springs from the same overload of scruples that made him eccentric to the society that produced him. What he did not recognize was the ironical consolation that the form his work took as a whole was itself as near the actual representative of unity as the individual mind can come; which is what we have now to show.

Henry Adams's mind acquired, as his work stretched out, a singular unity of conception and a striking definiteness of form. It was the idiosyncrasy of his genius to posit unity in multiplicity, and by exploring different aspects of the multiplicity to give the effect, known to be false or specious but felt as true, of apprehending the unity. In reading *The Life of Albert Gallatin,* so successfully is the effect of Gallatin's career composed, we have to think twice before realizing that it is meant to show one aspect in the story of the failure of the democratic process to unite American society. Published in 1879, when Adams was forty-one, it so well struck the theme of Adams's whole career that it can be bracketed with Adams's own autobiography and be called "The Education of Albert Gallatin."

As important here, striking his theme gave Adams his first mature prose. The previous essays had been comparatively metallic, brittle, and rhetorical, and carried a tone of intermittent assertiveness rather than of cumulative authority. It was the subject perhaps that matured the style: Gallatin was the best in character, ability, and attainment that American history had to offer. At any rate, the biography of John Randolph, which came in 1882 and portrayed the worst waste in ability and personal disintegration in American history, showed a reversion to the earlier immature style. If Adams was, as Hay said, half angel and half porcupine, then it was altogether the porcupine that got into this book. The tragedy of Randolph was personal eccentricity, his constant resorts hysteria and violence, and Adams brought those elements over into his own style. Later, in his History, Adams repaired his injustice and treated him with charity of understanding, as an energetic sample of his times.

Meanwhile and just afterwards, in 1880 and 1884, Adams published his two novels, *Democracy* and *Esther*. These suffer about equally from Adams's incompetence as a novelist, and the reader can take them best as brilliant documentary evidence of Adams's insights and preoccupations. To intrude the standards of the art of fiction would be to obviate the burden the books actually carry. *Democracy* exhibits a political society full of corruption, irresponsible ambition, and stupidity, against the foil of a woman's taste and intelligence. So brilliant and light is Adams's execution, it is hard to decide which vice is worst of the three.

Madeleine Lee, Adams's foil, is struck a heavy blow in the face by her first and only presidential reception. She stands fascinated and aghast at the endless wooden procession. "What a horrid warning to ambition! And in all that crowd there was no one beside herself who felt the mockery of this exhibition. To all the others this task was a regular part of the President's duty, and there was nothing ridiculous about it." It was Adams, not Mrs. Lee, who felt the full force of the blow. He remembered what he had seen at Devonshire House a few years back when Madame de Castiglione, the famous beauty of the Second Empire, entered.

How beautiful she may have been, or indeed what sort of beauty she was, Adams never knew, because the company, consisting of the most refined and aristocratic society in the world, instantly formed a lane, and stood in ranks to stare at her, while those behind mounted on chairs to look over their neighbors' heads; so that the lady walked through the polite mob, stared completely out of countenance, and fled the house.

In *Democracy,* Mrs. Lee received a second blow, which we may obscurely feel as a consequence of the first, when, after his corruption is discovered to her and she taxes him with it, her suitor, Secretary of the Treasury Ratcliffe, defends himself by minimizing his offense, passing it off as commonplace, and asks her to purify American politics through marriage to him and with his aid.

The audacity of the man would have seemed sublime if she had felt sure that he knew the difference between good and evil, between a lie and the truth; but the more she saw of him, the surer she was that his courage was mere moral paralysis, and that he talked about virtue and vice as a man who is color-blind talks about red and green; he did not see them as she saw them; if left to choose for himself he would have nothing to guide him.

Which blow was the harder to bear? Was corruption, like stupidity, only an atrophied form of intelligence? Given the system and the society, did not the practice of politics necessarily produce one form or the other?

Adams himself did not feel the full force of the second blow until twenty years later when Theodore Roosevelt inherited office from McKinley. Secretary Ratcliffe in *Democracy* was the archetype of all he hated and Roosevelt represented an approximation of a good deal he admired. Ratcliffe was about the worst you got and Roosevelt was the best you could expect. But the lesson the two men taught about the disease of power was much the same, however they taught it on different levels. At heart Roosevelt, as a type, was more source of despair than Ratcliffe.

Power is poison. Its effects on Presidents had always been tragic, chiefly as an almost insane excitement at first, and a worse reaction afterwards; but also because no mind is so well balanced as to bear the strain of seizing unlimited force without habit or knowledge of it; and finding it disputed with him by hungry packs of wolves and hounds whose lives depend on snatching the carrion. Roosevelt enjoyed a singularly direct nature and honest intent, but he lived naturally in restless agitation that would have worn out most tempers in a month, and his first year of Presidency showed chronic excitement that made a friend tremble. The effect of unlimited power on limited mind is worth noting in Presidents because it must represent the same process in society, and the power of self-control must have limit somewhere in face of the control of the infinite.

"Here," Adams goes on, "education seemed to see its first and last lesson." Certainly it is part of the lesson of the second Roosevelt as well as of the first; and certainly it is a lesson that in one form or another can be drawn not only from Presidents, but from every concentration of power in single hands. Power is greater than the hands that hold it and compels action beyond any tolerable volition. No wonder men make a game of it, as they make mathematics of time and space, since it is only as converted into a game that the experience of fatal struggles is commonly found tolerable.

But the lesson had other forms, as the energy it attempted to express took other forms than the political. There is the well of character, the abyss of science, and the aspiring form of religion, all expressions of human energy, and a wakened and scrupulous mind was compelled to respond to them all. Experience is only separated into its elements in the *tour de force* of expression, and as in *Democracy* Adams separated the bottom level of political experience, in *Esther* he separated the highest level of religious experience he could find in America and measured it against the response of a woman's intelligence. The question asked and the lesson to be learned were simple and fundamental and desperate. Assuming the Christian insight in its highest contemporary form, could the Church supply a sense of unity, of ultimate relation with God or the sum of energy, to which intelligence could respond? If the Church couldn't —and the Church had no other motive for being—nothing else could, and the soul was left on its own and homeless. Or so it seemed to Adams; hence the desperateness of the question; and hence the disproportionate importance relative to its achievement that Adams himself assigned to the book. Writing to John Hay from Japan in 1886, he suggests that it was written in his heart's blood, and again to Elizabeth Cameron from Papeete five years later, he says: "I care more for one chapter, or any dozen pages of 'Esther' than for the whole history, including maps and indexes." The nine-volume history represented the predicament of the society he had abandoned, and *Esther* represented his own predicament in relation to that God or unity the hope of which he could never in his heart altogether abandon. Like Spinoza, Adams was god-intoxicated, like Pascal god-ridden. His heart's hope was his soul's despair.

That the responding intelligence in *Esther* as in *Democracy* should have been a woman's, only reflects a major bias of Adams's imagination. Women, for Adams, had instinct and emotion and could move from the promptings of the one to the actualities of the other without becoming lost or distraught in the midway bog of logic and fact. Impulse proceeded immediately to form without loss of character or movement. More than that, women had taste; taste was what held things together, showing each at its best, and making each contribute to a single effect. Thus the argument of a woman's taste dissipated every objection of logic, and at its highest moments made illogicality itself part of its natural charm. Taste was the only form of energy sure enough of itself—as all non-human energies may be—to afford beauty; elsewhere the rashest extravagance.

Thus Adams tried everywhere to answer great questions in terms of a woman's taste and intelligence. Who else but Esther Dudley could form the center of the book she named? Only the strength of her instinct could accept the Church if it showed itself alive, and only the courage of her taste could reject it if it proved dead or a shell. That she might be confused in instinct and unconscious of her taste, only made the drama more vivid and its outcome more desperate. The problem was hers, but an artist could help her solve it, and perhaps a scientist, too, if he felt the struggle as an artist feels it. So Wharton, the artist, puts the question to her and answers it. "It all comes to this: is religion a struggle or a joy? To me it is a terrible battle, to be won or lost." The object of the battle is Nirvana or paradise. "It is eternal life, which, my poet says, consists in seeing God." The poet is Petrarch, and his words: *Siccome eterna vita è veder dio.* Strong, the scientist, for his part tells her: "There is no science that does not begin by requiring you to believe the incredible. I tell you the solemn truth that the doctrine of the Trinity is not so difficult to accept for a working proposition as any one of the axioms of physics." Between them—between art as it aspires to religion and science that springs from the same occult source—Esther might have been able to accept religion as that great form of poetry which is the aspiration of instinct and informs the whole of taste; but the Church itself, in the person of the Reverend Mr. Hazard, her lover, failed her both in persuasiveness and light. Power in politics and pride in the Church were much alike.

The strain of standing in a pulpit is great. No human being ever yet constructed was strong enough to offer himself long as a light to humanity without showing the effect on his constitution. Buddhist saints stand for years silent, on one leg, or with arms raised above their heads, but the limbs shrivel, and the mind shrivels with the limbs.

There is a kind of corruption in the best as well as the worst exemplars of each—which I suppose the Church would admit sooner than the state; a corruption in each case that makes for the self-falsifying effort of fanaticism. Hazard in his last argument appeals neither to instinct, intelligence, nor taste; he appeals to Esther's personal desperation and fear and so shows the ruination of emptiness within him. Esther can only answer him from the depth of revolted taste. "Why must the church always appeal to my weakness and never to my strength! I ask for spiritual life and you send me back to my flesh and blood as though I were a tigress you were sending back to her cubs." Although she loves him, the inadequacy of his church to its own purpose compels her to dismiss him, but neither for science nor for art, but for despair. That is the blood in which the book was written.

As *Democracy* foreshadowed the major theme of the *Education,* the theme of *Esther* is given deeper expression throughout *Mont-Saint-Michel,* and, as well, in at least one place in the *Education. Esther* is a representation of the failure in fact of American society to find God in religion. As he grew older, especially after the tragic death of his wife, and felt more and more that society had abandoned him, Adams grew more preoccupied with the ultimate failure of imagination itself, as illustrated in every faculty of the mind, than with the mere indicative failure of fact. Not facts which could be met but their meanings which could not be escaped were his meat. The meaning of *Esther* is intensified and made an object of inexhaustible meditation in the meanings Adams found in the monument Saint-Gaudens made for his wife in Rock Creek Cemetery. Part of the meaning lay in its meaninglessness to most of those who saw it, and part in the horror of the clergy who saw in it their defeat instead of their salvation. In a letter, Adams gave the monument the same motto he had embedded in *Esther: Siccome eterna vita è veder dio;* you could, in a gravestone, if you had the will, see what life needed but never provided. In the *Education* Adams suggests that the monument mirrors to the beholder whatever faith he has.

In *Mont-Saint-Michel and Chartres* the problem of *Esther* is made at once more universal and more personal. There Adams made an imaginative mirror of his own effort toward faith in terms of the highest point of faith—that is, of effective unity—the world had ever seen: the Christianity of the great cathedrals and the great intellectual architecture of the schools. The Virgin dominated the cathedrals as a matter of course; and Saint Thomas dominated the schools by an effort of will; but without the Virgin the schools would merely have paltered, as the cathedrals would never have been built. The Virgin was pure energy and pure taste, as her spires and roses were pure aspiration. Adams's book is the story of her tragedy; not that she was destroyed or even denied, but that men no longer knew and loved her, so lost their aspiration with the benefit of her taste, and no longer felt any unity whatsoever. The Virgin herself is still there, "but looking down from a deserted heaven, into an empty church, on a dead faith." She no longer gave orders or answered questions, and without her the orders and answers of Saint Thomas were useless; and similarly, for Adams, the orders and answers of all later authorities.

Thus the education that led Adams to the Virgin was the greatest failure of all; the highest form of unity was, in effect, for the modern man, only the most impossible to recapture. Where Esther had very simply repulsed the church because it appealed only to her weakness, Adams was in the worse ail of having no strength with which to seize it when it called for all the strength there was: he had no faith, but only the need of it. The Virgin's orders were the best ever given; obeyed, they made life contribute to great art and shine in it; but he had nothing with which to accept her administration. Her answers to his problems were final; she was herself the cumulus and unity of energy, and she removed, by absorbing, all the contradictions of experience; but seven centuries of time had made life too complicated for the old answers to fit. The same energy would need a new form to give the same meaning.

The failure of education was the failure of the unity which it grasped; the pupil was left with a terrible and weary apprehension of ignorance. Thinking of the Virgin and of the Dynamo as equally inexplicable concentrations of energy, Adams was led into the last phase of his education in the application of the mechanical theory of the inevitable change of all energy from higher to lower forms. What he wrote may be found in the later chapters of the *Education,* and in his two essays "A Letter to Teachers" and "The Rule of Phase Applied to History." It was, I think, the theory of a desperate, weary mind, still scrupulous in desperation and passionately eager in weariness, in its last effort to feel—this time in nature herself—the mystery in energy that keeps things going. It was the religious mind applying to physics on exactly the same terms and with exactly the same honest piety that it applied to the Virgin.

The nexus between the two was shown in the need for either in that fundamental condition of the mind known as ennui; and Adams quotes Pascal, the great scrupulous mind of the seventeenth century.

> "I have often said that all the troubles of man come from his not knowing how to sit still." Mere restlessness forces action. "So passes the whole of life. We combat obstacles in order to get repose, and, when got, the repose is insupportable; for we think either of the troubles we have, or of those that threaten us; and even if we felt safe on every side, *ennui* would of its own accord spring up from the depths of the heart where it is rooted by nature, and would fill the mind with its venom."

Nature was full of ennui too, from star to atom. What drove it? What made energy change form in *this* direction and not that? Adams tried to find the answer in the second law of thermodynamics—the law that assumes the degradation of energy; the law which sees infinite energy becoming infinitely unavailable; and he tried hard to *feel* that law as accounting for change in human society. The attempt only put his ignorance on a new basis. As analogues, the laws of physics only made the human predicament less soluble because less tangible. You might learn a direction, but physics prevented you from feeling what moved.

Reason, in science, as Adams had discovered earlier in *Esther,* deserted you rather sooner than in religion; and the need of faith was more critical. Had Adams had the advantage of the development of the quantum theory from the thermal field to the whole field of physics, had he known that all change was to come to seem discontinuous and that nature was to reveal a new and profoundly irrational face, he would have given up his last effort before he began it. A *discontinuous* multiplicity cannot be transformed into unity except by emotional vision. Adams had earlier said it himself. "Unity is vision; it must have been part of the process of learning to see. The older the mind, the older its complexities, and the further it looks, the more it sees, until even the stars resolve themselves into multiples; yet the child will always see but one." In 1915 Adams wrote to Henry Osborn Taylor that "Faith not Reason goes beyond" the failure of knowledge, and added that he felt himself "in near peril of turning Christian, and rolling in the mud in an agony of human mortification." But he had not the faith; only the apprehension of its need which made him struggle toward it all his life.

Failure is the appropriate end to the type of mind of which Adams is a pre-eminent example: the type which attempts through imagination to find the meaning or source of unity aside from the experience which it unites. Some artists can be content with experience as it comes, content to express it in the best form at hand. Adams gives LaFarge as an instance. "His thought ran as a stream runs through grass, hidden perhaps but always there; and one felt often uncertain in what direction it flowed, for even a contradiction was to him only a shade of difference, a complementary color, about which no intelligent artist would dispute." Shakespeare is another instance. In such artists failure is incidental, a part of the experience expressed. But Adams, by attempting to justify experience and so to pass beyond it had like Milton and Dante to push his mind to the limit of reason and his feeling to the limit of faith. Failure, far from incidental, is integral to that attempt, and becomes apparent just so soon as reason falters and becomes abstract, or faith fails and pretends to be absolute. Aside from the question of magnitude, one difference between Adams and his prototypes is, to repeat once more, just this: that his scrupulous sophistication made him emphatically aware of his own failure; and this awareness is the great drive of his work.

Here is our third emphasis. The failure of Adams in society—or society's failure to use Adams—was perhaps self-evident when stated. The singular unity of Adams's subsequent efforts to express the unity he felt has, I hope, been indicated. There remains the question of Adams's special value in the light of his avowed failure. The value is double.

The greatness of the mind of Adams himself is in the imaginative reach of the effort to solve the problem of the meaning, the use, or the value of its own energy. The greatness is in the effort itself, in variety of response deliberately made to every possible level of experience. It is in the acceptance, with all piety, of ignorance as the humbled form of knowledge; in the pursuit of divers shapes of knowledge—the scientific, the religious, the political, the social and trivial—to the point where they add to ignorance, when the best response is silence itself. That is the greatness of Adams as a type of mind. As it is a condition of life to die, it is a condition of thought, in the end, to fail. Death is the expense of life and failure is the expense of greatness.

If there is a paradox here, or an irony hard to digest, it is not in the life experienced or the failure won, but in the forms through which they are conceived, in the very duplicity of language itself, in the necessarily equivocal character, earned by long use, of every significant word. Thought asks too much and words tell too much; because to ask anything is to ask everything, and to say anything is to ask more. It is the radical defect of thought that it leaves us discontented with what we actually feel—with what we know and do not know—as we know sunlight and surfeit and terror, all at once perhaps, and yet know nothing of them. Thought requires of us that we make a form for our knowledge which is personal, declarative, and abstract at the same time that we construe it as impersonal, expressive, and concrete. It is this knowledge that leads to the conviction of ignorance—to the positive ignorance which is the final form of contradictory knowledge; but it is the triumph of failure that in the process it snares all that can be snared of what we know.

The true paradox is that in securing its own ends thought cannot help defeating itself at every crisis. To think straight you must overshoot your mark. Orthodoxy of the human mind—the energy of society in its highest stable form—is only maintained through the absorption into it of a series of heresies; and the great heresy, surely, is the gospel of unity, whether it is asserted as a prime mover, as God, or, as in art, as the mere imposed unity of specious form. In adopting it for his own, Adams knew it for a heresy. Again and again he describes unifying conceptions as working principles; without them no work could be done; with them, even at the expense of final failure, every value could be provisionally ascertained. That is the value of Adams for us: the double value of his scrupulous attitude toward his unifying notions and of the human aspirations he was able to express under them. To feel that value as education is a profound deliverance: the same deliverance Adams felt in the Gothic Cathedral. "The delight of its aspiration is flung up to the sky. The pathos of its self-distrust and anguish of doubt is buried in the earth as its last secret." The principles asserted are nothing, though desperate and necessary; the values expressed because of the principles are everything. For Adams, as for everyone, the principle of unity carried to failure showed the most value by the way, and the value was worth the expense.

1936

7

The Everlasting Effort

A CITATION OF T. E. LAWRENCE

"Either forced good or forced evil will make a people cry out with pain."
—Feisal to Lawrence in *Seven Pillars.*

In thinking of T. E. Lawrence we are bound up in the web of action and event—of the war, the air force, the motorcycle—which made the man a legend while he yet lived, a myth, and almost a Cause, lost but lurking: as who should call a king great because his country perished during his reign. The fate of Arabia, of Europe, the no less irrelevant fate of Lawrence himself: these as they work together to the merest look of recognition make the image that goes before us—Will o' the Wisp if you will—in our present adventure, shared or imminent. Lawrence wrote it down himself in the introduction to the Oxford text of the *Seven Pillars of Wisdom:* "We were wrought up with ideas inexpressible and vaporous, but to be fought for. We lived many lives in those whirling campaigns, never sparing ourselves any good or evil: yet when we achieved and the new world dawned, the old men came out again and took from us our victory, and remade it in the likeness of the former world they knew. Youth could win, but had not learned to keep, and was pitiably weak against age. We stammered that we had worked for a new heaven and a new earth, and they thanked us kindly and made their peace. When we are their age no doubt we shall serve our children so." Lawrence wrote it down as a statement of fact, but on the advice of

Bernard Shaw omitted it from later editions; for Lawrence was docile, in the very measure of his scrupulousness, and in imagination as well as act, to those whom he admired. He walked always with pebbles in his boots.

But he put it down and we put it back. It is there: all the power—of persuasion, of enactment—that comes from the ability to put things down: the power without which Lawrence could not have become a legend or a myth, for without that power he could not have revealed his cause, its strength, its weakness, its necessity. At least he could not have done so in our Western world, however it may be in the East; for in the West the old men habitually obliterate every power short of the rational imagination: imagination rising from a Cause through the written word. Lawrence would have been made nothing or wholly falsified, as at the Peace Conference or in the newspapers, if he had not written a book. Whether fable or fact, there is justice in the tale that the first manuscript of the book was stolen from the train at Reading Station, presumptively by the agents of the old men, almost as soon as it had been written, in November 1919 when the old men had taken over the world again not to let it go: we may think they recognized with what, some day, policy could not cope. Which is so. The subtitle of the book calls it A Triumph. Lawrence may have meant it, ironically enough, as the liberation of the Arab nations; for us only the third step in irony is needed to make it mean the liberation of the actual, Arab and otherwise, by the imaginative power of the written word; for so only has it transpired.

Let us turn away from the action of event and policy, the plot of the book, and turn directly, as Henry James would say, for the sake of the moral involved, to the book itself: first to the prose style, the general means of the writer, then to the whole sensibility which it both enriches and feeds on. Event and policy will return; indeed, they will never have been absent, only abjured for the time being—as in the diagnosis of bodily ills and resources one abjures the personality one wishes to save, which yet inhabits the body, at the least look, pat and regardless.

It may be as well to begin with an emphasis upon Lawrence's own view of himself as a craftsman: his love of the minute mechanics of writing and his aspiration toward major form—toward what he called, along with many, the architecture of his book. The emphasis cries for plain citation. Here are a few sentences and phrases isolated from the letters, of which the first set deal with words.

That frenzied aching delight in a pattern of words that happen to run true. . . . My deepest satisfaction [is] in the collocation of words so ordinary and plain that they cannot mean anything to a book-jaded mind: and out of some such I can draw deep stuff. . . . Prose depends on a music in one's head which involuntarily chooses & balances the possible words to *keep tune* with the thought. The best passages in English prose all deal with death or the vanity of things, since that is a tune we all know, and the mind is set quite free to think while writing about it. . . . Only occasionally in things constantly dwelt upon, do you get an unconscious balance, & then you get a *spontaneous* and perfect arrangement of words to fit the idea, *as the tune*. Polishing is an attempt, by stages, to get to what should be a single combined stride. . . . The worst of being a habitual translator is that one gets in the way of trying to squeeze every sponge dry—and so few authors ever really *intend* all the content of their sponges. Words get richer every time they are deliberately used . . . but only when deliberately used: and it is hard to be conscious of each single word, and yet not at the same time self-conscious. . . . What you say about the emphasis I get on simple words like Moon or chocolate bisquits, mayn't it be partly because I do try & feel every article and emotion that comes into the book? I tie myself into knots trying to re-act everything, as I write it out. It's like writing in front of a looking-glass, and never looking at the paper, but always at the imaginary scene. That, and a trick of arranging words, so that the one I care for most is either repeated, or syllable-echoed, or put in a startling position.

So much for the craft of words. The citations are emphatic, it seems to me, of the high degree in which Lawrence was a deliberate craftsman. It is not easy to make the emphasis as plain with regard to the more formal aspects of craft, because the citations seldom appear in compact phrases or sentences. Any reader of the letters may find for himself instance after instance of Lawrence's effort to shape his books for sequence and balance and drama.

The chief labor that went into *The Mint,* for example, seems to have been the labor of rearranging its items so as to reach a satisfactory pattern. As it happens, there is one passage about *The Mint* compact and self-complete enough to quote. "You are right about the absence of flowers in *The Mint*. There is a severe beauty in some buildings, which would only be reduced if creepers were grown over them. I tried—deliberately—for that. You see, as I suppose every writer who reads it will see—how deliberate the construction and arrangement of *The Mint* is. I called its proportions the worst side of *The Seven Pillars:* and was determined that (what Siegfried Sassoon calls the architectonics of) whatever else I wrote should be, at any rate, calculated." We shall see later the irredeemable fault which made the proportions of *The Seven Pillars* what Lawrence called their worst side. Meanwhile we can note that Lawrence was quite aware of the worth of a few flowers on even the severest of buildings; for he continued the letter just quoted with this paragraph. "Your liking for the first-afternoon-football-match pleases me. That page was meant like a seat for anyone tired with the idea of effort. So was the whole third book put in like a benediction after a commination service: and the very occasional landscapes and lyric paragraphs, between stresses."

Finally, just as a general statement selected from among many for the ambiguity at its center—for just that ambivalence and sense of defeated judgment which has afflicted so many writers—there is this paragraph, taken from the letter containing the quoted passage about words as sponges. "I mustn't slip again into the technique of writing. Writing has been my inmost self all my life, and I can never put my full strength into anything else. Yet the same force, I know, put into action upon material things would move them, make me famous and effective. The everlasting effort to write is like trying to fight a featherbed. In letters there is no room for strength."

This is the declaration of vocation at the strongest value Lawrence ever reached: the co-operative sentiment of doubt was here no stronger than the sentiment of vocation. Conviction, which alone makes mastery possible, he never reached; for reasons of sensibility which it will be the main effort of these notes to show. His general sentiment was more nearly at the level of the following statement, which he made in a letter to Robert Graves shortly before he died. "Almost I could be an artist, but there is a core that puts on the brake. If I knew what it was I would tell you, or become one of you. Only I can't."

The everlasting effort nevertheless went far before the brake was felt. It was forced writing, seldom discovered writing, never the writing of momentum. Lawrence *forced* his eyes into the looking-glass with all the impetuosity which is characteristic of the complex dread of letting go, of missing, and of going forward. His writing acquired ease, I think, only in the sense that impetuosity became a habit. Usually his best effects are conspicuously either struck off or seized at, snatched from a near physical collision of his sensibility with the object. How strong his predilection was for violence of imagery is perhaps suggested by his choice of a first paragraph for *Revolt in the Desert.* It is taken from the second paragraph of chapter VIII of *Seven Pillars,* where the first, in a more composed writer, would have served more masterfully. "When at last we anchored in Jeddah's outer harbour, off the white town hung between the blazing sky and its reflection in the mirage which swept and rolled over the wide lagoon, then the heat of Arabia came out like a drawn sword and struck us speechless."

It is an excellent passage in its kind, but it is quoted here because of the initial position Lawrence assigned to it in the *Revolt:* which leads us immediately to understand in *Seven Pillars* that it is the violence of the first two pages there that gives them their principal relevance to the book, for, without the yoking consideration of violence, they deal with matters not otherwise explored. I refer particularly to the description of casual homosexuality among the Arab troops. A "cold convenience" he called it, and proceeded: "Later, some began to justify this sterile process, and swore that friends quivering together in the yielding sand with intimate hot limbs in supreme embrace, found there hidden in the darkness a sensual coefficient of the mental passion which was welding our souls and spirits in one flaming effort. Several, thirsting to punish appetites they could not wholly prevent, took a savage pride in degrading the body, and offered themselves fiercely in any habit which promised physical pain or filth."

The reader will remember that these sentences occur in a general consideration of the Arab revolt and Lawrence's relation, as an alien Englishman, to it. They come down like a fist struck on a table during an otherwise steady argument, without significance to it but the contrary, yet forcing attention upon it beyond the confines of logic. Memory is invested; whether the shock or the argument is better remembered is no question, the association is permanent: kept, say, as the sense of smart. This mode of persuasion is well recognized, whether in conduct or in art; is often the deliberate substitute for mastery (the more inviting because in the instance it amounts to mastery); and Lawrence furnishes an extreme, perhaps a heroic, example of a writer for whom it constituted a chief resource. It overcame in the act one of his major obstructive obsessions —which we shall come to in another form; it overcame his sense of "many humiliating material limits" by declaring that there were "no moral impossibilities," and overcame too, by enacting it, that "physical shame of success" which was the reaction to victory. It gave him the means to say, or partly say, what he at once knew and did not know, otherwise unsayable.

If his reliance on this mode marked a limit, in the sense of barrier rather than boundary, to the major aspect of sensibility, and was the outward sign of an inward cripplement, it yet gave him for detail—for any detail short of the largest—a constant principle of growth; and made, indeed, an excellent showing forth of his own observation, "that the rules of action were only snares of action till they had run out of the empty head into the hands, by use."

There are at least three easily separable sub-species of writing in which Lawrence reached through the rules of his mode into handy use. One is the expression of atmosphere, landscape, setting, through imagery which, by coupling close observation, that might be dead, with far-fetched simile, that might often be *distrait,* gave a created effect of actuality. The strain of sensibility becomes thus equivalent to the tension of the object. Citation of this species is easy because brief examples offer. One is the figure of the heat and the drawn sword quoted above. Another, especially apt here, is when Lawrence remarks of tactics that nine tenths are teachable, "but the irrational tenth was like the kingfisher flashing across the pool, and in it lay the test of generals." He proceeds immediately, and here is the characteristic interesting point: "It could be ensued only by instinct (sharpened by thought practicing the stroke) until at the crisis it came naturally, a reflex." The reader will note how vivid, and useful, and how created out of whole cloth is General Kingfisher. Again, when Lawrence told the Arabs of Allenby's successes: "My hearers' minds drew after me like flames. Tallal took fire, boasting." Here the apposition seems at first sight so logical that no amount of analysis—which the reader may make for himself—will reduce its aptness to the level of yoked superficies where logically it belongs. What was created by the first stroke cannot afterwards be cut down, except by an uncalled for act of will. *Seven Pillars* is full of such strokes, some simple and some complex, e.g., balls of dead thistle "careered like run-away haycocks across the fallow"; an airplane "climbed like a cat up the sky"; and "black-white buildings moving up and down like pistons in the mirage"—which last gains its virtue perhaps precisely because it will not bear analysis at all.

One of the slightly more complex examples of this type of trope may be cited, an example where it is the sensibility rather than the language that betrays the signs of force in our present sense. It seems that "to an Arab an essential part of the triumph of victory was to wear the clothes of an enemy." Thus the dead were stripped naked. After one such victory Lawrence went out onto the field:

> The dead men looked wonderfully beautiful. The night was shining gently down, softening them into new ivory. Turks were white-skinned on their clothed parts, much whiter than the Arabs; and these soldiers had been very young. Close round them lapped the dark wormwood, now heavy with dew, in which the ends of the moonbeams sparkled like sea-spray. The corpses seemed flung so pitifully on the ground, huddled anyhow in low heaps. Surely if straightened they would be comfortable at last. So I put them all in order, one by one, very wearied myself, and longing to be of these quiet ones, not of the restless, noisy, aching mob up the valley, quarrelling over the plunder, boasting of their speed and strength to endure God knew how many toils and pains of this sort; with death, whether we won or lost, waiting to end the history.

Here what was seen—better, what Lawrence forced himself to see—is the trope of imagination. The language itself is calm and reserved; the overt attitude is controlled: but the vision is violent, an extreme effort to exhibit a face of that aspect of life which is intolerable from within rather than from without. It is an example of Yeats's "uncontrollable mystery" of which the terms always have to be created since they cannot exist. *Convenit esse deos et ergo esse creaemus.* Yeats—of whom Lawrence said that his later work was the ash of poetry—returned to the image of the Christ-child; Lawrence straightened the bodies of the immediate dead. One arrives where one is driven.

It is not easy to cite either of the other two principal sub-species in Lawrence's practice in his natural forced mode. The difficulty is partly in length and partly in clear identification. The best citations will therefore be fragmentary and themselves forced. One sub-species is to be found in the series of Arab portraits that extend through *Seven Pillars*—the full-dress characterizations of such men as Hussein, Feisal, Abdulla, and Auda, given sometimes all at once, but more often a page or so at a time as the history called for comment. My point is that these portraits are marvelous forced creations, quite removed from but parallel to their unrealizable originals: pictures Lawrence kept with him, let us say, to remind himself of the complete men with whom he had to deal—preach to, persuade, and command.

The connection between the picture and the man is analogous to that between the minds that drew after Lawrence like flames and Tallal taking fire, not logical but putative. For Lawrence, they were limited acts of forced attention, for us they are created possibilities of human character, violent and incomplete, not open anywhere to analysis. They are characters not achieved or discovered, but asserted. Lawrence lacked the power, or the rare abiding charity, to make, or even to see, character complete; but he had inexhaustibly the power to make a willed substitute for it. To put it unkindly, his Arabs, and his Englishmen, and himself, too, all play character parts; they all work on formulas, however unpredictable and unusual; but, to make it praise, the formulas are intensely felt and the working out all fits into the game recorded. Two things need hardly be added, one that these remarks have no bearing on Lawrence's private intuition of character, which may have been perfect, but apply only to what he put down; the second, that what he did put down has only a lesser value, in the experience of character, than the productions of those who have put down, not so much more, but what was more complete. What is said here only makes another clue to help us discriminate the class of writer to which Lawrence belongs. Let us say merely that he was a man of feelings, which are fundamental, and of emotions, which are sometimes perfect products of feelings; but that, as a writer, he was governed by a driven and imperfect intellect, an intellect not ever his in the sense that his feelings were his, and not ever completing his feelings as his emotions might have completed them, and, as he knew, they were meant to. It is a matter of dominance, of hierarchy, of productive order, and not a matter of whether or not he owned the various talents; which he did, uneasily.

The remaining, or third principal sub-species in which Lawrence shows himself characteristic of his mode, has been saved till now because its great complexity is everywhere based on the relative simplicity of the first and second sub-species, and because it makes up, if we can cite it, evidently the very blood-stream of his imagination: the medium—the food and the habitat—of what he had to say. It will be understood that we speak really of the whole *Seven Pillars* and of *The Mint,* too, at least by extension, and that it is merely to focus attention that we bring up on a single passage: namely, chapters XXXI to XXXIII of *Seven Pillars.*

These chapters contain Lawrence's account of his journey from Wejh to Wadi Ais to find out why Abdulla had done nothing with his army for two months. During the journey he is sick with dysentery, boils on his back and heavy fever, commits judicial murder, and discovers the major strategy by which the Arab revolt can be successfully conducted. The sickness—the physical suffering and the biological dismay—together with a concomitant sense of landscape and quotidian actuality may be said here to furnish what I. A. Richards calls the coadunating power of imagination and so give meaning and location to the murder, and the strategy, and compose, on top, a new meaning possible to these pages alone. Certainly not the sickness only, and impossibly the landscape only, made these images their fertile apposition. Lawrence's wilderness had need to be spiritual as well as physical before it could breed vision out of observation, and the pang of conceptual feeling needed a direct base in bodily pain before it could be forced, by imagination, into emotion or, as it happened, the plot of action.

We can say if we like, looking for the technical aspect of these chapters, that we have just an example of old-fashioned straightforward first-person narrative, limited by the historical facts and enriched by the forced data of a special sensibility. Lawrence went, was sick, did murder, and conceived strategy; these things were so; this is how they were seen; no more. But this is to remove both the sense of the deliberate artist and of the driven intellect, which furnish the true setting of the narrative and produce the true meaning. So far as Lawrence was aware of his writing—and in terms of precision of feeling he was supremely aware—what he wrote was not narrative at all, but a re-seizure, highly selective and deeply canalized, of the focal material of experience: to which the mere narrative line can never be more than apposite. That is why the sickness and the landscape count for so much, while the narrative counts relatively for so little in defining the murder and enforcing the strategy come upon. Any other narrative would have done as well or as poorly; for Lawrence did not compose by narrative means, the story does not come first. In fact the composition comes the other way round: the story, the events, serve to enrich and to prune a little the native superabundance of the sensibility engaged. The events, say, served as a mechanical closing focus—the iris of a camera—upon the actual material of experience, just as his intentions, the residual pattern or habituated eyesight of his sensibility served as the evaluing focus. They reduced, and thereby concentrated, the scope of his attention sufficiently to permit the valuing act to occur.

This is, I think, the only way Lawrence knew how to write; it explains the predominance of the fragmentary and the violent over the evidently integrating and reserved factors in two books which had the express aim of presenting whole pictures. Wholeness, for Lawrence, lay in the sensibility; so far as its elements could be expressed, they would make a unity that might be taken as complete if taken at all: the unity of obsession.

The problem of Lawrence, if there needs to be a problem, is the problem of the obsessed sensibility, which beyond or beneath its obsessions is disparate, without conviction, altogether homeless, nearly lost. What can it make for itself, what must it miss? With these questions, locked as they must be in the arms of *Seven Pillars* and *The Mint,* the remainder of these notes is concerned.

Nothing could better introduce the bottom sensibility of *Seven Pillars* as we think back on it and feel into it than the first paragraph of Doughty's *Arabia Deserta.* The reader will remember that Lawrence leaves his proper story with an account of the first days after the Arabs' triumphant entry into Damascus. "A new voice hailed me of an old friend," said Doughty, "when, first returned from the Peninsula, I paced again in that long street of Damascus which is called Straight; and suddenly taking me wonderingly by the hand 'Tell me (said he), since thou art here again in the peace and assurance of Ullah, and whilst we walk, as in the former years, toward the new blossoming orchards, full of the sweet spring as the garden of God, what moved thee, or how couldst thou take such journeys into the fanatic Arabia?'" Lawrence called his book A Triumph; and so it was, but of the imagination, and terminating in an ambiguous, intolerable, because somehow alien emotion—an emotion the counterpart of which is raised somehow in the phrasing of Doughty's paragraph. In his Introduction to *Arabia Deserta,* Lawrence quotes Doughty that "if one live any time with the Arab he will have all his life after a feeling of the desert," but there is a richer phrasing in Doughty than that, which marks better the substantive feeling in Lawrence's emotion. "Here is a dead land, whence, if he die not, he shall bring home nothing but a perpetual weariness in his bones."

A part of the man died, as a motive canceled out, and survived only as emotion, so powerful or so pervasive, being now groundless and without object, that it sometimes alienated all that had survived. Emotion which has lost its motor is the true disease and disorder of spirit, infecting like the ragged, ejaculatory after-weakness of violence every remaining movement in the degree of its initial force.

This Lawrence knew, or partly knew; for there is a tailpiece to the Triumph, which doubles while undermining its value. "The strongest motive throughout had been a personal one, not mentioned here, but present to me, I think, every hour of these two years. Active pains and joys might fling up, like towers, among my days: but, refluent as air, this hidden urge re-formed, to be the persisting element of life, till near the end. It was dead, before we reached Damascus."

It had died; but death is a partial act in these senses, a mere pruning punctuation or breach of order; and what survives is re-enforced, sometimes in the direction of integration, sometimes not; but always leaving disruptions, gaps that may be found: which are the present object of search, though if we find them we shall probably not realize them, so embedded they must be in the continuing pattern of the man: so much a general stain of the sensibility, not anywhere startling stigmata. For it needs to be emphasized that only sensibilities of great strength and of a deep-seated order are capable of devastating weakness and actual disorder, and we are likely in looking at a man like Lawrence to mistake at critical points the one aspect for the other, just because of the greatness and the strength involved. That is why the matter is here introduced by the indirect means—assays of bias—of unconnected quotations, in the hope that the atmosphere they make when taken together will suggest to the reader the substantive feeling that brought them to mind: our feeling of Lawrence's emotion—a feeling full of ignorance and waywardness and imprecision—is all we can expect to manage, short of the attempt to share the emotion itself, which is a pathetic tame-goose chase not here to be commended however commonly self-applauded. It will be quite enough to absorb the full power of attention if we simply feel what disturbed and deprived Lawrence and drove him on, in his life and in his writing, to acts and images—to the unrelenting deed and deliberate vision—that he could not abide.

Except Swift, Lawrence is the least abiding writer of magnitude in English (short of Shakespeare in *King Lear*), and like Swift chose in his difficulty the subject matter of his art. The type is not uncommon outside the arts; the world is full of men and women who practice distraught endurance and press for chances to make stoicism absolute and dull. It is imagination that animates endurance into a vice and makes stoicism, as Henry Adams called it, a form of moral suicide; imagination concentrates endurance into a supreme kind of attention, and compels stoicism to declare the values it destroys. In this respect—in this type of sensibility—imagination operates analogously to religion upon the world which both deny; only, if as in Lawrence the imagination be without religion, the balance of heaven is lacking, the picture projected is incomplete and in an ultimate sense fails of responsibility. It is thus, I think, that we get from Lawrence a sense of unsatisfied excitement, inadequate despair, and the blank extreme of shock. But it is excitement, is despair, is shock; made actual; disturbing us; finding room within us in our own tiding disorder. On the imaginative level, perhaps on the moral level—or on any level except the social—order is only a predicament accepted. It is the strength of an imagination like Lawrence's that it removes the acceptance and leaves the predicament bare. The weakness, which is basic only, lies in the absence of any effective anterior conviction to supply a standard of disclosure; and there, it is suggested, is the limitation, the constriction, the stress, the missing urge, which we feel chiefly as a dislocated but dominant emotion throughout Lawrence's work. To change the context from religion to sensibility or character, the weakness amounts to an immaturity in the compositional habit, which Lawrence, had he gone on living in this slow age—slow in growth, not revolution—might well have made up for. The late letters, written as he left the Air Force, show intimations of the recovery of conviction; and, more important, looking back, his work had all along shown quick material enough to require any amount of composition, the deepest degree of conviction.

This is not all, and exhausts nothing, this weakness. To repeat for emphasis, the weakness is basic only; and in the worlds of the mind what is basic is not necessarily conclusive, what totters at the bottom does not always fall: the towers of imagination fling up, like Lawrence's active pains and joys, out of quicksand, and stand, firm in light and air. It may be there is a type of imagination, of which Lawrence would be an exemplar, incapable equally of the bottom reality and the top ideal, yet tortured by both, which exhibits its strength solely in the actual confronting world—the flux—and is confounded only in those terminals which, so to speak, it could never reach. Surely there is nothing that so illuminates the validity of imagination as when we find ourselves assenting to an imaginative process whose beginnings shift under us as we look for them and whose ends we must feel as alien. Something like this is the case with Blake (to whom it is noteworthy here that Lawrence when young was much attracted), with Donne, El Greco, Proust, Baudelaire, but which is not the case, to make a rough standard of comparison, with Shakespeare, the early Tolstoy, Mann, or Dante, where assent is carried one way or another beyond the actual. When we think of Lawrence we do not think of Shakespeare, but we might well think of Baudelaire and again of Proust. Writers like Shakespeare shape, predict, and sometimes embody our sensibilities, so vast their work is. Writers like Lawrence dislocate, unseat, but always stretch and freshen our sensibilities. The difference is not in subject matter or in expressive ability but in a limitation of imaginative process under the control of a distracted attention. That is why at distraught moments or times, writers like Lawrence seem especially rewarding: we see in them the minutia—the actuality—that is distraught. Distress seems better than any placation because more *immediately* honest. Besides, there is the recurrent, fearful question —more an emotion than a question—whether distraction is not as far as the mind can go.

It may some day be said that such an unconvicted belief was idiosyncratic of the experiment of our times. What else the suicidally distrustful epidemic ideologies, everywhere about us, that may be said rather to rage than to prevail, to promote rather than to meet catastrophe. Even this day—late summer 1940—shows chiefly the clinical picture of shock. It is almost nowhere the tragic sense, it is almost everywhere the perfidious sense that is encouraged. It is not impossible that a combination of these characters of the public sensibility may explain the extraordinary popularity of *Seven Pillars,* which must number by now a million readers. The public understands everything but the indictment, feels everything but the loss. Lawrence expressed—glamour is the refluent air in which it was received—an image on the great level of what many men would like to be so long as they know they cannot. That Lawrence showed also the actuality, which was part of his greatness, and that in his showing was a full sense, in Eliot's phrase for the poet's advantage, of "the boredom, the horror, and the glory," which is the rest of his greatness, together make the value both behind and beyond the popular fashion. His weakness—his radical distraction—only qualifies and canalizes the value.

Both the value and its qualifiers will clear up considerably if we measure the force of *The Mint.* In that work Lawrence recounted the daily life of an enlisted man in the Air Force during the first months of training, and followed it with an account of a short period some time later, at another post, when the burden of fatigue drill had been replaced, to a degree, by schoolwork, and the individual soldier participated in his work instead of submitting, so far as compulsion could go, to personal obliteration and the exhaustion of sensibility. The tale is flat autobiography, composed, Lawrence said, entirely of notes made at the time, later rearranged, but textually unaltered; nothing was taken out and nothing added. It constitutes, in the first part, a record of animal debasement, and in the second much shorter part the intimation of spiritual release through a disciplined and surrendered life. It is thus an essay in moral immolation and intellectual asceticism, religious in prompting, escapist in enactment; so that its final significance, while religious, is the significance of an irrational, restricted religion; which is to say that it is abnormal in the sense of being *merely* individual. It is the perfect fruit, true to sport, of Lawrence's enlistment in the Air Force, which took the influence of a Prime Minister to bring about.

It is not easy to discuss a work which cannot be counted as familiar to more than a few hundred persons and from which it is forbidden to quote; confidence which cannot be checked ought not to be felt in the critic, and certainly cannot be demanded by him. But there are several aspects of *The Mint,* related closer than cousins to aspects of *Seven Pillars,* that may be emphasized without recourse to the text. These are the aspects that show in Lawrence the development, or deepening, of his identity, and by the connections exhibited persuade qualities otherwise overlooked—in the *Letters* or *Seven*

Pillars—to transpire: and these just the illuminating qualities we want.

The first of these aspects is the overt theme, fresh-pressed in the title, which had by temperament obsessed Lawrence for years, and which by his enlistment he strove to enact and by his book to express: it was a question. What was the intrinsic value of the common coin pressed by the mint of His Majesty's Armed Forces? The extrinsic value varied about a norm from war to war and peace to peace; the intrinsic would be found partly in the transformation of material wrought by the pressure of the mint, and partly in what, if anything, remained unmodified, and was indeed brought out and firmed by the minting process. The difference between the civilian and the enlisted man was extreme. The civilian, for example, is presumed to choose and exalt his leaders, and is able to change them: he shapes the purposes of his society. The enlisted man is degraded beneath the level of choice and is expected, except in liquor and sex on leave, to reduce his personal abilities to a minimum: he exists to serve a purpose shaped beyond barriers which he cannot hope to cross except by his suicide as a soldier. Yet the material of which soldier and civilian are made is identical. How does the civilian become a soldier, and what keeps him so—what bars the restoring suicide—once he is there? There must be a deep and complex struggle involved, and some reward, not in sight but positive, some compensating, some fructifying release from the personality that has been lost. The interim period—the minting—will be an agony willfully maintained and attended, at least in peacetime, though it is not commonly understood or enjoyed as such. Lawrence himself had perhaps not at first thought of the experience as an agony—the obsession was too close—but when the word was offered him he snatched it. David Garnett, after reading the typescript, wrote that as the *Seven Pillars* was a Triumph, *The Mint* was an agony, and Lawrence wrote back: "You have it in one word. I should have written *an agony* after the Title," and indeed, two weeks later, writing to Jonathan Cape, he referred to his "second book *The Mint,* an agony of the Royal Air Force." An agony it was.

Lest the reader think that the agony had entirely a dramatic or religious emphasis—which is merely the emphasis we keep—it should be observed that Lawrence had also the motive of reforming and lightening the waste burden of discipline on enlisted men, just as he worked for the abolition of the death penalty for military cowardice. The practical concern was distinguishable from the imaginative concern, but not separable: his integrity, like his humanity, was touched in different ways. We see the involvement clear in chapter CXVIII of *Seven Pillars,* which is toward the end, just before the entry into Damascus, when some Indian troops worked in conjunction with Lawrence and the Arabs. Lawrence had not been close to any body of "civilized" troops for some time, and the contact struck him. "My mind felt in the Indian rank and file something puny and confined; an air of thinking themselves mean; almost a careful, esteemed subservience, unlike the abrupt wholesomeness of Beduin. The manner of the British officers towards their men struck horror into my bodyguard, who had never seen personal inequality before." Two pages further on is a passage which ties *The Mint* and *Seven Pillars* together, and on all levels, in the center of Lawrence's sensibility.

> But these others [British, Australian, Indian as compared to Arabs] were really soldiers, a novelty after ten years' irregularity. And it came upon me freshly how the secret of uniform was to make a crowd solid, dignified, impersonal: to give it a singleness and tautness of an upstanding man. This death's livery which walled its bearers from ordinary life, was sign that they had sold their wills and bodies to the state; and contracted themselves into a service not the less abject for that its beginning was voluntary. Some of them had obeyed the instinct of lawlessness: some were hungry: others thirsted for glamour, for the supposed colour of a military life: but, of them all, those only received satisfaction who had sought to degrade themselves, for to the peace-eye they were below humanity. Only women with a lech were allured by those witnessing clothes; the soldiers' pay, not sustenance like a labourer's, but pocket-money, seemed most profitably spent when it let them drink sometimes and forget.

The significance of this passage and what led Lawrence to write it would be worthless to any reader not aware, as Lawrence was aware, of the other side, of the theory and practice of war in the mass—of compound or social war. Lawrence showed his awareness often enough, but nowhere more clearly than when, in a paper called "The Evolution of a Revolt," he compared regular armies with his Arab bands with regard to discipline. One paragraph needs to be quoted entire.

> Consequently we [the Arabs] had no discipline, in the sense in which it is restrictive, submergent of individuality, the lowest common denominator of men. In regular armies in peace it means the limit of energy attainable by everybody present: it is the hunt not of an average, but of an absolute, a 100-per-cent. standard, in which ninety-nine stronger men are played down to the level of the worst. The aim is to render the unit a unit, and the man a type, in order that their effort shall be calculable, their collective output even in grain and bulk. The deeper the discipline, the lower the individual efficiency, and the more sure the performance. It is a deliberate sacrifice of capacity in order to reduce the uncertain element, the bionomic factor, in enlisted humanity, and its accompaniment is *compound* or social war, that form in which the man in the fighting line has to be the product of the multiplied exertions of the long hierarchy, from workshop to supply unit, which maintains him in the field.

Here is the overt justification, the administrative logic—with its *preliminary* disregard of the human material—for the humiliation of the self which must precede either humility or grounded pride: the hell through which alone access is afforded to paradise or personal triumph. But the overt is never enough for the intensive sensibility; for what is overt is incapable, construed alone, of minting the soul: that which drives forward or outward from within, searching a pattern to fill out, a circulating system to follow. Faith, philosophy, fanaticism—some vehicle of conviction—serves indifferently to supply the deficiency, blood to the veins, inward justification: and *declares* the material to be minted. Lawrence lacked such a vehicle, except insofar as others by some mode or vestigial habit of their own, assumed that he possessed one. One might say in passing that Lawrence constantly reached out for the precarious support of those who made such assumptions; that on the whole, Jacob's Ladder led downwards, each rung clutched with inhuman resolution, let go with utter weakness. It is as if the faculty of attention craved, was satiated, and then disgorged. We say that Dante was a master of disgust; lacking St. Thomas and Aristotle, Lawrence is a master of disgorgement—but not alone of what was disgusting, but also of what might otherwise, swallowed, have been delight. *The Mint* is a running example of such disgorgement—of the continuous cultivation of the intolerable; like Baudelaire's poems about corpses—evil in the bestial, flaunted sense—without Baudelaire's intermittently recurring spiritual control, but with a mastery of the actuality which Baudelaire never reached. Lawrence could have cried with Baudelaire, and indeed did many times, *Je jalouse du Néante;* but the nothingness was worn with a difference. Baudelaire's nothingness was of insensibility, and he longed unavailingly for the haven of *Nombres et des Êtres,* Pascal's refuge of mathematics and mysticism. Lawrence's nothingness was rather represented by complete disgorgement of the details of sensibility. Nowhere in Lawrence is the least presence felt of *Luxe, calme, volupté,* nor is there any place, even in the furthest ideal offing, where all is order. Baudelaire was damned; Lawrence deprived; both exposed themselves deliberately and at a maximum tension to the sense of their fates. Another way of putting it may be risked: that Baudelaire was reminded always of original sin—of radical imperfection; where Lawrence was engaged always in terminal sin—ultimate inadequacy. Thus we are furnished with another version of the effect of the lack of conviction: a deeply engaged perfidy to the experience which produces the last as well as the least sentiments. Lawrence put it all down, again and again: the very inner press of *The Mint,* the imaginative outcropping motive of *Seven Pillars,* and occasionally as a bitter bossed rubric in the letters. Let us put them together, with a letter, as both more self-conscious and it may be thereby the less candid, coming first.

Lawrence wrote a series of letters to Lionel Curtis during 1923 when he was in the Tank Corps—the very worst period of the minting—and in one of them, evidently in answer to an urgent plea that he leave the army and come to his senses, there is the following passage. "And the blackness of your letter? Because it tempts me to run away from here, and so doing it marches with my wishes against my will. Conscience in healthy men is a balanced sadism, the bitter sauce which makes more tasteful the ordinary sweets of life: and in sick stomachs the desire for condiment becomes a craving, till what is hateful feels therefore wholesome, and what is repugnant to the moral sense becomes (to the mind) therefore pure and righteous and to be pursued. So because my senses hate it, my will forces me to it . . . and a comfortable life would seem now to me sinful. . . . When I embarked on it, a year ago, I thought it a mood and curable: while today I feel that there is no change before me, and no hope of change." In a letter of two weeks previous, after describing both his hatred of and submission to bodily activity, he went on: "This sort of thing must be madness, and sometimes I wonder how far mad I am, and if a mad-house would not be my next (and merciful) stage. Merciful compared with this place, which hurts me, body and soul. It's terrible to hold myself here: and yet I want to stay here till it no longer hurts me: till the burnt child no longer feels the fire."

Thus the resolution, the devouring appetite, as it appeared to Lawrence when addressing a friend in the combined terms of self-justification and expiation. What the food was, and condiments as well as food, cannot be reproduced here, though it comes as near objective justification as possible; for *The Mint* may be read only privately, and, in this country, in the Congressional Library; but a neighbor taint of it may be presented, a leaf which fell in the same pile.

Lawrence left behind him some penciled manuscript, called *Leaves in the Wind,* meant to be notes for a final section of *The Mint;* some of these are printed in Garnett's edition of the letters, and of these one may be examined for our present purpose: to characterize the process of minting to which Lawrence yielded himself for some twelve years; but, more, to vitalize the references made here to the book itself, which was finished during the first three or four. The passage chosen finds Lawrence in the troopship *Derbyshire* on the way to India, as sentry in Married Quarters posted in the corridor leading to the women's latrine. The stench is bad; there is a splashing in the latrine, and peeping in Lawrence discovers the drain is clogged and the floor awash. The Orderly Officer makes a visit at this moment, and Lawrence tells him about the latrine:

The grimy-folded face, the hard jaw, toil-hardened hands. An ex-naval warrant, I'll bet. No gentleman. He strides boldly to the latrine: "Excuse me" unshyly to two shrinking women. "God," he jerked out, "flooded with shit—where's the trap?" He pulled off his tunic and threw it at me to hold, and with a plumber's quick glance strode over to the far side, bent down, and ripped out a grating. Gazed a moment, while the ordure rippled over his boots. Up his right sleeve, baring a fore arm hairy as a mastiff's grey leg, knotted with veins, and a gnarled hand: thrust it deep in, groped, pulled out a moist white bundle. "Open that port" and out it splashed into the night. "You'd think they'd have had some other place for their sanitary towels. Bloody awful show, not having anything fixed up." He shook his sleeve down as it was over his slowly-drying arm, and huddled on his tunic, while the released liquid gurgled contentedly down its re-opened drain.

I think it will be clear from this passage—which is not entirely exemplary—that the drive behind it was not simple disgust, nor even the forced will of disgusted attention; there is a drive toward satiation, toward a complete absorption of the material in hand upon the outer film of the whole sensibility. The risibilities, too, are somewhat engaged, and the sense of verbal decoration. There is here that sentiment which is the posthumous and irresponsible achievement of shock; even sentimentality in reverse. Lawrence was rather vain of his achievements in this line: he realized perfectly the effect of his hospital chapter in *Seven Pillars,* which is queried up several times in letters; and the quality here meant to be emphasized may be illustrated by a few sentences from that chapter, followed by a sentence of Lawrence's own comment.

"I stepped in [from blazing sunlight to a shuttered lobby], to meet a sickening stench: and, as my eyes grew open, a sickening sight. The stone floor was covered with dead bodies side by side, some in full uniform, some in underclothing, some stark naked. There might be thirty there, and they crept with rats, who had gnawed wet red galleries into them. A few were corpses nearly fresh, perhaps only a day or two old: others must have been there for long. Of some the flesh, going putrid, was yellow and blue and black. Many were already swollen twice or thrice life width, their fat heads laughing with black mouth across jaws harsh with stubble.

Of others the softer parts were fallen in. A few had burst open, and were liquescent with decay." The scene proper ends with this sentence: "The trench was too small for them, but so fluid was the mass that each newcomer, when tipped in, fell softly just jellying out the edges of the pile a little with his weight."

The reader who can separate himself from the subject matter, which is extremely adhesive, should notice the vocabulary: the relish with which words were found to present the horror. The relish is the cement; the condiment of which Lawrence wrote to Curtis as desired by the sick stomach; condiment which not only promotes the appetite but forces feeding beyond capacity.

There are other examples on different or higher levels of tension, as it were, of the moral morass, to which we shall come. Here the concern is to point the difference between the quality of the text as quoted and the quality of Lawrence's feeling about it. In the latter was no relish. Writing to Edward Garnett, who had evidently complained more than once because Lawrence had omitted the chapter from *Revolt in the Desert,* Lawrence argues himself right in these terms: "No, I have not changed ground on the hospital chapter. I have been firm from the start that it was totally unsuited, because of its power, its bitterness, its length, its late position, for inclusion in a popular abridgment. I kept my horrors further back, where the blood was hot, and let the book just run down to its conclusion. . . . To overweight the last pages with matter emotionally more powerful than anything in the body of the book would be to finish up with a bang. Whereas the bang comes in the third act, properly.

Disregarding Lawrence's obvious overestimation of the chapter (in another, earlier letter to Edward Garnett he thought that the *inclusion* of the chapter would have prevented the *Revolt* from being a best seller), it is yet plain that Lawrence put an excess value on the expression of physical disgust and the revulsions, guided by the attending mind, of the flesh, without or with but little respect for the intrinsic significance of the agent. This is another point in the distinction between him and Baudelaire; for the latter even in his most exorbitant submissions to casual evil knew with *what* disciplined imagination he was submitting and thereby always extracted from the grossest material at least a connection and often an intensification of *that* imagination. Lawrence was driven perhaps further: to exploit the grossest material on those terms only in which it actually declared itself and regardless of the terms, if any, of the envisaging imagination. Hence—with a lack of control equaling the lack of conviction—the presence, which must either be ignored like vulgarity or taken as intrusive impertinence, of the "relishing" words in the passages quoted above. Lawrence called *The Mint* pure observation; but like most pure observation it had better be called uncontrolled or ungrounded idealism.

Which is a phrase, this last, that gives us a foothold of transition to what seems to me a central declaration, along the lines already laid down, of the intent, scope, and magnitude of Lawrence's sensibility. The declaration is double, to be discerned in an apposition made by the critic, rather than by Lawrence, to establish as well as state the identity of the two ends, expressive and receptive, of the engaged sensibility. Let us remark, as a renewed clue for attention, that Lawrence was severely addicted to all that we think of in the phrase, trial by ordeal; which is meant not only as a convenient summary of moral attitude, but also to suggest that the emotion of justice, and the feeling of justness, appeared to Lawrence chiefly masked as annihilation.

Both passages come from *Seven Pillars,* and the first carries as running heads to its two pages the phrases "Midnight Sermon" and "A Full Conversion." Lawrence had come back from the "clarifying wilderness" to find that his allies, the Serahin, were lacking in spirit to continue the revolt. Lawrence exhorted them in "a halting, half-coherent speech, struck out desperately, in our extreme need, upon the anvil of those white minds round the dying fire." The second and third paragraphs out of four in which the speech is recounted are here quoted.

To be of the desert was, as they knew, a doom to wage unending battle with an enemy who was not of the world, nor life, nor anything, but hope itself; and failure seemed God's freedom to mankind. We might only exercise this our freedom by not doing what lay within our power to do, for then life would belong to us, and we should have mastered it by holding it cheap. Death would seem best of all our works, the last free loyalty within our grasp, our final leisure: and of these two poles, death and life, or, less finally, leisure and subsistence, we should shun subsistence (which was the stuff of life) in all save its faintest degree, and cling close to leisure. Thereby we would serve to promote the not-doing rather than the doing. Some men, there might be, uncreative; whose leisure was barren; but the activity of these would have been material only. To bring forth immaterial things, things creative, partaking of spirit, not flesh, we must be jealous of spending time or trouble upon physical demands, since in most men the soul grew aged long before the body. Mankind had been no gainer by its drudges.

There could be no honour in a sure success, but much might be wrested from a sure defeat. Omnipotence and the Infinite were our two worthiest foemen, indeed the only ones for a full man to meet, they being monsters of his own spirit's making; and the stoutest enemies were always of the household. In fighting Omnipotence, honour was proudly to throw away the poor resources that we had, and dare Him, empty-handed; to be beaten, not merely by more mind, but by its advantage of better tools. To the clear-sighted, failure was the only goal. We must believe, through and through, that there was no victory, except to go down into death fighting and crying fo failure itself, calling in excess of despair to Omnipotence to strike harder, that by His very striking He might temper our tortured selves into the weapon of his own ruin.

There are so many things of interest here—things so alien or so fundamental to our common experience—things fundamental *made* alien—that it is hard to determine where the seat of interest stands. Death as leisure; subsistence as the stuff of life; failure as goal; human despair as God's ruin. Let us take them, and the rest, as they work together; for it is, or ought to be, Lawrence's relation to the whole that counts most. Is it not a relation to the feeling of conviction?—conviction by debasement?—conviction without humility?—debasement that comes, as Lawrence says, by "the slow humbling of the Serahin" which ended in "their flashing eagerness to ride with us whatever the bourne." Here is where the seat of conviction shakes; and mastery is felt as self-nullity.

It is, the whole passage, the labor of the sensibility to bear, on its own, the new thing. That is to say, only by an intensive denial can you come *down* to affirmation. (There is another route, not down; but Lawrence was incapable of taking it.) One thinks, perhaps this is the heritage of Christianity tottering; the heritage irrecoverable except in terms of close denial. But might it not be more appropriate to think, *That* half of Christianity always tottered, and only existed by tottering. The ascetic insight, brought into the Western world, must needs totter; partly because its alienship in a temperate climate makes it a forced growth, so that it essentially wrings away from its unnatural soil; partly, and rather, because the other half—of Christianity, of the human spirit—constantly leaps into the saddle. There is no one like your European ascetic for awareness of the sensual, for riding upon it and being ridden, for spurring and being roweled. If the merely ascetic, which is here to say the personal, aspect of the insight is dropped, the whole man or at least the whole sensibility emerges, restored to that balance wherein asceticism is of the heart rather than the brain, is the motor rather than the motivation. Lawrence could not drop it; his brain needed it to get on with; but he transformed it, using it on uncommon considerations—death as leisure and creation, the flesh as drudge. Hence both the force and the incoherence of his reactions.

It is as if a man needed to be insane in order to act, needed to destroy himself in order to express himself. We see him here, above, in the passage quoted, bringing men (and most himself) to the point of action by denying every worth to action except the worth of failure. The goal is *hubris* through *denial,* through *abandonment* as an actively and resolutely secured state. Faith, to him, could not be the substance of things hoped for, but of things conceived as impossible. There is here, it may be, the rancor of experience when understood through an ungrounded idealism. It is the nothing-heart at work, humbled, in the pejorative and oppressive sense, by the blind pride of its own heroism: without humility; and to say so reminds us again of Baudelaire, and the distinction we made between him and Lawrence. It makes itself again. Baudelaire's cry,

> *Et mon esprit, toujours du vertige hanté,*
> *Jalouse du néant l'insensibilité*

was very different from Lawrence's because based on a conviction, inherited and mastered. Lawrence's conviction was unequal to his experience; or his experience was superior to his conviction. In either case, he could only judge experience by annihilating its values.

If his exhortation to the Serahin represented the maximum value of sensibility on the high plane of action, we have hardly to turn a page to find its maximum value on the bottom plane of personal reaction. It is exactly the same driven, committed asceticism which led Lawrence to the imaginative recapitulation *and* sensual actualization of the collective sexual assault made on him in the Turkish station, which might otherwise, as commonly, have just horribly happened, but which to Lawrence meant that the citadel of his integrity "had been irrevocably lost." The reader will remember the narrative—the stripping and the knife, the whip, the delicious warmth—and will know that Lawrence did not *mean* any of the words in his summary declaration, except in terms of his ascetic recapitulation. Yet one knows through them what he did mean: human defilement as final humiliation. If we put this together with the final pride of the midnight sermon to the Serahin, they will make what perhaps is the measure of Lawrence's contribution.

It is not an inch measure nor a yard stick, but a compass bearing: the focus of scope, great enough initially to absorb any amount of attention, wide enough eventually, one thinks, to command a full horizon, though it need not be just the closing night horizon Lawrence himself actually envisaged, but perhaps—however *manqué, deraciné,* and without term—still the horizon Lawrence once said —for imagination—that he desired to show. Writing to Edward Garnett in 1922 in answer to a letter of praise for *Seven Pillars,* he made his best intention plain. "Do you remember my telling you once that I collected a shelf of 'Titanic' books (those distinguished by greatness of spirit, 'sublimity' as Longinus would call it): and that they were *The Karamazovs, Zarathustra,* and *Moby Dick*. Well, my ambition was to make an English fourth." One barrier to satisfaction—perhaps the only barrier—was in the limiting factor of subjectivity. Lawrence wrote always about himself, the individual who, ultimately, could not cope—with nothing, no plan or frame or conception, to fit himself into to make his tale objective in immediate import. His plain ambition is, as it were, untested; he could not steer for it, whether instinctively or deliberately; which is the difference in value between his books, and his life, and the books of the "Titans" he desired so to emulate. The ungrounded idealism which was fatal to him as a man comes out in his writing as compositional weakness, and is indeed the rough counterpart to what we feel as the lack of an abiding conviction. What is meant here by composition is the sum of those inner modes and outward manners by which the materials of experience are set together so that they make a whole so secure that the mere intention of the writer becomes immaterial to the book. In Lawrence, the intention everywhere counts, which is to say is questionable: uncomposed. It was his only operative weakness; other weaknesses hardly count, hardly exist, so tenaciously, with such strength of sensibility, did he fasten upon just those major aspects of experience which he could not compose. Few with that strength *and* that weakness—for it is a weakness that inhabits especially the whole class of great but eccentric sensibilities—few in the measure of Lawrence have done more. Not Melville, certainly not Nietzsche; only Dostoevski on Lawrence's list, and he by that inexhaustible charity of imagination which produced, quite superior to the insult, the injury, and the humiliation which attracted Lawrence to him, a vast host of what we call "characters." Characters are an end-product, an objective form, of imaginative composition, and their creation depends on the deepest-seated of human convictions, so humanly full of error, by the occasion of genius so superhumanly right. When we say that Lawrence never produced a character, not even his own, if we add that he produced nevertheless almost everything that makes for character, we have said very nearly what is necessary. It was his everlasting effort.

1940

8

The Craft of Herman Melville: A Putative Statement

This essay proposes to approach Herman Melville altogether gingerly and from behind the safe bulwark of his assured position—whatever that is—in American literature,—whatever *that* may be. The tacit assumption will be all along that Melville is a sufficiently great writer in a sufficiently interesting literature to make the sidelong look, the biased comment, and even a little boring-from-within, each valuable in itself, if perhaps only as characterizing an inadequate response on the part of one reader. We need, of course, a preliminary assertion to get us under way; and the last thing we want is anything in the direction of reducing Melville's greatness to subhuman terms. What we want is an assertion that, pursued, will elucidate one aspect of the work actually performed, irrespective of its greatness.

If we assert that Melville was an imaginative artist in the realm of fiction, then it is legitimate to think of him as he was concerned with the craft of fiction in his two most interesting works, *Moby Dick* and *Pierre*. As a further limitation, let us think of the craft principally under two heads: dramatic form with its inspiriting conventions, and the treatment of language itself as a medium. Other matters may come in by the way, and further matters may suggest themselves in conclusion; but the mode of discovery will be everywhere at bottom in the consideration of the tools by which Melville himself secured his effects: the tools of craft.

It is of preliminary interest that Melville never influenced the direction of the art of fiction, though in *Pierre* he evidenced the direction, and it is astonishing, when you consider the magnitude of his sensibility, that he never affected the modes of apprehension, the sensibilities, of even the ablest of his admirers. He added nothing to the novel as a form, and his work nowhere showed conspicuous mastery of the formal devices of fiction which he used. Unlike most great writers of fiction, he left nothing to those who followed him except the general stimulus of high and devoted purpose and the occasional particular spur of an image or a rhythm. It is not that he is inimitable but that there was nothing formally organized enough in his work to imitate or modify or perfect. It is easy enough to say on this score that Melville was a sport, and unique, and perhaps that is the right thing to say; but it would be more useful if we were able to say that Melville's lack of influence at least partly arose from a series of technical defects in persuasive craft—from an inefficient relation between the writer and the formal elements of his medium. None of us would want to recommend his wares along the lines of Melville's strategy. To adumbrate such a statement is a part of this essay's purpose.

Of secondary, but deeply contributory interest is the fact that though a young man still as writers go, Melville wrote nothing of major significance in the forty years he lived after writing *Pierre*. (I mean that only a lesser case could be made out for *The Confidence Man* and *Billy Budd* than for *Pierre,* not that the later books were uninteresting; they could not fail of interest as forced through Melville's sensibility.) It was not that his mind rotted or that insight faltered. It was not, I think, that the poor reception of *Pierre,* nor the long aggravation of his private life, dried his desire as a novelist. It was, I think, partly bad luck—the luck of the age, if you like—though it was no worse than Dante's luck and not so bad as Villon's, as Melville himself knew; and it was partly that his work discovered for itself, if we may say so, and in the very process of writing, that it was not meant to be fiction. Melville was only a story teller betimes, for illustrative or apologetic or evangelical purposes, and when the *writing* of *Pierre* proved that the material of illustration had been exhausted in *Moby Dick*—which is one way of noting the breakdown of *Pierre* as a story—there was no longer any need to tell a story. His means determined, as they always do, not the ends in view, but the ends achieved; and Melville had never predominantly relied upon the means of the novelist, had never attempted to use more than the overt form of the novel, until he attempted to compose *Pierre*.

What is really interesting, and what this essay intends to make most use of in this corner, is the light that *Pierre,* technically considered as a novel, casts upon the means, quite different from the means of fiction, which Melville actually employed both in *Moby Dick* and *Pierre* itself. For these books with their great effects, if they were not written out of the means of the novelist, were written out of great means of some other mode or modes of the imagination. It will most likely appear that there is an operative connection between Melville's lack of influence upon following writers and his forty years of comparative silence; and it is, again, a connection, as moral as may be, that can best be seen as a technical consideration. Similarly, the problem of the inarticulateness of *Hamlet* is better accounted for technically than philosophically. We shall see, or try to see, what modes determined what ends—but always provisionally within the modes of the rational imagination.

There is, again on this train, a dubious kind of consideration which in the very doubtfulness of its nature exerts its great attraction. In our literature we are accustomed to the question precisely because it gets itself asked at every turn. It is a coroner's question: what devilish thing did his age do to Melville? What malevolence was there in the current of American life that struck from the heights of possibility writer after writer, even those most satisfied with the American scene?—for the Longfellows, the Whittiers, the Holmeses were as fatally struck as Hawthorne and Melville and Mark Twain. But does an age act? Is not an age itself a long action, an unfolding, a display, a history, with limits set by the discernment and capacity of the observer, never by Clio herself? And is not every age an enemy of every artist it cannot directly use, an enemy not out of antipathy but of inner necessity? An age moves; it is momentum felt. An artist expresses an arrested version of movement, expresses it at the level of actuality. But this is pushing consequence intolerably. We are all enemies of our age the moment we begin to tamper with it, whether we arrest it to take its picture, hasten it toward its end in the guise of leadership, or just consciously live in it our own lives. Consciousness is the agent, not the age.

It is the whole consciousness, not its mere miniscule conscience, that makes us cowards. Hence in all large doings we are adept at removing compassion from our experience by at once inserting it in the formula of a dead convention; and so are often enabled to skip consciousness, along with conscience, altogether. How otherwise could we attend the Christian service of Holy Communion, quite aside from the matter of faith and for the "poetry" in it merely, without terror and dismay and the conviction of inadequacy. How could we attend *King Lear* on the stage if we did not commonly channelize our attention upon the obscuring details of the performance, letting the actual play work in us, if at all, unawares? This is precisely what the artist cannot substantially do if his work is to live; and this is precisely what society compels him to seem to do if his work is to succeed in the open—that is, be widely persuasive upon the consciousness of the great audience most artists aim at. Upon his skill and luck in performing this equivocal act depends all that part of an artist's achievement which rests on a firm relation with his age.

Here we have a crux in the deliberately maintained, willfully heightened consciousness of the artist. It is the crux in which we see that the conceptual faculty of consciousness is honesty if we can manage it, but that the executive faculty of consciousness must be hypocrisy. I do not wish to strain or seem far-fetched, but I believe this to be a technical matter in so far as we think of the arts—whatever it may be in religion or politics, which are not always condemned to actuality but can often play free havoc with the ideal. What it comes to in practice is that the artist must dramatize his theme, his vision, his observation, his "mere" story, in terms of existing conventions however adverse those conventions may seem to his intentions, or however hollow or vain they ring when struck. The deadest convention was meant for life—to take its place; and if by putting life into it the artist does not always change it for the better, he at least shows it for what it is. Instinctive artists commonly resort to the nearest conventions susceptible of dramas. Consider the Negro spirituals or the anonymous architecture of the twelfth century. Highly individualized artists have done the same. There is Dante who mastered the conventions of Thomistic Christianity to represent the actuality—far from Thomistic—of fourteenth-century Italy; and there is Henry James who resorted to the "social" conventions so well that many people for long believed he was taken in by them, when his predominant concern was to dramatize the actual good and evil of his time in terms of the conventions through which he most saw good and evil operating.

The point here is, for us, that Melville either refused or was unable to resort to the available conventions of his time as if they were real; he either preferred or was compelled to resort to most of the conventions he used for dramatic purposes not only as if they were unreal but also as if they were artificial. Artificial they surely were to the kind of philosopher Melville was—though they would not have seemed unreal to Montaigne or Plato; but to the dramatist of any description they would have glowed with the possibility of every reality. As for Melville's case we have his own words, put in extremity, for his attitude toward all conventions of the mind.

For the more and the more that he wrote, and the deeper and deeper that he dived, Pierre saw the everlasting elusiveness of Truth; the universal lurking insincerity of even the greatest and purest written thoughts. Like knavish cards, the leaves of all great books were covertly packed. He was but packing one set the more; and that a very poor and jaded set and pack indeed.

Here we see the ineptitude, for the artist, of moral preoccupation with what ought to be as compared with the equally moral obsession with what is. As thought, we can leave Melville's text alone, and insist merely that as an artist Melville misunderstood the import of his own words. The "universal lurking insincerity" he spoke of, is just the most fascinating aspect of the face of dramatic truth; and the conviction of it should liberate the artist's honesty among his material generally, as the preposterous fables of *Lear, Othello,* and the *Merchant of Venice* particularly liberated the profound honesty of Shakespeare, or as the *smallness* of life in Emma Bovary's town liberated Flaubert's honesty. Melville apparently felt that his insight condemned him to a species of dishonesty. Feeling the necessity—feeling the condemned state as unreprievable—he proceeded to employ conventions of character and form in which he obviously and almost avowedly did not believe. Had he been a convicted and not a condemned novelist he would have felt his insight of insincerity on the same level that he felt the convention in the following lines, in which he never detected the insincerity at all.

It is a thing most sorrowful, nay shocking, to expose the fall of valor in the soul. Men may seem detestable as joint stock-companies and nations; knaves, fools, and murderers there may be; men may have mean and meagre faces; but man, in the ideal, is so noble and so sparkling, such a grand and glowing creature, that over any ignominious blemish in him all his fellows should run to throw their costliest robes. That immaculate manliness we feel within ourselves, so far within us, that it remains intact though all the outer character seem gone; bleeds with the keenest anguish at the undraped spectacle of a valor-ruined man. Nor can piety itself, at such a shameful sight, completely stifle her upbraidings against the permitting stars.

At his best—his best as a novelist of character and aspiration—this sentiment controlled Melville's perception of dramatic fate. Had he felt the immaculate manliness as Henry James, say, felt his perception of the Sacred Fount, as a germinal, copulative, and plastic principle in every human relation, and also as the very prod and forward stress toward form, then his sentiment would not only have opened up inexhaustible subject matter, but would also have required of him that in his execution every resource, every trick, every mediate insincerity, either of craft or of social pattern, be used for the utmost there was in them. That would have been to work on the representative, the dramatic level. What he did, as we shall see more particularly below, was to work on the putative level. His work constantly *said* what it was doing or going to do, and then, as a rule, stopped short.

As it happens, Melville's is not a putative smallness but a putative immensity, and he puts it with such eloquence that the mere statement produces a lasting tone in the general atmosphere. He was without knowing it in the habit of succumbing to the greatest insincerity of all, the intoxicating insincerity of cadence and rhythm and apt image, or, to put it on another plane, the insincerity of surrendering to the force of a single insight, which sometimes amounts to a kind of self-violation. Who can measure for example the effect of the preparatory statements about Ahab upon our actual reception of him when he appears? For instance, in chapter XVI there is a paragraph about the greatness of some whaling men rising from a combination of Quaker blood and the perils of the sea. "Nor will it at all detract from him, dramatically regarded, if either by birth or other circumstances, he have what seems a half wilful, overruling morbidness at the bottom of his nature. For all men tragically great are made so through a certain morbidness. Be sure of this, O young ambition, all mortal greatness is but disease." . . . This is but one of the many preparatory, almost minatory statements that Melville made about Ahab. Many directly named him; many more, like this one, were purely indirect and putative in character. Ahab is not mentioned, but the reader who remembers the passage will know that it was he who was meant all the same; and if the reader does remember it may well occur to him that Melville meant his sentences about greatness and disease to spread throughout the novel. They were planted of a purpose, whether by instinct or intention, to prefigure in the general atmosphere the specific nature of the burden Ahab wore.

The interesting thing is that Melville preferred to make his statement, in which one version of the whole theme of the book is expressed, not only baldly in isolation, but out of place and rootlessly; which is how the reader will ultimately remember it. It worked, indeed; but it worked outside the story. A dramatist would have been compelled to find the sentiment of these sentences in a situation, an action, and they could have been used only as the situation called for them and the action carried them along; and a novelist when he can should follow the example of the dramatist. Melville, as we have said, preferred the nondramatic mode. To put it sharply, he did not write of characters in action; he employed the shells of stock characters, heightened or resounding only by the eloquence of the author's voice, to witness, illustrate, decorate, and often as it happened to impede and stultify an idea in motion. This is, if you like, the mode of allegory—the highest form of the putative imagination, in which things are *said* but need not be *shown* to be other than they seem, and thus hardly require to *be* much of anything. But successful allegory—*La Vita Nuova* and *Pilgrim's Progress*—requires the preliminary possession of a complete and stable body of belief appropriate to the theme in hand. Melville was not so equipped; neither was Hawthorne; neither was anyone in nineteenth-century America or since. That is why Melville's allegorical devices and patterns had to act *as if* they were agents in a novel; and that is why we are compelled to judge Melville at his most allegorical yet formally as a novelist.

Perhaps the point needs laboring. Many critics—many students of Melville—have done a good deal to make an allegorical interpretation of *Moby Dick*, and I am sure they are right and accurate in the form of what they say. Melville certainly had allegorical intentions. My argument—again it is technical—is that the elaboration of these intentions was among the causes that prevented him from the achievement of enacting composition and the creation of viable characters. He mistook allegory in *Moby Dick* as a sufficient enlivening agent for the form of the novel. Actually it was a chief defective element which, due to the peculiarly confused, inconsistent and incomplete state of belief he was in, he could not possibly have used to good advantage. In the craft of writing, in any form of expression, artificial allegory, like willed mysticism (of which Melville showed a trace), is a direct and easy mode only in that it puts so much in by intention as to leave nearly everything out in execution. Bad allegory, even to the allegorist, comes very soon to seem not worth doing; which is why charades and political parties break down. Melville's allegory in *Moby Dick* broke down again and again and with each resumption got more and more verbal, and more and more at the mercy of the encroaching event it was meant to transcend. It was an element in the putative mode in which, lofty as it was, Melville himself could not long deeply believe.

We have so far been concerned mostly with what Melville did not do as a practitioner in the novel and with certain possible causes which, technically, prevented him from doing what he wanted to do. Let us now examine particular instances of what he did do under the two heads first mentioned: dramatic form with its inspiriting conventions, and the treatment of language itself as medium. If anything so far said has made its point it will be in the degree that it certifies and illuminates what follows—in the degree, that is, that it makes it seem natural and just and necessary to find so much fault in a genius so great.

The dramatic form of a novel is what holds it together, makes it move, gives it a center and establishes a direction; and it includes the agency of perception, the consciousness set up in the book upon which, or through which, the story is registered. Dramatic form cannot in practice be wholly isolated from other formal elements; form is the way things go together in their medium—and the medium itself, here language, may properly be considered the major element of form; but we may think of different ways in which things go together in a given work, and strangely, the labor of abstraction and violation will seem to deepen our intimacy with the substance of the work and, more valuable, to heighten our sense of how that substance is controlled. The sense of control is perhaps the highest form of apprehension; it is understanding without immersion.

The question we have here to ask then is how did Melville go about controlling his two novels, *Moby Dick* and *Pierre?* The general, strictly true, and mainly irrelevant answer would be: haphazardly—that is, through an attitude which varied from the arrogance of extreme carelessness to the humility of complete attention. It is not that he attended only to what seriously interested him, for he was as careless of what he thought important as of what he thought trivial, but that apparently he had no sure rule as to what required management and what would take care of itself. His rule was vagary, where consequential necessities did not determine otherwise. And even there, Melville's eye was not good; he did not always see that if you took one series of steps your choice of further directions was narrowed, and that you could not step in two directions at once without risk of crippling yourself. It is perhaps his intellectual consistency, which he felt putatively omniform, that made him incorrigibly inconsistent in the technical quarter. For example, in *Moby Dick,* after setting up a single consciousness to get inside of, he shifted from that consciousness at will without sense of inconsistency, and therefore, which is the important thing, without making any effort to warrant the shifts and make them credible. Ignorance could not have excused him, because he had the example of Hawthorne, who was adept at shifting his compositional centers without disturbing his gravity, plumb in front of him. Not ignorance, but ineptitude and failure to discriminate. For the contrary example, I can think of only three occasions of importance in *Pierre,* if we except the digressions of the author himself in his own voice, where the consciousness of the hero is not left the presumed sole register of the story. Of these occasions, two are unnecessary to the story, and the third, where in the very end the perceiving center is turned over to the turnkey in the prison, funks its job. Yet in *Pierre* the theme cried out, one would think, for as many and as well chosen centers of consciousness as possible, all to be focussed on Pierre himself, the distraught and ambiguous, otherwise not measurable: the principle being that the abnormal can only be seen as viable, as really moving in response to the normal world, if seen through normal eyes.

Meanwhile we have approached a little nearer the composition of the two novels. Melville was right, granting the theme of *Moby Dick,* in choosing Ishmael the novice, to represent a story in which he had only a presumed and minor but omnipresent part; he was only wrong where he breached his choice without covering up. Ishmael, not otherwise ever named, is as mysterious as Ahab, but he is credible because he tells us not what he is but what he sees and what he sees other people see. The mere interposition of a participating consciousness between the story and its readers, once it has been made logical by tying the consciousness to the story, is a prime device of composition: it limits, compacts, and therefore controls what can be told and how. The only error Melville made is that he failed to distinguish between what Ishmael saw and what the author saw on his own account. If an author is to use digressions, which are confusing but legitimate by tradition, he ought to follow Fielding and put them in inter-chapters, and especially where the narrative is technically in the first person. Otherwise, as with Ishmael, the narrator will seem to know too much at a given time for the story's good; it will tend to tell itself all at once, and the necessary modicum of stupidity in the operative consciousness will be blighted by excess intelligence. As Ahab said to the carpenter who handed him a lantern: "Thrusted light is worse than presented pistols." Ishmael of course is Melville's alter ego, which explains why so much is imputed to him, but does not condone the excess.

On the whole the mode of Ishmael is a success exactly where the mode of Pierre (another alter ego of Melville) is wrong. Ishmael is looking on, and able to see; Pierre is in the center of his predicament, and lost in the action. Ishmael represents speech; Pierre represents rhetoric. Ishmael reports the abnormal, driven and demonic Ahab, either through his own normal sensibility or through the reported sensibilities of the mates and the crew. Pierre is seen principally without the intervening glass and focus of any sensibility whatever—so that he falls apart into a mere voice whenever he speaks, whereas the voice of Ahab, equally eloquent and rhetorical past belief, rings true in ears that have actually heard it.

It should be noted, curiously, that Ishmael is the only character in the book not "characterized" by Melville; he is merely situated in the center, explained a little, and let speak his part of recording angel. The curiosity is that all the other characters except Ahab and Queequeg near the beginning (the night at the inn), although given set characterizations as they appear, are far less viable and are far less *present* in the book than Ishmael. The reason may be that the other characters are only pulled out at intervals and are usually given stock jobs to do, set speeches to make, whereas Ishmael, sacking his creative memory, is occupied all the time. Which suggests two or three things: that character requires the sense of continuous action to show continuously, that the mates and crew were not *in* the book substantially but that their real use was to divide up the representation of the image of Ahab. There is nothing illegitimate about such characters, but to be successful and maintain interest they must be given enough to do to seem everywhere natural, and never obviously used, as here, *only* to make the wheels go round. One suspects, therefore, that Ahab comes out a great figure more because of the eloquence of the author's putative conception of him, and Ishmael's feeling for him, than from any representational aids on the part of the crew. The result is a great figure, not a great character. Ahab is as solitary in the book as he was in his cabin.

Pierre was in his way as compositionally isolated as Ahab; he was so situated, and so equipped as a consciousness, that he recorded his own isolation to the point of solipsism. If Pierre was real, as he was asserted to be, then nothing else properly in the novel was real except in terms of his perception or through the direct and unwarrantable intervention of the author. That is the risk attached to making the protagonist record the action in which he participates to the exclusion of other agents and while the action is going on. Melville instinctively tried to get round the difficulty by resorting to a series of dramatic scenes in which Pierre was chief interlocutor. The device was the right one—or one of the right ones—but it failed to work for a number of reasons, of which the chief was that Melville had no talent for making his dramatic scenes objective except by aid of external and unrelated force—as in *Moby Dick* he was able to resort to the ordinary exigencies of life on a whaling ship. In *Pierre* the White Whale was entirely in the protagonist's own inadequate perception of it; and the real weight of the book—what it was really about: tragedy by unconsidered virtue—was left for the author's digressions and soliloquies to carry as it could; which is to say that the book had no compositional center at all.

Something of the same sort may also be true of *Moby Dick*. Is it not possible to say that Ishmael, the narrator, provides only a false center? Is it not true that a great part of the story's theme escapes him, is not recorded through his sensibility, either alone or in connection with others? Then the real center would lie where? It would lie variously, I think, in the suspense attached to the character of Ahab and the half imputed, half demonstrated peril of the White Whale—the cold, live evil that is momently present. If we think of the book in that way, we may say that its compositional form is a long, constantly interrupted but as constantly maintained suspense, using as nexi or transitions the recurring verbal signs of Melville's allegory, Ahab's character, and the business of whaling. The business of whaling, including both the essays on anatomy and those on butchery, takes the most space and provides the most interest. All the reader has to do is to *feel* whaling as interest and he will recognize it as a compositional device mounting to the force of drama. Indeed we speak of the drama of whaling, or of cotton, or of gold without substantial injustice to the language; and I cannot for the life of me see why the drama of whaling should not be as efficient an agent of interest, if well felt, as the drama of who fired the second shot; and with Melville there is the additional advantage that the business of whaling points to the everlasting assassin instead of the casual and no doubt remorseful murderer. Interest is the thing of prime importance as any artist and any audience will tell you. If it takes up time and prepares for life, it does not matter how it is secured and does not fatally matter if it is overdone or vulgar in its appeal as it is in *Moby Dick*.

But is the real interest in the whaling or in the firing of the shot? Is it not always partly in the presentation, the feeling of detail and design, and partly in the image toward which the design points? Melville was lucky in *Oomoo* and *Typee,* to a less degree in *Mardi* and *White Jacket,* and most of all in *Moby Dick;* he was lucky or it was his genius that he had material in perfect factual control with which to take up time and point toward an image—in *Moby Dick* a profound and obsessive image of life. As it happened, it was in each case the material of a special and vanishing experience, dramatic enough in its own right to require very little fictionizing—very little actualizing—to exert the invaluable hold of natural interest over the average reader. If to interest, you add eloquence, you have all the essentials of the great novel below the first order. Many readers will be deceived and think the provision greater than it is. I have discovered a number of readers who on being asked reported enjoyment of a great story in a book of which Henry James would have said that it told no story to speak of; which indeed it does not.

In *Pierre* we are in a different box; a box quite empty of special material of objective interest to do for compositional strength otherwise lacking. There is no sea, or ship, or whale, or unique tradition of behavior, no unusual daily life—most precious of all—to give atmosphere, and weight and movement to carry the book toward the image of its chosen end. Melville was required to depend more than ever before upon the actual technique of the craft, and nothing much else, to make the book hang together. What is most illuminating is most pitiful. The glaring weaknesses of *Pierre* show up the hidden weaknesses of *Moby Dick,* and each set of weaknesses shows the other as essential—at least in the critical context in which we here provisionally place both books.

That one novel may criticize another is a commonplace when we think of different authors, as when we say that the novels of Henry James form a criticism of the novels of Flaubert and Turgenev, or that, in a way, the *Comédie Humaine* is a critique of the Waverly Novels. I think it is equally true that a consideration of the failures of a single author will often form the severest criticism of his successes, and a consideration of his successes may relatively improve our estimation of his failures. A great author is of one substance and often of one theme, and the relation between his various creations is bound to be reciprocal, even mutual; each is the other in a different form. So with *Pierre* and *Moby Dick*. If we wish to take up thinking of the two novels together in this way—which is the purpose of this essay—the alert consciousness will be struck with the repetition of the vices of *Pierre* in *Moby Dick,* or struck the other way round with the fact that the tragedy of *Pierre* fails to come off as well as *Moby Dick* only because the later book lacked the demonstrable extraneous interest of whaling. The efforts at plot in the two books are as lame; narrative runs as often offside. Dramatic motive on the subordinate level is as weakly put; Starbuck's tentative rebellion against Ahab and the threatened revenge of Glendinning Stanly and Frederick Tarton upon Pierre are equally unconvincing. The dialogue is as by turns limp and stiff and flowery in one book as the other. The delineations of character are almost interchangeable examples of wooden caricature. And so on. More important, the force and nobility of conception, the profundity of theme, were as great in either book—not from the dramatic execution but in spite of it, in the simple strength of the putative statement, and in the digressions Melville made from the drama in front of him, which he could not manage, into apologues or sermons, which he superbly could.

The strength of the putative statement is only simple when

thought of abstractly and as appealing to the intellect—to the putative element in appreciation: as if we read lyric poetry solely for the schematic paraphrase we make of it in popular discussion, or as if, in contemplating war, we thought only of political causes or in terms of the quartermaster's technique alone. What we want is to see what is the source of putative strength and how deeply its appeal is asserted; and in that pursuit we shall find ourselves instantly, I think, in the realm of language itself. Words, and their intimate arrangements, must be the ultimate as well as the immediate source of every effect in the written or spoken arts. Words bring meaning to birth and themselves contained the meaning as an imminent possibility before the pangs of junction. To the individual artist the use of words is an adventure in discovery; the imagination is heuristic among the words it manipulates. The reality you labor desperately or luckily to put into your words—and you may put it in consciously like Coleridge or by instinct as in the great ballads or from piety and passion like the translators of the Bible—you will actually have found there, deeply ready and innately formed to give objective being and specific idiom to what you knew and did not know that you knew. The excitement is past belief; as we know from the many myths of heavenly inspiration. And the routine of discovery is past teaching and past prediction; as we know from the vast reaches of writing, precious and viable to their authors, wholly without the conviction of being. Yet the adventure into the reality of words has a technique after the fact in the sense that we can distinguish its successful versions from those that failed, can measure provisionally the kinds and intensities of reality secured and attempted, and can even roughly guess at the conditions of convention and belief necessary for its emergence.

Melville is an excellent example for such an assay. We have only to relate the conception of the reality of language just adumbrated to the notion of the putative statement to see whence the strength of the latter comes; and we have only to relate the conception of language to its modifying context of conventions in order to understand the successes and at least excuse the many shortcomings and over-leapings of Melville's attempts at the paramount and indefeasible reality that great words show. For Melville habitually used words greatly.

Let us take first an example not at all putative and with as little supporting context of convention as possible: an example of words composed entirely of feelings and the statement of sensuous facts, plus of course the usual situating and correlative elements which are the real syntax of imaginative language.

To a landsman, no whale, nor any sign of a herring, would have been visible at that moment; nothing but a troubled bit of greenish white water, and thin scattered puffs of vapor hovering over it, and suffusingly blowing off to leeward, like the confused scud from white rolling billows. The air around suddenly vibrated and tingled, as it were, like the air over intensely heated plates of iron. Beneath this atmospheric waving and curling, and partially beneath a thin layer of water, also, the whales were swimming. Seen in advance of all the other indications, the puffs of vapor they spouted, seemed their forerunning couriers and detached flying outriders.

This is the bottom level of good writing, whether in prose or verse; and a style which was able to maintain the qualities of accurate objective feeling which it exemplifies at other levels and for other purposes could not help being a great style. The words have feelers of their own, and the author contributes nothing to the emotion they call forth except the final phrasing, which adds nothing but finish to the paragraph. It is an example of words doing their own work; and let no one think it is not imaginative work, or does not come to an emotion, because the mode is that of close description, and neither directly expressive nor enacting. Let us compare it, with achieved emotion in mind, with a deliberately "emotional" description taken from the chapter called Enceladus in *Pierre.*

Cunningly masked hitherto, by the green tapestry of the interlacing leaves, a terrific towering palisade of dark mossy massiness confronted you; and, trickling with unevaporable moisture, distilled upon you from its beetling brow slow thunder-showers of water-drops, chill as the last dews of death. . . . All round and round, the grim scarred rocks rallied and re-rallied themselves; shot up, protruded, stretched, swelled, and eagerly reached forth; on every side bristlingly radiated with hideous repellingness. . . . 'Mid this spectacle of wide and wanton spoil, insular noises of falling rocks would boomingly explode upon the silence and fright all the echoes, which ran shrieking in and out among the caves, as wailing women and children in some assaulted town.

This is, if I may insist on the term, putative description. It asserts itself to be description and passes for description until it is looked into, when you see that it is primarily the *assertion* of an emotional relation to landscape, and through effects of which landscape is incapable. Its force depends on the looseness, vagueness, and tumultuousness of the motion of the words. As a matter of fact the words are so chosen and arranged that they cannot contribute any material of emotion beyond that which may be contained in a stock exclamation. The primary point of our comparison is that the second passage dilutes and wastes an emotion assumed to have existed prior to its expression, whereas the first passage built up and united the elements of an emotion which exists only and actually in the words employed. The first passage discovers its meaning in words, the second never reached the condition of meaning. The first passage reminds you of Gerard Hopkins, the second of Ann Radcliffe; a contrast which brings up the secondary point of our comparison.

The spirit of the gothic novel ran frothily through the popular literature of America in the first half of the nineteenth century, ending possibly with its own travesty in *The Black Crook*. Melville, faced with the bad necessity, as it must have seemed to him, of popularizing the material of *Pierre* and *Moby Dick,* adopted outright the gothic convention of language with all its archaisms and rhetorical inflations. The effect in the two books was similar in fact though not quite the same in effect. Some of the soliloquies in *Moby Dick* seem more like tantrums than poetry, but they were the tantrums of a great imagination fed with mastered material. In *Pierre,* without any fund of nourishing material, the dialogues, soliloquies, and meditations got lost in the flatulence of words.

Now, the gothic convention is not susceptible of reality in itself, as we see in Beckford and Peacock and Brontë—perhaps in Poe and occasionally in Hawthorne—but it requires on the part of the author unconditional assent to it as a convention. This assent Melville could not give; he used it, so far as I can see, as a solemn fraud and hoped for the best. In *Moby Dick* the fraud passed preliminary muster because the lofty "unreal" terror that rode the *Pequod* made it seem at least plausible, even in its greatest extravagance, as a vehicle of response. And there is the further defense, often made, that the worst excesses of langugae and sentiment are excusable because of the poetry they are supposed to hold. To which the answer is that the poetry would have been better without the excess; when Melville dropped the mode and wrote in a language comparable to the passage first quoted above, as in Ahab's last soliloquy, better poetry was actually produced. But no one, so far as I know, unless it be Foster Damon who writes *con amore* of anything both American and gothic, has defended the excesses of *Pierre,* of which the passage quoted above is a tame example.

It may be said in passing that what is often called the Elizabethan influence in Melville's prose might more accurately be called the gothic influence heightened by the greatness of Melville's intentions. If I may have the notation for what it is worth, I suspect that in "the three boats swung over the sea like three samphire baskets over high cliffs," while the samphire baskets undoubtedly came from *King Lear,* still they had got well spattered with gothic mire on the long journey. Again, the sister-brother crux in *Pierre,* while it may be found in John Ford has a very different reality of expression from that in Ford's verse.

> The menacings in thy eyes are dear delights to me; I grow up with thy own glorious stature; and in thee, my brother, I see God's indignant ambassador to me, saying—Up, up, Isabel, and take no terms from the common world, but do thou make terms to it, and grind thy fierce rights out of it! Thy catching nobleness unsexes me, my brother; and now I know that in her most exalted moment, then woman no more feels the twin-born softness of her breasts, but feels chain-armour palpitating there!

These lines, spoken by Isabel in response to similar declarations on the part of Pierre on the occasion of their second conversation, could not have been matched in Ford, but they could be matched a hundred times in the popular gothics. As for the minor effects of Elizabethan influence, where it has been said, by Mumford among others, that Melville's prose is Websterian—and perhaps it sometimes is—yet it far more often supplies us with Marlovian tropes. For every phrase such as "the cheeks of his soul collapsed in him," there are a dozen on the tone of the following: "With a frigate's anchors for my bridle-bitts and fasces of harpoons for spurs, would I could mount that whale and leap the topmast skies . . . !" This is the Marlowe of *Tamerlane,* and the unregenerate Marlowe letting himself go, not the Marlowe remodeled and compacted of *Faustus* and *The Jew*. Occasionally there is such a triumphant meeting of rhetoric and insight as the passage which contains the famous phrases: "To trail the genealogies of these high mortal miseries, carries us at last among the sourceless primogenitures of the gods"—a passage more mindful of the *Urn Burial* than of anything in *The Duchess of Malfi,* but which is mindful most of Melville himself.

If it was the gothic excess that gave occasional opportunity for magnificent flashes, we should be grateful to it that much: it is at least a delight by the way; but it far more often produced passages like the speech of Isabel, which are perhaps collector's items, but not delights. Besides, what is most and finally illuminating, when Melville really had something to say, and was not making a novel, he resorted to another mode, which was perhaps the major expressive mode of his day, the mode of the liberal Emersonian sermon, the moral apologue on the broad Christian basis. There Melville's natural aptitude lay; when he preaches he is released, and only then, of all weak specifications. That the sermon was to say the best of it an artificial mode in fiction mattered nothing, and emphasizes the fact that Melville was only a novelist betimes. He made only the loosest efforts to tie his sermons into his novels, and was quite content if he could see that his novels illustrated his sermons and was reasonably content if they did not; or so the books would show. He preached without scruple, and with full authority, because he felt in full command of the mode he used: he believed in its convention of structure and its deeper convention of its relation to society with all his heart. Father Mapple's sermon on Jonah and Plotinus Plinlimmon's lecture—it is really a sermon—on Chronometricals and Horologicals are the two sustained examples of self-complete form in his work. The doctrine might not have appealed to Channing or Parker, but the form, the execution, the litheness and vigor and verve, the homely aptnesses, the startling comparisons, the lucidity of presentation of hard insights, the dramatic and pictorial quality of the illustrations, and above all the richness of impact and the weighted speed of the words, would have appealed as near perfection.

The curiosity—and Melville looked at is all curiosity—that needs emphasis here is that the vices of his style either disappeared or transpired only as virtues when he shifted his mode to the sermon, and this without any addition of insight or eloquence, but simply, I believe, because he had found a mode which suited the bent of his themes, which allowed the putative statement to reach its full glory without further backing, which made room for rhetoric and demanded digression, and which did not trouble him, so great was his faith in it, with its universal lurking insincerity. Consider the following lines, which form the counter sermon to Phinlimmon's lecture in *Pierre*.

All profound things, and emotions of things are preceded and attended by Silence. What a silence is that with which the pale bride precedes the responsive *I will,* to the priest's solemn question, *Wilt thou have this man for thy husband?* In silence, too, the wedded hands are clasped. Yea, in silence the child Christ was born into the world. Silence is the general consecration of the universe. Silence is the invisible laying on of the Divine Pontiff's hands upon the world. Silence is at once the most harmless and the most awful thing in all nature. It speaks of the Reserved Forces of Fate. Silence is the only Voice of our God.

Nor is this so august Silence confined to things simply touching or grand. Like the air, Silence permeates all things, and produces its magical power, as well during that peculiar mood which prevails at a solitary traveller's first setting forth on a journey, as at the unimaginable time when before the world was, Silence brooded on the face of the waters.

The author of these paragraphs was at home in his words and completely mastered by them; and he had reached in that language, what Pierre never reached, the "sense of uncapitulatable security, which is only the possession of the furthest advanced and profoundest souls."

In our present context there seems little more to say. The consideration of Melville as a novelist should have shown, at least in the superficial aspects which this brief essay has been able to touch, that it was precisely the practice of that craft that put his books, and himself, at a loss, and left him silent, stultified, and, before the great face of possibility, impotent for forty years of mature life. I trust that it will have been shown as at least plausible that Melville suffered the exorbitant penalty of his great failure, not as a result of the injuries inflicted upon him by his age, but because of his radical inability to master a technique—that of the novel—radically foreign to his sensibility. The accidents of his career, the worse accidents of his needs, brought him to a wrong choice. Yet had he made a right choice, the accident of his state of beliefs might well have silenced him altogether. Judging by the reception of his two serious books, he would have been anathema as a preacher and unpublishable as an essayist. We should be grateful for his ill luck in only a lesser sense than we are for Dante's, or we should have lost the only great imagination in the middle period of the American nineteenth century: a putative statement to which all readers must assent.

1938

9

Humanism and Symbolic Imagination

NOTES ON RE-READING IRVING BABBITT

When a man has been dead some time and his works have pretty well died after him, when his mark, so to speak, has been nearly effaced, it is a little shameful to try to resurrect him, to brighten up his mark, merely for the legerdemain of it. Earth is the choice sarcophagus, not the critical essay. But there are figures of men, quite dead in themselves and whose work is quite finished, who yet survive by implication, not actively through what they were or what they did, but as representatives, unusually pure in type, of being and work more wholly achieved by others. Such men, prominent or notorious in life, are quickly seen afterwards to have been of small magnitude and without fertility, but with the beautiful advantage, thus scaled down, of simplicity carried to the point of the commonplace. In thinking of them we know almost exactly where we are in relation to what they stood for. They have become immediate formulas through which vastly complex and far-reaching considerations are amply dealt with for the moment. Nothing is dearer to the mind than such formulas, so dear indeed that we usually hide them in the broad cloak of some symbolic or philosophical term. Such a figure was Irving Babbitt, whose formula was hidden, by his own insistence and help, in the very superior, quite aristocratic cloak of Humanism. It is the purpose of these notes to see what the formula was and why it was tragically necessary for it to be hidden in Humanism. That is the opportune interest; our real interest lies in the fact that formulas similar to Babbitt's, and if anything more sterile, are like to fly in our faces in every window and must be dealt with, not by pulling down the shades, but by the deep exorcism of the effort of understanding. We must restore something of the complexity which the formula under his Humanism began by getting rid of.

This is of course to begin by saying that Babbitt's mind operated by rote, a method which has great initial advantages of knowing beforehand what is going to be said and of making available such a fund of ignorant energy that opposition—the non-routine picture—is put down before it is seen. The rote-mind, when powerful, is good for teaching up to a point. If we think of teaching at Harvard below the point of William James (a name chosen because he stood for the experimental, the ambiguous, the possible, all of which Babbitt detested), then Babbitt was by universal report as stimulating a teacher as the College ever had. Nobody could study under him and fail to do a vast amount of co-ordinated reading. Nobody could listen to him without a sense of participation in the end-process of learning: intellectual assimilation. Indifference to what he taught was as impossible as, to him, indifference to the problems which he treated. He taught not by sympathy or persuasion or personality, by stretching the student mind, but by force. He limited mind where James stretched it. But one thing he had in common with James; he not only communicated his own energy but he roused the native energy of his students, though more often in revolt than in growth. Knowing well that he taught against the temper of his time he laid about him like an evangel, no doubt hoping to convert by zeal—that is, at the expense of the other fellow—and no less expecting to create opposition. He taught, he thought, he fought against the odds; his converts were few, though singularly his own, and the opponents he created were many and emphatically heretical or alien in their interpretation of the point of view which he had himself hammered into their heads. His best students, men like T. S. Eliot for example, could not help going beyond him, where only some deep privation of imagination, some paucity of sympathy, some racking poverty of sensibility, kept him from going himself. It was as if he taught music, and taught it magnificently, but only in the written score. He was right, everlastingly, about everything which may occur before the playing begins.

The figure is not as forced as it may sound. For what did he teach—what in all the enormous mass of literature that he read did he praise—but those great dead writers whose works we know precisely only as scores, with an imperfect clue to the notation even there, and which we cannot play at all. These are the writers whose ideas have survived and can be dealt with as formulas, as abstractions of the middle way, but whose poetry, what happened when their ideas got into drama, or got lodged in actuality, we must through ignorance for the most part let go by the board, unless in ourselves, in our own imaginations, in the literature of our own times, we can see the poetry refreshed. Sophocles is nothing without his violence; Antigone a mere mechanical fanatic without her folly; Creon an ineffectual ranting without his stupidity; Ismene a mere vapor without her double charge of fear and love. In short, the whole Greek drama is nothing but exemplary if we do not ourselves supply the violence, the folly, the stupidity, the mixture of fear and love. Babbitt was not only content with the exemplary, he insisted on its dominance at the expense of every other interest. That is why he never seemed inside his examples.

He was a praiser of gone times because he had none of his own. His mind dwelt where it fed among the bones of the chosen past and when it came out to try the daylight it saw the present fleshless. His classicism was in effect primitivism in reverse; almost with the violence of direct experience he insisted upon invoking the thin shades of the classical lot *as shades*. He never saw afresh in the imaginative field. He never, so far as I can find, attempted to revive the turbulence of the flesh—the fury and the mire, to use Yeats's phrase, in human veins—which alone made the shade of Oedipus, say, truly ancestral. He never realized that we inherit only in the flesh, that the spirit is nothing without the letter. He knew nothing, in short, or at any rate never took account of the chthonic underside of things which the topside only keeps down. His interest, to repeat, lay almost entirely in what could be made to seem exemplary within the terms of a formula.

We strike here upon the most startling professional feature of

Babbitt's mind; that he was a professed literary critic, and was interested only in the abstractable elements of literature, only in what it had in common with the general abstractions which go to make the focus of human significance, and not at all in what literature concretely did to its abstractions. With the consequences of this attitude upon his actual critical writing, and with the transactions between his literary criticism and his political criticism, we shall be later concerned. Here let us see rather if we can further characterize the type of mind which, confronting itself with literature, would show such a feature. For it was a typical mind, and from its typicalness if anywhere his followers gathered the sense of solidity, security, of individuality as men, and, what was more important, a renewed sense of the Human—something very near the divine—in Man. Babbitt was representative—exemplary in the sense that we have just been using the word—on the intellectual side, of a central and fecund human attitude, mixed in the making like any attitude, but historic, ancestral, and permanent; an attitude which we must be concerned to enrich rather than to destroy.

It was, then, this central attitude, the attitude that there is always an ascertainable order, very near an absolute order in the moral world, which is the only right human order. That is an unfair description of the Babbitt brand of Humanism, but it is very hard to be fair to the achievement of Babbitt, at least for me, because in almost the exact measure that he secures assent to his main position he rouses antipathy by the blows—blind, brutal, and arrogant—which he strikes from it. His main position—his Humanism—is impregnable by nature, for it is in the middle, the product of maximum, and concentric, pressure from all sides. One would like to be, as a mind, where he thought he was, at the median, focusing, balancing point, at the fulcrum of higher and lower, the one and the many, the intuitive and the rational, the inner and the outer, the expansive and the contractive tendencies of the human imagination at work, yet at once immersed in the imperfection of human nature and having access, within the self, to the will of God. To feel oneself at the center of every human conflict, to feel the conflict as one, and to feel it so settled in the self as to be able to say, as he said toward the end of his life, that he "ranged" himself "unhesitatingly on the side of the supernatural"—surely such a feeling of centricity, of rightness, of power, is heroic to the classic extreme; it tempts the gods. For to perfect the human role is fatally to surpass it, and leaves only the possibility of tragedy.

The tragedy of Irving Babbitt for himself may well have been his isolation—the utter desolateness of the center. For us the tragedy appears as the damnation, the attendant mutilation, of every foray, every footstep of his faculties outside the center. He was sound motionless, in position; in motion, in the restless, driven effort to gather the world of experience home to his position, he was ruined. To summon the tragic sense to the consideration of a critical mind is perhaps to stain our appreciation with raw colors, but if we do not think of the absolute activities of the mind as tragic we have only a flat affair, a thing merely to reject. It is the special vividness, the life-giving quality of the tragic sense that it gives perspective, background, both to the ambition achieved and to the actuality consequently uncovered.

The tragic sense questions more than it answers. From what was Irving Babbitt isolated? What was the condition of his desolation? What of the rich material world, what representative filings attached themselves to the lodestone? What was excluded? In short, what kind of order did Babbitt envisage, and what was its cost, applied? Here is tragedy at the nub. The effort to create order out of imagination permits the triumphs of civilization and ordains the tragedies of individuals—just as the assertion of order without imagination demolishes civilization and makes the individual impossible altogether. What imagination does outside the terms of order no one knows, since without order it never transpires; it is its order by which we keep hold of it. Thus in dealing with an intellectual or philosophical critic like Babbitt, we must get hold of, for ourselves, his notion of order before we can judge how much it was a product of his imagination and how much it was, desperately, merely an asserted formula.

But order is not single. Order is various and of various value depending on the kind and the intensity of the impact of the disorder which is its concern; and if there is an order of orders it is more likely to be discovered in solution than as a precipitate: one would not recognize it till *after* one had experienced it, and it might well seem only a new and overwhelming kind of disorder. There is nothing in the notion of order that requires that it be rational except the limitations of human reason; an admission found eloquently in most frames of human thought but almost totally absent from Humanism, which takes no stock in the unaccountable whether in magic or physics. In fact Humanism, or Babbitt's brand of it, pretty well limits itself to a single kind of order for which it claims supremacy over such other orders as it recognizes.

This order has nothing to do with what for present purposes may be called the *primary* kinds of order, namely the descriptive and statistical kinds of order which rest on the notions of sequence, repetition, development, and by the aid of which things and affairs are seen to declare themselves and become realizable in the mind as if they were just themselves. When St. Augustine declared—and no doubt St. Francis would have agreed with him—that the love of God consisted in knowledge of His creation, he was only expressing the maximum function of this type of order. To Babbitt it would have seemed a low, even a degraded order, in that it lacked transcendence. His deliberate concern was with the *secondary* kinds of order which are bound up with the notions of the moral, the prophetic, the ideal. Here every orderly movement—and other movements are ignored—ends in judgment. The power of discrimination discredits all that does not meet the requirements of judgment. It is the circle of formula at work rather than the line of observation; reaction is an enclosing rather than a meeting force, an agent of exclusion rather than inclusion, of shutting rather than opening. Things are exhibited in opposition, rather than combination, one good the other evil, not mixed, as good *and* evil. These are the orders of the complementary, the completing, the transcending. They make up, in short, the order of human aspiration; and they have the tragic tendency, in the consequent motions of thought, to make aspiration the source rather than the end of effort. The tragedy, of course, consists in the prejudgment of experience which follows necessarily once the direction of aspiration is reversed. To prejudge—which is the great temptation of intellect—is to make experience sterile whether judgment is, in the instance, right or wrong. The mind recoils upon itself unless it partakes of what it judges.

This is what happened to Babbitt as an active critic. His Humanism, by acting as if it were complete, as if it were itself the unity of what it saw, became in effect a methodology of prejudgment, a barrier between the mind and the sensibility in which it lodged, between the score of the music and its performance. How this happened, not only to Babbitt but to half the articulate minds of his time and ours, is a matter of both immediate and profound interest. How is it that minds may be so virile in principle and so emasculated in act, so fecund in pattern and so sterile in texture? I do not profess to know the answer, but I am firm in the suggestion that the decay of Christian imagination, the voiding of religious imagination of any description, has a great deal to do with it. It is the religious imagination, more than anything else, that unites the actuality of a culture, or of a man's life, with its principles, or its standards of judgment; for the religious imagination requires for its functioning a continuous act of piety, a steady consciousness of charitable understanding, all the way from top to bottom, and without prejudice of balance or proportion, of the human gamut. The habit of such imagination may not be acquired as a by-product of an intellectual mediation of extremes, as the Humanists attempt it, for intellectual mediation leads merely to decorum, and decorum, except by accident, excludes charitable understanding. Neither can what is called the intuition of the Higher Will—transcendent intuition, or what you will—invoke such imagination, for such intuition starts too near the top of aspiration to reach the bottom undistorted. It is only the religious imagination which has the advantage of including the traditional standards of life along with a minute knowledge of its immediate experience; hence it commonly keeps, along with its principles, escape from them through intercession, repentance, sacrifice, grace, as forms of behavior with which the Humanist will usually have little to do. The important thing about religious imagination, as with religion itself, is that it is only secondarily concerned with the problem of conduct and the problem of moral order which as a rule exhaust the attention of the Humanist; its primary concern is at one end with the worship of God on this earth and at the other end with the shape and the significance of the experience of life whether above or below the level of conduct. I hope T. S. Eliot would agree with me if I say it is because of considerations like these that Humanism cannot substitute for the religious imagination, that Humanism without religion is sterile, but that the religious imagination of our world—what is left of Europe and the Americas—is not likely to survive without the aid of an enriched Humanism. Mr. Eliot has his own arguments, which are best read by those of his own persuasion. Here I make no need for a profession of faith, nor for any psychological substitute for the experience of conversion; I do not believe either to be generally possible, and what is not generally possible will not greatly affect our culture; but I do insist that it is both necessary and possible that we make a secular equivalent of the religious imagination. It was human need and aspiration that created supernatural religion; the same need, and perhaps only a reduced aspiration, are now in the process of creating a merely superrational religion, in which the great care must be that nothing is deified but God. The difference between a supernatural religion and a superrational religion is no greater than that between Christianity and Buddhism in the eyes of a non-professing Christian; the difference being that to him Christianity seems a transgression of the rational faculty where Buddhism seems rather a development beyond the rational faculty. To a Buddhist, of course, the thing would appear the other way round. A better example, to our eyes, might be the religious imagination we find in Greek mythology, of which the poetry seems to crown, without ever infringing upon, the full reach of reason.

The word poetry has crept in here unannounced, and needs to be qualified lest he become a usurper, or worse a restored monarch. Poetry is by no means to be understood as anything but an *inadequate* substitute for religion; and it is because we can take Greek mythology—or Buddhist, or Egyptian—only as poetry that we cannot take it as religion. More important, while the religious imagination is poetic, the poetic imagination is only rarely religious and when it is so is something else as well. What that something else is cannot be said of an individual, for it is what the individual draws from, but we know its connections well enough when we speak of a race or a culture in the aspect of its religion. It is the power of creating or discovering symbols which are the sources as well as the reminders of meaning, and which, once recognized, are inexhaustible, and are, so to speak, fertile in themselves. The man—and whether he be poet, philosopher, priest, or some other accident of consciousness, makes no matter—the man who uses the symbolic imagination must find the most part of his poetry already written for him out of the live, vast waste of disorder of the actual, out of those myths which as Jung says somewhere we may think of as the dreams of the people—the needful vision of the tribe. He must write deliberately out of the anonymous, contributing only the name, the order, of the given instance. The symbolic imagination perhaps can be put as the means of bringing to significance, to order, the knowledge we have above and below the level of the mind. It is, in short, the chief mode of participation in the life common to all men at all times.

A merely rational imagination cannot reach and can hardly envisage such knowledge and must tend to abhor, to distrust, such participation; often rejecting the instance in favor of the ideal which never comes. Babbitt's Humanism—positive, critical, thoroughgoing, individual—is like that; refusing to acknowledge its subject matter unless it appears manifestly in an ideal order. Consider, for example, the lines of Burke which Babbitt tirelessly repeated as a central statement of his conviction: lines to the effect that all the good things in our civilization are the result of a combination of "the spirit of a gentleman and the spirit of religion." The spirit of a gentleman produces decorum, and the spirit of religion produces, for Babbitt, the will to refrain. These are the texts from which Babbitt preaches, for Babbitt is a preacher rather than a thinker. He struck down too much for discrimination, and he ignored too much for judgment. He was very near a fanatic against fanaticism, and quixotic, too, for he always saw his opponents as much bigger and far more evil than life, and was zealous never to let the dimension grow smaller. Thus he was able to attack Rousseau as the devil who promoted Bolshevism with the same vigor as he had attacked Rousseau as the devil of the French Revolution—poor Marx never getting more than a thumbed nose. Thus, too, we find him in the chapter of *Democracy and Leadership* called "Democracy and Standards," attacking those who would socialize justice through the means of equity as destroying the strict letter of the law, where the trouble is that Babbitt does not realize that the theory of equity has always been to provide remedies for all wrongs not remediable at law, which ought, one would think, to be the very critical part of the Humanist concept of law. Again, to make an end of this sort of example, in speaking of the disappearance of the will to refrain, he for a moment excepts Goethe, and then goes on: "Any one who thinks of the series of Goethe's love affairs prolonged into the seventies is scarcely likely to maintain that his *Entsagung* was of a very austere character even for the man of the world, not to speak of the saint."

What led Babbitt to such singular aberrations of Humanism—such backslidings of balance—was precisely, one supposes, his obsessive addiction to a literal interpretation of his formula about the spirit of Christianity and the spirit of a gentleman. The outward irregularity, the breach of decorum, the mere wrongness of sin, in short the mere orderliness or lack of it in the outward world became for him the sole applicable standard. He had a mind contaminated by the lust for order, a lust which amounted at times to a trembling bodily infatuation which if it did not destroy order certainly dismantled it, rendering it incapable of the great primary virile act of composition. It is at this point that the reader feels the fatal lack of the religious or the symbolic imagination, the lack indeed of any imagination at all.

Babbitt was aware of the lack, though not of its consequences, himself; and there are two passages of great interest which illustrate the profound character of that awareness. One passage deals with the doctrine of grace and may be found in the chapter "Europe and Asia" in *Democracy and Leadership*. He has been talking about the insoluble difficulty of using the intellect to the utmost without insubordinating it and in general about the conflict between—in Pascal's sense of the terms—the head and heart, and remarks that the general cure has been usually some kind of obscurantism. He then goes on to examine the conflict between the primacy of grace and the primacy of mind, as if he held (as I do not) that this conflict were parallel to the others. "It can be shown," he writes, "that the doctrine of grace was the keystone of the whole edifice of European society in its medieval form. It is not as clear as one might wish that European civilization can survive the collapse of this doctrine." To this I assent, but I wish I were surer of Babbitt's version of what it is I assent to; he says nothing that I can discover either in the locus of this quotation or elsewhere to expand or define what he meant by the doctrine of grace. Perhaps he was unable; grace being far more of a condition of being than a doctrine, it is not easily susceptible to translation to the medium of general ideas where Babbitt could alone have handled it. It can be risked here that grace—the saving grace, the grace of God, the saying of grace, the grace in light and the grace in darkness when these are balm, the grace in dying, the grace indeed that suddenly inhabits all things deeply realized—is expressed if at all through the symbolic imagination. As a clue to the commoner apprehensions of grace one risks the further suggestion that the beauty which we feel in passages of nature or, more consciously, of art, not themselves handsome, pleasant, well-proportioned, things even intolerable in themselves, might better be called grace than beauty. One thinks of Gulliver or Lear.

Babbitt thought of neither. He thought rather, faced with the collapse of the *doctrine* of grace, that the thing itself had collapsed, and turned to the East, to Buddhism, in order to suggest a means of restoring peace to the ethical will, in order to secure what he called the centripetal element in liberty. These are of course excellent goods to restore or secure, but I do not see for the life of me that they have any bearing on either the warfare of the head and heart or the doctrine of grace, and if Babbitt thought they had, then his thought amply demonstrates that he had no access to the experience of grace. Babbitt had barred himself off, it would seem, from the very intuition, the imagination, which he needed, and knew that he needed, to make his decorum in fact, what it is etymologically, the outward habit of grace.

In order not to seem unfair, a parallel example of the failure of imagination may be given in passing from the same chapter, where Babbitt was dealing with the Logos as the Christian mode of subordinating the divine reason to the divine will, which is all to the good. But then he goes on: "The truth of the incarnation, to put the matter on purely psychological grounds, is one that we have all experienced in a less superlative form: the final reply to all the doubts that torment the human heart is not some theory of conduct, however perfect, but the man of character"; which is good till the conclusion, and the conclusion is shocking. Babbitt saw and argued that the transformation of Christianity into a religion of service was its ruin, but to reduce Christ to a man of character is to make a second and sterile crucifixion. Babbitt could not deal with the symbolic imagination without reducing it to its merely intellectual level. No wonder such men are hopeless of their own times when they save, in actuality, nothing of the past times they revere.

To come now to the second passage of great interest, we move away from the imaginative realms of grace abounding and reason subdued, into the homelier region of the conscience. Conscience was for Babbitt the mainspring of positive criticism and out of its decisions individual acts were formulated as expressions of personal liberty; but what is most interesting is Babbitt's view of the source of conscience. It is found in the discussion of Rousseau and the Idyllic Imagination. He has been arguing various dualisms of man as political animal, and has gotten off, as so often, into the subject of the general will, when the following sentences suddenly occur. "Any one who traces the subject historically will acquire the conviction, as I have already said, that the Christian religion founded something of which not even a Plato or an Aristotle had any adequate notion—personal liberty. By its separation of the things of God and the things of Caesar, it established a domain of free conscience, in which the individual might take refuge from the encroachments of the omnipotent state." These sentences ought to have been the nub of all Babbitt's Humanism, but like the remarks on grace, this notion of the conscience and personal liberty are hardly pursued, either here or throughout the works. One reflects how magnificently the notion of humility might have been modified by the notion of the free conscience as a refuge, and likewise how the notion of humility (which in Babbitt consists partly in looking up in order to be safe in looking down, and partly in strenuous meditation) could have enriched the function of the free conscience. Instead, Babbitt uses both to strike down the Civil Religion of Rousseau as sentimental and utilitarian and in general a mere vanity of intellect. We can add for him, then, what he did not see, that as he did not possess grace neither did he possess the refuge of a free conscience, whether Christian or its equivalent. It seems almost superfluous to say that had he possessed either he could not have said that "Circumstances may arise when we may esteem ourselves fortunate if we get the American equivalent of a Mussolini; he may be needed to save us from the American equivalent of a Lenin." That the remark was made in 1923 eases its folly but does not reduce either its arrogance, its extravagance, or the failure to understand American history which it implies. Even in 1923 the castor oil cure for political opposition was no more humanistic than it was humanitarian, and castor oil, street fighting, murder, and sabotage of spirit, made up the features of fascist decorum.

The point is, that Babbitt was willing to enslave his conscience in fact, to make it a prison rather than a refuge for individual liberty, at the dictation of a merely intellectual order. How is it that he could not apply to himself the judgment that he made of the best Greeks, that their failure to make a sound individualism was due partly to the inadequacy of their treatment of the allied problems of the imagination and the higher will, and partly because of their obstinate intellectualism. That to intellectualize the imagination and the higher will (the will of God) is precisely what the intellect is prone to do the moment it begins asserting an order as literally efficacious, apparently never occurred to Babbitt, in his own case, at all. Yet that is what happened, and very nearly all that happened. The moment of action was the moment of relapse. How right, how accurate even, Babbitt is until you look to see what action he proposes as a consequence of his thought. It is then that his thought shows as mere thought, the exercise of a formula upon the basis of undeclared and largely unconscious prejudices. He is a first-class example, the perfect cliché, of the man who provides the right answers to the wrong questions. For what is almost a free example, consider how he complains of "the solid darkness of this enlightened age," and goes on: "By the dismissal as mere prejudice of the traditional forms that are in no small measure the funded experience of any particular community, the State loses its historical continuity, its permanent self, as it were, that unites its present with its past and its future." Surely nothing could be finer or righter to argue; but how awkward, how disconsolately disjointed and disgruntled are the elements of this prose thought, when once we discover that Babbitt is most anxious to preserve the Supreme Court (as of 1920), to put down labor unions, and that he is most afraid of the least infringement upon private property. Once more we have it indeed in evidence that the style is the man.

Which end came first I will not say, but, to repeat—for it is the whole burden of these notes—it was either the style that reduced the man or the man that impoverished the style to the condition of order, so that every consideration that did not either clearly oppose or naturally fall into that order was ignored. This is to say that Babbitt made for himself a mind that was restricted to general ideas, and general ideas that could not refresh themselves, such was the severity of their order in the monkish sense, in the fount of disorder. In fact, one had better say that Babbitt's mind was fitted only to attack general ideas by means of his own generalized ideas. That which is generalized is a convenience in thinking, a sign, empty itself, employed to save time or to telescope effects. Excellent themselves, it is only when they become laws—that is, when they become predictors of thought or behavior—that they become evil because sterile, mere headstones on the bodies of dead thought.

This is the consequence, which he did not see, of the felt lack of a doctrine of grace, of the actual lack, however described, of the symbolic imagination. If evidence is wanted, it is rife in the various essays in literary criticism; evidence which appears irrefutably if we merely describe the essays. It is not, that is, so much a matter of a difference of opinion or judgment, but the limits of interest outside which Babbitt refrained, to use his own word, from ever poaching. There is not, I think, in the whole long list, a single essay upon an imaginative writer as such—the nearest perhaps being the paper on the Correspondence of George Sand, which dates from 1898, and which comes nearer than Babbitt ever afterwards came to an appreciation either of an imaginative figure or of the imaginative predicament. The essays deal rather with the intellectual apparatus which, one way or another, impaired the approach of other critics to literature but which dominated their views of life. There is no evidence to show that Babbitt ever saw the imagination at work at all despite his avowed major interest in balancing intellect and imagination. He was content in practice to examine the machinery others used in the attempt at such balance and to show the various odd detrimental things that got in by the way when the machinery was used automatically.

Such writing is not illegitimate, is indeed necessary, for nothing will puncture the pretensions of critics like showing how much of their work is the mere grinding, however well oiled, of gears and *genres,* and it is useful, too, in detecting those areas in literature itself where merely intellectual formulations masquerade as organic themes. That is to say, such writing is a good weapon of rejection. Two further functions may be discriminated for Babbitt's practice. There is a sense in which literature, or any of the arts, illustrates the history of general ideas, and another sense in which it exemplifies the development of patterns of life, and if you remember that the ideas are merely primary and that the patterns are merely prior to the literature, then you can legitimately use literature in these senses in your work as a historian or a philosopher. But you must not think that thereby you have touched the content of literature itself, or criticized it, or gotten rid of it.

There is the curiosity. Babbitt evidently felt that he did touch literature, did criticize it, and did, for the most part, get rid of it, by means of his intellectual standards put into operation upon the current of general ideas he found in it. To deal with literature as a current of ideas is about as rewarding, compared to the possibilities, as dealing with the plays of Shakespeare as the current of the plots which he begged, borrowed, or invented and which often impeded or obfuscated rather than aided the true movement of his drama. You get only the most available order, the outside order, the intellectually formulable order, and only by accident touch on the intimate actual orders—for there are many, not one—which kept things going.

The fact may be that these intimate orders are not susceptible of verbalization on the intellectual level; and it may be that this fact is responsible for the confusion and sterility of the relation of Humanism and literature. The Humanist feels that he must capture the content of literature, and as he tries to do so by intellectual means gets only an intellectual content, which naturally seems to him pretty thin; then he begins to feel that the thing would be better the other way round, that literature needs humanism in order to have any content in the sense that he can understand it, so that he rejects literature that does not declare itself immediately as humanistic—as Greek drama, by definition or by habit, happens to do. Here is the radical confusion—caused entirely by his retreat upon the intellectual formula—into which the Humanist drives himself, whether in relation to politics or literature or religion or any great movement of the mind. He has made his Humanism absolute instead of conditional, active instead of residual, assertive instead of responsive. Any literature, so far as it can be understood, which is to say digested, should be good food for Humanism; any literature, any politics, any religion, any movement of the symbolic imagination, seen and realized as actual, should bring the intellect of the Humanist nearer the condition of grace. Any failure, any rejection, merely deepens, to remodel Babbitt's own phrase, the solid dark of intellectual enlightenment by willfully enclosing it. No stronger argument could be made for the Humanist insistence upon the necessity of the religious imagination—or as I have called it the symbolic imagination —than the lack of grace, in any definition of that word, in the Humanist practice without it.

Neither to argue nor to insist is to secure the good named; virtue rises out of knowledge no more in the intellect than in morals; these are commonplaces of Humanist doctrine, and Babbitt rehearsed them, for purposes of adverse judgment, over and over again, turning always for cure to the resources of the inner life, the higher will, the citadel of character, in short, self-discipline. Now if Babbitt is representative, as I think he is, of a frame of mind which for convenience we call Humanism, though most of its devotees do not call it at all, believing it to be just the operation of thought at its purest or best, then self-scrutiny, a recognition of the nature of its own will and of the limits of its own character, should be its best, because native, cure. It should hospitably make room for what it lacks. Intellect is but the manners of the mind, and the Humanist who inadvertently makes himself, as Babbitt did, all intellect, is all manners and no man. Hospitality, on the other hand, is imaginative, plastic, responsive, symbolic, and to practice it enriches one's manners and gives them being. That is what self-scrutiny should do for the Humanist; by making him perennially re-experience the source of his manners, the rigid order into which they had solidified would freshen and become open.

Well, then, the true business of Humanism, since it works from intellectual bias in even its most imaginative moments, and since it takes for itself the function of mediation, is to mediate the ravenings of the intellect; to feel the intellect as elastic, plastic, absorptive; to feel the experience upon which intellect works as ambiguous, present only provisionally, impinging, vanishing, above and below, known far beyond its own mere grasp; and thus to restore to the intellect its proper sense of strength and weakness in necessity, that in setting up its orders and formulas of order, it is coping with disorder. It should remember that an order is not invalidated by disorder; and that if an order is to become imaginative it must be so conceived as to accommodate disorder, and indeed to desire to do so, to stretch itself constantly to the point where it can envisage the disorder which its order merely names. If Humanism can do that, it will do so by something very like the symbolic imagination. But if it does that, it will not be only Humanism any longer.

1941

10

In the Hope of Straightening Things Out

If you think of the body of Eliot's criticism as if it were completed you will see several things more or less clearly, especially if you use your official eye. It has, for example, a vital relation to all the monuments of criticism from Aristotle's *Poetics* to Wordsworth's *Preface* and Coleridge's *Biographia.* It is in vital reaction to Arnold and Pater: the fight with, and use of, Matthew Arnold is life-long, the fight with Pater is more with his "cause" than with his judgments and is more a foray than a war. Again, Eliot's criticism "owes" a good deal to George Santayana, Rémy de Gourmont, Irving Babbitt, and Ezra Pound. Still again, there is the continuous struggle—the honest wrestling—with the work of I. A. Richards, which it seems to me becomes more intense the more the two men show that their purpose is common. And so on: anyone who wished to do so could trace the literary history of Eliot's criticism to the certain conclusion that it is a part of the general literary history. No doubt this work will be done, along with another job about the relations of Eliot's mind to the Christian religion and to the classical world. In short, Eliot as critic is in pretty full and pretty specific relation with all the things a critic ought to be in relation with: the conventional elements of the traditions he supports. With us the type is less common than we believe it used to be.

But there are other accounts of Eliot's criticism which it might be more immediately valuable to take up. There is his indissoluble connection with human behavior; there is his radical allegiance to language; there is his sense of the constant pressure into the mind—

into life—of forces with which neither behavior nor language can cope but to which they must respond.

What I am saying is that Eliot's great concern with order and tradition and hierarchy is in part a result of his direct and constant perception of disorder or of unknowable orders. He knows that human orders are what you do with disorder; he knows that no order remains vital which has lost its intimate contact, at some point, with the disorder or the unknown order which gave it rise. That is why his second thoughts are often better than his first: as in his successive essays on education and the classics, or on the structure of culture or society, or his successive judgments on Milton and Shelley. The *thought* perhaps remains the same but in its second form the thought has renewed and deepened contact with the underlying disorder or unknown order. I could wish, with this in mind, that Eliot might rewrite his paper on Hamlet and his problems, and above all I wish he might write once again on Baudelaire and Pascal. For it is in these three papers, which have been so attractive to so many, that he has too much *rationalized* his attitude toward disorder and the unknown order. In these papers, neither is the fog in the fir trees nor is the salt on the briar rose.

I would suppose such an account of Eliot's criticism could have major interest, but it ought not to be made without some attention to two other matters. After all, we do live and work and have part of our being in our conscious intellectual tradition; and from it we borrow much of our light. In some sense Eliot has lived all his life—in his phrase, all the damage of a lifetime—in intellectual awareness of Coleridge's "three silent revolutions in England." These revolutions were (in Saintsbury's citation from *Table Talk*): "When the professions fell off from the Church; when literature fell off from the professions; and when the press fell off from literature." I think it is the sense of the damage of these revolutions that explains both the tory polemic and the tory rebelliousness of Eliot's mind, what is excessive and what is vital about it .Though of course there are those who believe that the tory lives on, like the Auk, only in the degenerate razor-billed form, yet the truth is that the tory is a permanent not a devolving type. And this (which is my other pertinent matter) I will illustrate in Eliot's own words from his essay on Dante.

It is when he begins to get really into the *Purgatory* and runs hard on the problem of beliefs in poetry. It is too bad, he says, that the problem has been exaggerated. "But the question of what Dante 'believed' is always relevant. It would not matter, if the world were divided between those persons who are capable of taking poetry simply for what it is and those who cannot take it at all; if so, there would be no need to talk about this question to the former and no use in talking about it to the latter. But most of us are somewhat impure and apt to confuse issues: hence the justification of writing books about books, in the hope of straightening things out."

As this last phrase is the least debatable claim for criticism in general I have yet run into, so I trust it will justify the rest of these remarks. It is always the hopeless things, short of futility, that deserve justification most.

There is surely a great deal in Eliot's criticism which can stand straightening out: so many have used it to their own warp. That is why I am so much more interested in putting that criticism together than in taking it apart. This is partly because Eliot—both as poet and critic—has entered into that period of his career when those who will come after him are in reaction against him. It is much more because Eliot's criticism, despite its great influence (he has more than anybody *named* his time, just as in another way he has *undermined* his time, and in another way has *preserved* it), has lacked a general character, and has lacked even the intention of sustained generalization. His essays have been almost entirely topical: what was given him to write about or talk about for money or for a cause; and when they were not, his method has been conversational, for he begs off both the talent and the bent for abstract thought. Even when he undertakes an authoritative air, it is as a short cut, such as a man takes in an argumentative conversation; and there is likely to be a joke or a fresh start or an old memory or an obsessive image in the next sentence. No; the order in Eliot's criticism is that of conversation; and I mean this, as I think he would take it, as a pleasing characterization of a critic so deeply concerned with matters of general order, and I believe it is a characterization that leads to a sense of the unity of his mind.

In support of this characterization, there is a passage in his obituary tribute to Charles Whibley. Whibley, he wrote, had a unity of personality. He goes on:

> In attaining such unity, and indeed in attaining a *living* style, whether in prose or in verse, the practice of conversation is invaluable. Indeed, I believe that to write well it is necessary to converse a great deal. I say "converse" instead of "talk"; because I believe that there are two types of good writers: those who talk a great deal to others, and those, perhaps less fortunate, who talk a great deal to themselves. It is two thousand and two hundred years since, that the theory was propounded that thought is conversation with oneself; all literary creation certainly springs from the habit of talking to oneself or from the habit of talking to others. Most people are unable to do either, and that is why they lead such active lives. But anyone who would write must let himself go, in one way or the other, for there are only four ways of thinking: to talk to others, or to one other, or to talk to oneself, or to talk to God.

This was written in 1931. At another place he has said that a sound poetic style was the heightened conversation of the time, and in his latest book he has the wonderful remark—for our society—that if you know an author well enough personally you do not need to read him; and indeed that whole book—*Notes Towards the Definition of Culture*—is a warm plea for conversation, and a high sample.

That is why I want to put him together, to add together some of the elements of his unity of personality which have gotten conversationally into his critical writing. It is the order of his personality that gives force to his thought about literature, and it is not a logical, nor a theoretic, nor in any way a systematic order, except as these may enter into the topical and the conversational commitments of the mind. If you do not like the idea of unity of personality, you may try the unity that goes with successive relatively stable states of a deeply held point of view. What he says reflects or illuminates either the personality or the point of view, and you can value a single essay or passage only if you can keep in mind a good many other essays and passages; no one of them, however useful in itself, reflects or illuminates enough by itself. In this he more resembles his image of Montaigne than his image of Pascal: Montaigne is a substance, Pascal a set of orders.

Eliot is a substance besieged by orders. If we want to see this clearly we have only to think of how his criticism runs parallel to his poetry. There is a gap between, but the attraction across the gap is so strong that one train often runs on the other's track. *For Lancelot Andrewes* is only understandable when *Ash Wednesday* and *Little Gidding* have been well read, and I rather suspect that all three need, at some point but not at all points, the backward illumination of "The Hippopotamus":

> Although he seems so firm to us
> He is merely flesh and blood.

Better than that, it is the shocking characteristic of Eliot's mind that he brings his inner divergences, the division of his startling allegiances, rather nearer the surface than most minds, and sometimes they explode through. W. H. Auden put it very well when he said in *The New Yorker* that Eliot is a household with

> at least three permanent residents. First there is the archdeacon, who believes in and practices order, discipline, and good manners, social and intellectual, with a thoroughly Anglican distaste for evangelical excess. . . . And no wonder, for the poor gentleman is condemned to be domiciled with a figure of a very different stamp, a violent and passionate old peasant grandmother, who has witnessed murder, rape, pogroms, famine, flood, fire, everything; who has looked into the abyss and, unless restrained, would scream the house down. . . . Last, as if this state of affairs were not difficult enough, there is a young boy who likes to play slightly malicious jokes. The too earnest guest, who has come to interview the Reverend, is startled and bewildered by finding an apple-pie bed or being handed an explosive cigar.

Auden was right; but he should have said at once that these people live very close together, and are in either a conversational or poetic order of things one and the same: that is, in the unity of personality. There is an inner violence of this sort connected with every formidable assertion of order. It is even a type, with special emphasis on the small boy, in this country. Eliot differs from the type in the *quantity* of all three denizens of his jungle that get into his work: the quantity of behavior that gets into his language. Most get only a trace; Eliot gets the sense of the whole force. It seems to me that both the essays and the poems get their compositional strength through the succession of violent and tragic and formal gestures that inhabit them; they cry to each other, and are *together* a voice.

Let what has been said be taken as a particular preface to thinking about Eliot's criticism; here is a general preface, which has more to do with the nature of literary people (more smugly, the state of culture) than it has with Eliot. He wrote essays on the Metaphysicals and the Elizabethans with a serious running effort in mind to correct the estimation of the main course of literature, in short to correct Arnold. What happened was that the reputation of Marvell, the Herberts, Donne, Tourneur and Webster went up. What he wrote about Jonson seems to have been less effective, for it put Jonson into the Empyrean. And it is clear that what he wrote about Milton and Shelley and Swinburne had more effect than he intended, for certain classes of people quit reading these poets at all. People went out and read or refused to read what Eliot wrote about. They also took their Eliot neat, undiluted with other reading: as with Dryden, Samuel Johnson, and the seventeenth-century preachers. After *The Waste Land,* Jessie Laidlaw Weston went out of print. After *Ash Wednesday* the Book of Common Prayer had a *literary circulation,* as if like the Bible it too had become a monument of English prose; and indeed it may be said that there sprung up a whole literary generation whose only knowledge of Christianity was what they got by reading Eliot—I mean those who did not read the prayer book. Again, Eliot rebuilt Baudelaire on the rock of original sin, which is at least firmer ground than the perfumed swoon in which Arthur Symons had left him. Again, partly because of Eliot's quotations in his own poems from Dante and partly from the effects of his long essay on him, a "cult" for Dante spread through Bloomsbury and Cape Cod. No modern critic has had anything like the effect of Eliot on the literary people. How he got it I think lies partly in the force of the unity of his personality, some of it in the small-boy part: since he has persuaded so many people who had nothing but personality that the poet had only an impersonal relation to poetry. But his effect came partly, and more properly, from the pressure of the fact that he talked about literature as such, relating it only to life, to that old peasant grandmother of his, and because he has never failed in an extraordinary skill at quotation. In any case he became a literary dictator unexampled in our times: nobody but a dictator could make Ezra Pound *il miglior fabbro* by a simple dedication.

It is worth noticing about literary dictatorships that they only partly work. There is no police power in this dictatorship, only the power communicated through fashion, and fashion is impervious to what lies in the realm of tedious or too laborious change. Eliot as dictator failed in at least three of his Orders in Council: that the poetry of our time should resemble that of Ben Jonson when it got done resembling Webster and Marvell: that it should take up the power of statement found in Dryden: that it should take stock of Dryden's poetic successor, Samuel Johnson. It is notable that Eliot has not himself been in the least able to follow his own Orders in these respects. Not only the fashion but also the possibilities were evidently against it. But with these exceptions, Eliot has created and imposed a taste—a set of habits in reading and writing—of very high standards; has set going a serious criticism with respect to these standards; and has set abroad a current of ideas which has vitalized the profession of literature by reducing the claims made for it and then eloquently affirming the claim that was left. He did a great deal on a task which everybody wanted done but which most people concerned had doctrinal difficulties of Art for Art or of the New Knowledges to prevent them. This was the task of bringing literature back into the common enterprise. It was the archdeacon perhaps who thought he was up to that job; but it was a lonely job and he got the company, if not the help, of the violent grandmother and the malicious boy. Let us say that they both let him know what he had to deal with—themselves—and also, for their own part, kept things lively.

On this sort of statement no conclusion is possible except to stop; as a statement, it is too general. Luckily there is plenty left to tackle. No man not a fool or a saint is out of his time—or the ideas of his time. Eliot has been centrally concerned (we had an example above) in what Richards has called the great plague of contemporary poets, the relation between thought and feeling, the relation between belief and poetry; and Richards compelled the form in which Eliot undertook to deal with that plague. Richards took instinctively to the twinning of science and poetry, Eliot twinned poetry and religion. Poetry for both of them lay so to speak in the middle: the relation between the twins raised the question of belief. Richards wanted to get rid of belief in favor of pseudo-statement; Eliot did not want to get rid of belief at all, certainly not for pseudo-statement, yet he knew that poetry did not require the allegiance of belief; both the grandmother and the small boy told him that. Poetry was more like behavior than belief, and required only the kind of belief that behavior requires. What he did was simple; he excluded thought *as such* from poetry and said that poetry dealt with the experience or feeling of thought which might or might not—probably *not*—have been the poet's thought; and similarly he said that poetry dealt with belief as the experience or feeling of belief which probably had to be, from the nature of belief, the poet's own belief. This is not at all the same thing as the willing suspension of disbelief; it is a positive and poetic attitude toward belief and thought where both of them show the aspect of behavior.

I simplify and summarize from various places in the essays. The clearest single statements of Eliot's position may be found in the long essays on Shakespeare and Dante, and all that he says there strikes me as sensible so far as either poetry or criticism can be sensible. Eliot does not need the kind of sense that is needed by Richards's much wider and more philosophical enterprise. Eliot can afford, what Richards cannot, to bring his divided allegiances into the open precisely because his belief is a kind of behavior, and what a poet and critic can afford he must certainly do: it is his one possible extravagance.

One of the reasons he can afford it, I think, is because he has tradition, a slogan word and a slogan thing, but a real word and a real thing too. Tradition for Eliot is the weapon and resource of individual talent. Tradition is the positive cumulus, good and bad, aside from ourselves, and we have to find out for ourselves all that grandmother will not tell us of what it is. It is the hardest work to find out what is already there. It is also, when we have it, our means of protection against what we are not. It is what is impersonal in the personality, and it is the materials of which we make the form—the mask—of personality: the public shape which stands between the world and the denizens of our jungle. If we are really thinking of Eliot, and not of a doctrine which we dislike, the word tradition should always be associated with the idea of the individual and with the idea of personality. Otherwise we shall not understand Eliot's rich personal insistence on impersonality as the means of escaping the abuses of personality which pass for creation and authority and originality. As order is what we do with disorder, impersonality is what we do with personality. Eliot knows too well that what is called "personality" is the private creation out of the damage of a lifetime, just as he knows that "romanticism"—like a good meal or good whisky—often alone avails to make private life tolerable. Personality and romanticism cross loneliness and obscure isolation. But Eliot also knows—as the result of these things too much discussed—that it is the disorder within no less than the disorder without that requires the assertion of order and tradition and impersonality.

Thus Eliot has never repudiated the three doctrines found in the early essay, "Tradition and the Individual Talent." First that, by tradition, all literature forms one order and that each new work alters the whole order. Second, the different and later remark that orthodoxy exists whether we know it or not. The first is manifesto thinking which he needed to get work done; the second is deep observation about the structure of the mind. To these let us add a third from the book on the definition of culture to the effect that orthodoxy—right thinking or belief—requires the constant prodding of fresh heresy; which seems to me to put the first two together in the form of insight as to how tradition changes.

The second doctrine in the early essay was the doctrine of the poet as the filament of platinum, as the catalyst in whose presence, unaltered, combinations of emotions and feelings take place. I believe that what this says in essence is that the poet only uses language well by getting himself out of the way; that language is real, the result of a tremendous historical collaboration, and that its reality is somehow objective and ought so far as is possible to be submitted to: so that oneself—let alone the reader—might "know" what has been written. It has always seemed to me that Eliot must have heard read the same words I heard in Professor Wood's course in Indian Philosophy, for the notes were very old when I heard them used: "The reality in words, gentlemen, is both superior to and anterior to any use to which you can put them." These words were accompanied by a strenuous forward rubbing of the hands on the desk, as if somehow the reality of words was being rubbed both into the grain of the wood and the grain of our minds. Eliot's filament of platinum may well have an ancestor in words spoken in Emerson Hall.

The third doctrine from the early essay was the doctrine that, so far as the writing of poetry *itself* goes, but without regard to the kind of poetry or the extra-literary value of the poetry, one age, one stage of development of mind or spirit, is as good as any other. Feeling and emotion are absolute and final, and the poet of any age has enough to go on—even more in youth than later; he has only to improve his technical processes. This is rather like Croce's rule that it is the quantity not the quality of poetic gift that differs. For Eliot then, it was only technically that the poet could improve himself—in the theoretic form of feelings—in the means of communication. I see no reason to believe that Eliot would repudiate this notion if asked, but I suspect he might for once quote Shaw approvingly, that this situation is a grand example of how youth is wasted on the young.

It is in relation to these three notions that I want to consider the idea of the objective correlative as found in the paper on *Hamlet*. These are Eliot's words: "The only way of expressing emotion in the form of art is by finding 'an objective correlative'; in other words, a set of objects, a situation, a chain of events which shall be the formula for that *particular* emotion; such that when the external facts, which terminate in sensory experience, are given, the emotion is immediately evoked." This has been called a doctrine, and as a doctrine it has flooded the language of criticism. I would rather call it an observation put into the form of a notion: that is, an observation which was the result of numberless observations about the way the individual talent acts as a catalyst between the feelings and emotions, not necessarily his own, that he wants to write about and the language, the words, in which he must write. It is a metaphorical account of how feelings and emotions get into the words with the least interference by the "mere" personality. This metaphor does not in any way presuppose success: the observation was made in the course of an examination of *Hamlet* where the material of feelings and emotions was intractable and no satisfactory "objective correlative" was found. Eliot was making a metaphor about Shakespeare's failure, as he saw it, to give the right words and actions in the right relation or sequence to express the emotions and feelings that were already there in Prince Hamlet, in his mind and the impulses of his behavior. It was not, as I see it, a metaphor about the poet's own relation to *his* feelings and emotions and to *his* language. The inconsistency with his other notions about tradition and order and behavior and belief would make the acceptance of the objective correlative as a doctrine for poetry impossible even in a mind with such deeply divided allegiances as Eliot's. If I am right, most of the arguments about this notion as doctrine or principle take place only in the critics' own minds and concern Eliot only as a mistaken development of what he wrote in his book-review of Robertson on *Hamlet*. The whole situation lacks clarity.

Eliot's own doctrine of poetry, as he has united it in his personality, seems to me to turn up in what he says about the triad of feeling, emotion, and sensibility. While everybody and his dog seem able to play with the objective correlative, many people seem unable to understand the distinctions and the relations of this triad. They appear to me simple to understand by good will, though, since that commodity is short, awkward to state simply.

Feeling is the fundamental term: concrete, sensory, nuclear, somehow in experience, whether actual or imagined, always particular: the hand rubbing into the grain of the desk.

Emotion is feelings organized by a force whether within or without the psyche. Emotion is feelings, organized, generalized, abstracted, built into a form, theoretic or not. You can hurt a man's feelings, you cannot hurt a man's rage; but you can rouse his rage by hurting his feelings. And so on. A congeries of feelings may mount, may organize, may crystallize into the emotion of sexual love, or, by a twitch of phase, into the emotion of another kind of love. Art is full of particular emotions in the sense that the abstract or theoretic form, the emotion, is good only in that instance. Further, emotion in art, like life, is made sometimes out of feelings alone, sometimes out of feelings and emotions modifying each other, and sometimes out of one emotion working on another form of emotion.

> And so each venture
> Is a new beginning, a raid on the inarticulate
> With shabby equipment always deteriorating
> In the general mess of imprecision of feeling,
> Undisciplined squads of emotion.

Sensibility is the discipline of the squads, the precision of the feeling. Sensibility for the poet is his stock, his reservoir, his cumulus, of feelings and perceptions in various stages of organization; and thus represents his residual skill to respond sensibly. Sensibility is what you draw on to make fresh responses. Live language and particularly live poetry make the great objective reservoir of sensibility: the traditional and impersonal source of what power you have over your own sensibility.

It is as simple as that, and I hope it will not seem that I have twisted Eliot to my own purposes; I think I depend only on the language as it is in the dictionary and in usage and *thereby* in Eliot's own use; and I would say that the use depended on Eliot's own observation as an individual struggling with his talent—which of course differs from those of people of different education and temperament. It is the observation of the man who could write: The spirit killeth, the letter giveth life. That is the small boy's way of insisting on the genuine, but with a violence belonging to the grandmother, and in the vocabulary of the archdeacon.

But let us have some samples of other observations: all, so to speak, expert beyond experience. I think they will add up to an order dealing with disorder and with unknown order. But they will add differently for different people.

No verse is "free" for the man who does a good job. That is, there is real work in poetry like the work in carpentry.

Poetry is a mug's game. That is, no matter how hard you work, you are likely to find you have been taken in.

Crabs and sea-anemones. Imagination is full of memory. "Six ruffians seen through an open window playing cards at night at a small

French railway junction where there was a water-mill, such memories may have symbolic value, but of what we cannot tell, for they come to represent depths of feeling into which we cannot peer." That is, there is the unknown order struggling toward incarnation.

Poetry may have three meanings: what is immediate, what comes by study, and what only gradually reveals itself. The incarnation in poetry is slow.

Poetry sees beneath beauty and ugliness: it sees the boredom, the horror, and the glory. The incarnation of poetry is deep.

Poetry, by its music, by its discovered rhythm—which may come from the internal combustion engine in airplane or ship or car, as well as from river and sea and garden and wind—by its music poetry may persist, its meaning may persist, after the words have stopped. Though the incarnations in poetry may last, all incarnations are only partial.

Poetry may be legitimately concerned with the actual whereas one's prose reflections are concerned with the ideal. That is, poetry incarnates—manifests—only what of the ideal, of the ultimate real, can be found in the actual feelings and emotions.

I have been using, unexplained, the word *incarnation* in my appendages to Eliot's remarks; and I have done so deliberately as a means of getting at the important fact of Eliot's religion. Incarnation is a religious word: I am the more justified in using it here because Eliot in his book on culture has himself used it. Culture, he says, is essentially the incarnation of the religion of a people. Poetry is a part of culture when it exists and is certainly a part of what we mean by culture. The adventure of incarnating religion in poetry is what Eliot has been up to all along, and not only religion but the conditions of religion: as it is in the actual world, all that is under and aside and apart from it. It is this point of view which infects Eliot's criticism with its special problem and its final ideal. This is how he puts it in the book on culture:

> Aesthetic sensibility must be extended into spiritual perception, and spiritual perception must be extended into aesthetic sensibility and disciplined taste before we are qualified to pass judgment upon decadence or diabolism or nihilism in art. To judge a work of art by artistic or by religious standards, to judge a religion by religious or artistic stand-

ards should come in the end to the same thing: though it is an end at which no individual can arrive.

It seems to me that here is the feeling, the emotion, the justified impulse; it is how Eliot's mind works; it is how he finds it necessary to dine with the Opposition. Poetry is an act of incarnation; but the incarnation is slow, deep, partial, and only of what has been made actual. The real and the ideal are far off.

But what a relief it is not to have too many claims made for poetry. What a relief to read a man who never cheats on poetry, who insists on the gift and the genuine, but who is to this extent not fooled: He knows that poetry is only a part of the enterprise. He knows that poetry saves nobody, but shows rather the actual world from which to be saved or not, and shows also what has been made actual, what has been actually felt, of aspiration. A living language, for Eliot, has to do with a living religion. All this is in a remark which ought still to have the widest circulation: "Poetry is a superior form of amusement."

1951

11

The Lion and the Honeycomb

This paper proposes to examine into a certain section of the scholarship and criticism of poetry—the section to which I have been attached for some twenty years and which I feel I can understand—and further proposes a possibility of expansion or growth for it. Far from wishing to repudiate this scholarship and this criticism, my discontent is because I wish them to live their proper life. I believe they have completed a certain stage with honor; I do not wish the honor to become empty, and that means I wish the honor to be renewed for other services in consequence of and in relation to the first. And I fear that if new growth is not undertaken there may be only a false and sterile life. In criticism and scholarship this takes place when method becomes methodology; when a means becomes an end; and my discontent may be a sign that something of that sort is happening now to what is known as the "new criticism," and its scholarship.

Let us go afield to begin with, so we may see, when we come back, where we are located.

A small comparison may be made between what is now happening and a simplified account of what happened in classical society between Plato's *Phaedrus* and Quintilian's *Institutes*. In the *Phaedrus* three chief modes of understanding were at work modifying, supplementing, and criticizing one another: the poetic, the dialectical, the rhetorical; and there was no form of knowledge which was not in a state of growth and subject both to speculation and exploration. By poetic is meant: the creative action of the mind which has an eye to truth in the objects it makes. Dialectic has nothing to do with Hegel. By dialectic is meant: the reasonable conversation of the mind which has an eye to truth in ideas. By rhetoric is meant: the art of persuasion, properly, in the service of dialectic or poetic; improperly, in the service of argument on the pleading of a "cause"; *in extremis* or in abstraction, the art of persuasion uprooted, flourished for its own sake, with its eye on itself. The three together comprise the chief modes for the full play of the mind. So it was with Plato. By Cicero's time, the dialectical had been absorbed in the rhetorical; Lucretius does the work of Plato and Aristotle. In another century, in Quintilian, the poetic was absorbed along with the dialectical, and the rhetorical was left solitary and absolute. Society had become fixed and the substance of understanding had become absolute. It followed that the mode or method of the mind called rhetoric became a methodology—a set of rules and formularies—more and more independent in *both* validity *and* form from the material it manipulated. From dialectic, the great balancing mode of the mind, it kept logic, which it believed could prescribe truth. From poetic, the great discovering or originating or as we say creative mode of the mind, it kept the iamb, the hexameter and the figure of speech, which it believed could celebrate truth. It may be observed that the characteristic intellectual monument of the Roman Empire was law. The *Institutes* of Justinian took up the slack in those of Quintilian, and the law in its turn came to use the methodology of rhetoric; it is difficult to know where there is worse repute, in the term legalistic or in the term rhetorical.

No doubt society is immortal no matter what, and would have survived intellectually under the administration of law and rhetoric alone, but Rome never had to try that experiment; for these two methodologies had no sooner absorbed power unto themselves than theology appeared with the terrible urgency of interpreting the will of the living God. To the theoretically fixed world of the Rome of the Empire, which required only routine interpretation, there was added the equally fixed revelation of the Rome of the Church, where every word of scripture required poetic and dialectic and rhetorical interpretation if the means to salvation—that is to say, true survival—were to be understood and followed. It is in the fathers of the

Church, particularly in Augustine, that we see the maximum task the full human mind has been able to perform under the dominant modes of law and rhetoric, with poetic appearing only as the passion in the language. What theology would have been like under the dominance of different modes of the mind, is not a question we have the experience to ask; but we do have the experience—it is in the underground of all our intellectual habits—to see that there is a kind of *summa* of criticism and scholarship in the theology of the fathers as they used the methodologies of rhetoric and law, and that there is the opposite of a *summa,* whatever the term may be, some congeries of the bottommost, mostly nearly sterile form of the same methodologies, in the rule-books of the rhetoricians, and the closed speculations of the grammarians. Of course we can see this only by a kind of deliberate exaggeration. Theology never escaped the prescriptive *mortmain* of Quintilian and Justinian and never wished to do so; and on the other hand, no rhetorician ever escaped the living burden of language, even if it persisted only as an obstacle to perfection. But with a little exaggeration, and for our own rhetorical purposes, we can assume purity and fullness in either case.

It is an assumption that helps us in looking at the modes of understanding—both of criticism and scholarship—by which we use literature in our own time. It appears to me that what we are very largely up to in practice, and to a considerable extent in theory, is the hardening of the mind into a set of unrelated methodologies without the controlling advantage of a fixed body of knowledge, a fixed faith, or a fixed purpose. That is to say, we are following the tradition in the phase set up under a series of relatively closed societies after the authentic incentives of faith and intellect which brought the phase about have lost their affirmative existence, and when the specific momentum of that phase seems to have run down. I suppose Yeats's image of "The Second Coming" had something of the sort in mind in the first of its two parts.

> Turning and turning in the widening gyre
> The falcon cannot hear the falconer;
> Things fall apart: the centre cannot hold;
> Mere anarchy is loosed upon the world,

> The blood-dimmed tide is loosed, and everywhere
> The ceremony of innocence is drowned;
> The best lack all conviction, while the worst
> Are full of passionate intensity.

These lines should by now have the familiarity that once belonged to scripture, and, as we know, they require, but without the same authority, the kind of reading our ancestors gave to scripture. Yeats is writing about the dissolution of that authority; but his remedy—or his resolution—cannot be ours, or only partly ours, and only in the last instance; for his resolution is prophetic, and is also without authority, a mere piece of rhetorical incantation:

> Surely some revelation is at hand;
> Surely the Second Coming is at hand.

Yeats turned to prophecy and invoked revelation because he hated the characteristic methodologies of rhetoric and law that belonged to his age, and he was, so to speak, tragically content to envisage the whole enterprise of culture brought to fresh incarnation in the conditions of nightmare and with the birth of some rough beast. It may be that Yeats's image is right and the whole tradition is gone, but it seems to me a better act of will, and more conformable to our daily experience (in which after all we do live most of the time, with so much of what we ever were, surviving) to hold that only a phase of the tradition is gone. Thus it would seem that it was another phase of the old tradition, and not necessarily a new phase, into which we have entered, so that we should wish to keep of the last phase only what has survived it, what was always living; and —even there if we could we should, in Isaiah's language, eat the butter and honey of the imagination that we may know to choose the good and refuse the evil. It is not that I wish to go back and not that I wish to separate our adventure from the history of what we have been through; I am quite willing to ask what is the next phase of Christianity, and I am certainly prone to believe that whether Christian or not it will have a deep analogous relation to some phase or aspect of things in the understandable past.

It is indeed by analogy that I believe the mind makes its richest movements, and it is by analogy that I believe the mind makes its deepest use of what it has understood; or at any rate I believe this to be an appropriate way of looking at the labor of the mind in a society, like ours, without a fixed character, and operating under a revelation which turns out to have been imperfectly understood. It is through analogy, if at all, that the falcon can again hear the falconer, that things can come together again, and that again the center can hold.

The general area of analogy I propose is between ourselves and the Greek society of Plato and Aristotle, between ourselves and one of the ancestral forms of the phases of culture which have intervened; and the particular matter for my analogy lies in the vital mutual relationships which then existed among the poetic, the dialectic, and the rhetorical modes of the mind compared to the relatively defective mutual relationships among what corresponds to those modes today. I believe such analogies profitable in considering any mode of thought or action, and that belief is my warrant for applying them to the single field of literary scholarship and criticism, and to the one rather restricted section of that field, our own English and American practice, where I know anything at all; and even here I mean to make a very little stand for a great deal. You see by this I stand almost firmly upon our rhetorical tradition. I assume the truth of my premise—that there actually existed this vital mutual relationship in the modes of the Greek mind, I assume that our minds recognize the goodness of this truth; and I conclude that even in the contumacious field of literary scholarship and criticism our minds will hasten to master, with beautifully articulated skills, this good truth.

Perhaps I should begin by the assertion that scholarship and criticism make, when valid, a single field because there is necessarily a mutual relationship between them, and that either branch of the enterprise is in sorry condition when the relevant form of the other is not present. The relation, and the difference that is in relation, may be expressed grammatically, like so much else in the affairs of the mind. Criticism draws *from* literature that which it signifies or which is useful. Scholarship is *about* literature, describes it, surrounds it, identifies its content, and supplies what is lacking because of the movement of time or the shift in the conventions of the literary mind. Criticism is use; scholarship is the means of use. Criticism accords to the act of imitation or creation. Scholarship accords to the act of description or the refreshment of memory or history. Criticism is within, scholarship without, the work. Criticism deals with the experience of the ideas (or feelings, or what not) *in* the work. Scholarship deals with the ideas (or feelings, or what not), otherwise derived, that may or may not be in the work. Scholarship and criticism edge into each other; in the limbo between is that extraordinarily complicated thing called full appreciation short of judgment; for appreciation with judgment requires the ultimately simple act of scholarship and criticism combined in a single intuition—of which there has naturally never been enough for much to reach print, since it is more likely performed in an irrecoverable flash than in lucid prose. The distinctions that could be made along this sequence are not infinite but are empirically indefinite; so let these suffice as a random choice.

The point is, each depends on the other for its own validity, and each modifies the other for its vitality. Yet the characteristic excess of each is when it masquerades as the other without knowing it: I mean, when criticism resorts to description when ignorant of the facts; I mean, when scholarship believes it has made an interpretation by surrounding the work with facts. I mean also, when criticism substitutes personal history for the history of the work, or when scholarship substitutes general history for the history of the work. Everyone should be able to provide himself with examples which are not only glaring but explicable: we can understand how they came about and can expect that they will be repeated, for we see that they depend on the state of scholarship and criticism in a given figure in a given time. There is Dante on Vergil. There are Voltaire and Tolstoy on Shakespeare. There is Dryden translating Chaucer. There is Dr. Johnson on John Donne. There is the Variorum Shakespeare—especially the commentaries on "The Phoenix and the Turtle." And there are the standard commentaries—say a late Scartazzini—on Dante.

There is anything you like when you are looking for excess and very near as much when you are looking for defect; but I should like, with a view toward my analogy, to mention only one pair of characteristic defects: the pair composed by timidity in scholarship and arrogance in criticism, which result from either an under- or an overestimation of talent, and which have in both cases the effect of narrowing the talent that does exist. How many times have you not seen an extraordinarily able work of scholarship vitiated because the scholar did not dare transform his facts about the work so as to affect our sense of what we get from the work: the very sense of the work at a given moment. A vast amount of able scholarship is a vast understatement made not as a rhetorical device or a dramatic gesture but as a flat and aimless understatement which is the effect of training in caution, reserve, and the sin of over-scrupulosity in every matter not directly warranted by fact. It is mere facts that make mere scholarship; it is the mere facts about the work that fail to tell us what the work is about.

Similarly, in the corresponding case of criticism, have you not seen an otherwise able work devoted to finding out the use of an author quite vitiated and turned trash because the critic had not availed himself of the living burden of the scholar's facts. He was not able to say truly what his author was about because he had not taken the trouble to find the illuminating facts about his author: the very facts from which the author jumped to the act of creation. A vast amount of criticism is a vast overstatement made precisely as a rhetorical device or a dramatic gesture because of the critic's congeries of beliefs, and partial beliefs, that literature is independent, or autonomous, or pure art, from which he concludes that the critical act is also independent or autonomous if not quite pure and has therefore its own omnicompetent methods. There is a strong taint of original genius about many critics, which is the less surprising if you remember that it is the critics who developed that doctrine.

Another way of expressing these characteristic defects of timidity and arrogance lies in remembering both St. Paul's words: The letter killeth, but the spirit giveth life, and Eliot's paradoxical reversal of them: The spirit killeth, the letter giveth life; in which case Eliot was writing in the interests of criticism, St. Paul in those of scholarship. But for my own part, I should be glad if you would think also of my analogy with the mutually related and interinanimated modes of poetic, dialectic, and rhetoric as they play upon each other in the

Phaedrus of Plato; because this analogy applies to the excesses as well as the defects of scholarship and criticism, and indicates, besides, what the virtues of the complete scholar-critic if ever he came to exist would be. He would not resemble Matthew Arnold nor anything Matthew Arnold hoped to resemble, for none of his virtues would ever tell him that it was his job either to make literature a substitute for religion or a guide for right conduct or a set of magic touchstones. I do not suppose the complete scholar-critic would resemble anything we have yet seen, but I would say that of all men he must be the master-layman of as many modes of human understanding as possible in a single act of the mind. I do not say a master but a master-layman—a master of the sense, use, and scope of each mode, both each in itself, and each in its living fragmentary relation to the other modes; I say a master-layman because he is committed, not to the creation of experience, but to the response to experience no matter what the experience is of, and no matter how far short of direct knowledge of the experience his sensibility might come; and I say a master-layman, too, because this ideal monster the complete scholar-critic, as such, cannot permit himself properly the extravagant delight (though he may unawares fall into it) of making his response by means of any single method or mode of the mind exclusively. Whatever his own skills may be he must maintain a lay sense of the pressure of other skills as corrective and supplementary to his own. If he does not know what he ought to have done in a given job of work he will at least have a probable sense of how he abused it.

He will, in short, be a lover of everything that may be done in language conceived as an act of the whole mind; and he will conceive himself, as a lover ought, as only a layman with respect to his beloved, and at best a master-layman. This is not to make claims either for literature or for the scholar or for the critic that any of these have a unique or necessarily superior position in human affairs. I should like to believe that the day of apology or defense or hypostasis of any sort is done, at any rate for the scholar and the critic. I should like to believe that there is clear proof of the need, in our particular society a greater need than ever before, for both scholar and critic to do a particular job of work: the job of putting the audience into a responsive relation with the work of art: to do the job of intermediary.

Critic and scholar are go-betweens and should disappear when the couple are gotten together, when indeed there is no room left for them. That is why there are no statues to critics and scholars. That is why there is nothing deader than dead criticism and scholarship; only the stink remains, sometimes so powerful that it is mistaken for life. Who can tell between the lion and the honeycomb? Criticism, even more than scholarship, was a regrettable necessity in the first place; and what is most regrettable is that some criticism, and some scholarship, remains alive, for good or ill, long after the generation, or even the age, in which it was written. The job of putting the audience into relation to the work of art not only has to be done over again, which is to the good and a sign of vitality, but the job is often so difficult that we cannot do it ourselves, there being something lacking in our dominant methods, and we are compelled to rehearse an old job of work done in a different language in a different situation to a different tune.

Such would seem to be our situation, and I propose, again thinking of my analogy from the *Phaedrus,* two models for consideration. There is Coleridge [1] and there is Aristotle, who not only survive but who increment themselves and supplement each other. No one has finished mining Coleridge; no one has yet finished building on Aristotle; and no one has put them together. Coleridge seems the fellow most likely to provide means to do the job we did not find out till just now has to be done. Aristotle is certainly the fellow who when we look into him takes the words out of our mouths. Coleridge began the whole business of the special techniques of modern scholarship and criticism of poetry: all the expansions into the psychology of language and imagination. Aristotle is there to absorb and unite the excesses of these techniques in the terms and under the

[1] Coleridge because we are English-reading and because we get through Coleridge a great deal of Europe we have otherwise no name for. But we should think also of what happened on the continent, which took the same German source Coleridge took but came out in different trains of thought and sensibility. Think of Rivière, de Gourmont, Valéry, Du Bos; of Unamuno and Ortega; of Hesse, Dilthey, Curtius. *We* have Coleridge.

force of my analogy; the force and illumination of the joint presence of poetic, dialectic, and rhetoric. Aristotle is a sacred book, with its great unwieldy mass of misinterpretation, misunderstanding, and distortion, equalled only by Shakespeare and Dante, surpassed only by the Bible. Coleridge seems to be at least a secondary sort of sacred book, and I can imagine the spreading notion, in this little field, of another alliance of the two testaments. I can imagine, too, if the alliance is made it will be made through the rhetorical tradition of the European mind which reached its true heights of articulate imaginative richness in St. Augustine and Dante: to whom all the modes of the mind were equally parts and instruments of aesthetic experience, and each with a warrant to correct, modify, complete, and incarnate each of the other modes.

To make such an alliance seems to me a proper function of sacred books, the more especially as it might, in the sense that every marriage is a fight for life, restore to each its proper authority, that of the mind seen in direct action. There is an attractive force to mountain peaks; including the *apices mentis* which survive the floods by pure sature. The odd thing is that the force attracts even when we do not climb the peaks and our knowledge of them is something fusty and much garbled. The force is in the words that come into our mouths and in the daily actions of our minds.

I cannot suppose our present batch of critics spend much time reading Aristotle or Coleridge, and what they do read is in musty light. No matter; the *Poetics* and the *Biographia* are there just the same—and when one of them is read directly, and especially when the contact is forced by an urgency of the living mind, the explosion is violent, from one phase of mind into another. I. A. Richards read Coleridge in the early 'thirties; it was love in ambush; he became passionate, eloquent, memorable, that is, a part of our sensibility as well as of our theory. Intimate contact with Coleridge on the imagination of language brought a new reality to his own language, a new stage of ripeness, based, in his own phrase, on a new principle of "the sane growth of the mind." Well, Richards has since read Plato, another sort of sacred book, but not directly helpful to the task of criticism and scholarship. I wish he might now read directly and with only the impedimenta of his own vision, the *Poetics* of Aristotle. It would be another ambush, another explosion, another stage of ripeness and growth: perhaps a book called *Aristotle on Imitation* to complete the task begun in *Coleridge on Imagination*. Such a work, whoever did it, if he did it in the spirit of the sane growth of the mind, would help re-organize our critical sensibility, as well as add to it, so that it might again, without loss of concreteness, generalize, choose, and judge on fuller aesthetic grounds than it seems able to master at present. I advocate this because I believe that the shape and status of our times provide an opportunity for it: and the kind of opportunity which, looked at with the eyes of my ideal figure, the master-layman, may be construed as necessity. The criticism and scholarship of an age would seem most often to be determined by the minimum necessity seen in the twin problems of how to account for art and how to relate it to its audience, and I shall presently explain why I believe that the figures of Aristotle and Coleridge put into living relation constitute the minimum necessity of our time. It will be a layman's explanation.

But I ought of course first to say what I mean by the sacred books of Coleridge and Aristotle. By Coleridge I mean the notions in the set of three words—not any one or any two but the set of all three words: *esemplastic,* which means forming, shaping, at a rhetorical level if you take rhetoric as a creative agent; *coadunative,* which means having to do with the union of dissimilar substances, at a dialectical level if you take dialectic as an aesthetic agent; and *synergical,* which means having to do with working together, cooperative action where the total effect is greater than the sum of the effects taken separately, and all this done, of course, at the level of poetics if you can conceive poetics as applying to all the modes of the mind, including the most intellectual.

These are Coleridge's words, and I believe my definitions are conformable to the way Coleridge used his mind, and all the more so, rather than less, because I have brought into the definition my analogy about rhetoric, dialectic, and poetic. Nor would it hurt if the terms of my analogy were differently assigned; it would not hurt, it would be another help in understanding how deep the mutual relationship is of the modes of the mind in action. In Coleridge as he wrote these terms apply to the behavior of words and are the attributes of imagination in words; and for him they provided those occasions for poetry of "more than usual emotion with more than usual order." For us they provide a free heuristic psychology of poetry, a rich partial means for finding out what is in the words of poetry, and an equally rich partial means of putting the maximum meaning into the words we use ourselves.

By Aristotle, I mean the notions that still live in the following set of six terms, especially when they are returned to their Greek forms: *Praxis,* or action; *Mimesis,* or the imitation of action; *Mythos,* or plot, which is the soul of the work; *Ethos,* or the operation of character; *Pathos,* or the tragic incident through which action is felt; *Katharsis,* or the purging, cleansing, purifying of the *mythos* subject to *mimesis.* These are the six terms I would chiefly keep from Aristotle, but of course to use them I should also need the aid of the five more nearly formal terms, three for the action of the plot, and two addressed to the persons through whom the plot acts. The formal terms about the plot are *Desis,* or complication; *Crisis,* or turning;[2] and *Lysis* or unraveling. The formal terms about the persons are *Peripeteia,* or the reversal of roles or situation; and *Anagnorisis,* or shock of recognition. Together, the two sets of terms apply not to the behavior of words like Coleridge's terms, but to the behavior of the things indicated by the words. They fasten attention upon that momentum of life which the histrionic sensibility may grasp by the mimesis of action. Mimesis, I take it, is the mind's action, and there is no question that, richly understood, any single full mimesis operates in deep, but widely variable, relation to poetics, dialectic, and rhetoric. For myself, I see a sequence or relation whereby the mimetic act is the incarnation into actuality of what we can grasp of reality; which is the reason why we pay enormous salaries and devotion in Hollywood and why in my boyhood Bernhardt was the Divine Sarah, and which is also a good part of the reason for the lasting power—the greatness—of great literature. More technically, we seem to believe that the soul as the form of forms has a formative or creative power in the relation of mimesis which we call *Poiesis* or poem-making; and it is when we remind ourselves of

[2] This needs a little expansion. Turning is a kind of decision. *Crisis* is the intellectual act, *and* its occasion, of decision.

that, we know what Coleridge is really for: to find out the relation between the behavior of the words in the poem and the behavior of the things indicated by the words and imitated through them.

Under the influence of the Coleridgean criticism—or perhaps I should say "the new criticism"—a scholar, Robert Goheen, has written a book on the images in the *Antigone,*[3] which enquires precisely into the relation between these two streams of behavior; a work of scholarship which passes into criticism as it took its immediate incentive from criticism; and a work which, though novel and opening up a new field for the scholar-critic, is nevertheless characteristic of our time. Mr. Goheen has made without intending it a practical gesture toward making an alliance between Coleridge and Aristotle, and if he has done so under the aegis of the "new criticism," that is all the better to my purpose, for it is the extension, complementation, and purification of the "new criticism" that I want now to deal with. I want to protect its methods from its methodologies.

What is called the "new criticism"—now well enough established to have a public odor of disrepute about it—is, I should expect, a set of emphases in criticism and scholarship which have been objectively determined, like other sets of emphases in other times, by the literature, by the presumed reader, by the general state of culture and knowledge, and by the immediate history and tradition of critical and scholarly ideas and practice: all working unequally and more or less incongruously together. Let us look at some of these determinants, and then at the criticism.

The literature in this case is poetry, called variously the School of Donne, the School of Hopkins, Yeats, Eliot, Pound, Stevens, and Auden, the new Metaphysical School, and so on. The important thing is that it is a learned poetry, roughly the first in English since the seventeenth century, and with as many direct continental roots as old English roots. There have been learned poetries before. I suspect Chaucer was learned. There is Dante; there is Vergil; probably Sophocles; and of course the Indians and the Japanese. And I suspect, with any of these, that we do not know to what extent their learning is not ours. A learned poetry is new only to us. But this

[3] *The Imagery of Sophocles' Antigone* (Princeton University Press, 1951).

poetry is not only learned; it depends a great deal upon the conventions of language as image, conceit, metaphor—the whole complex of the connotative uses of language; it depends characteristically upon what has happened since the Renaissance to the old rhetorical tradition, and contains the poetic and dialectic modes in relatively subordinated and even hidden positions. I think in this poetry we have been witnessing a strange, less than conscious rebirth of the old rhetoric; it is a poetry which depends on the reality of words to carry all other reality. What kind of criticism would you expect of such a poetry?

The presumed reader in this great age of mass literacy—this even greater age of the division of the mind—turns out to be illiterate with respect to this poetry, which is natural enough, for it takes time to get used to any new poetry, and also turns out to be illiterate with respect to almost all poetry, which seems unnatural, and which requires great additional burdens in the job of education from both criticism and scholarship. At any rate we see that the difficulty of the reader with Eliot and Yeats only exaggerates the difficulty with all poetry. What kind of criticism and scholarship would you expect for such a reader?

The general state of culture and knowledge is of course reflected in the characteristic poetry and the presumed reader. Culture has become fragmentary, belief has become beliefs, as interests have become specialized and communities massive. The enormous heightening of self-consciousness is accompanied by the diminution and mutilation of available general consciousness. As our knowledge and understanding of the classics increase, both their study and use go out of fashion. We have the interesting relationship that as we intensify individuation the *society* of individuals tends to disappear; for a sociology is not a society. What we have, with respect to the older forms of our culture, is the disappearance of the man who by his education, his tradition, and his own responsive life, was the layman to all the forms of his society. The mind no longer feels omniform or that it knows its own interests. We have a society of priests or experts who are strangely alien to the great mass movements which they presumably express or control.—What would you expect the criticism to be which had the burden of relating Eliot and Yeats through our presumed reader to such a state of knowledge and culture?

Clearly with such a burden imposed upon it you would like to have expected a coherent, fully implicated, and fully committed body of criticism in sound relation to a similar body of scholarship: together something good for the sane growth of the mind: together, something with the authority of action not assertion. But you ought not to have expected such a thing from the history of criticism.

Very little since Aristotle and until Coleridge has been demanded of criticism, and not much more of literary scholarship. We are of recent need. The immediate history and tradition of critical ideas are unfortunately those of pure art—art for art's sake—the Arnoldian claim that poetry might substitute for religion or philosophy, along with the tremendous infusion into our general habits of mind of new ways of finding trouble, uncertainty, insecurity, ambiguity, irrationality through the techniques of psychology, anthropology, semantics, and physiology. None of these trains of attitude and idea help much to create, either in poetry or its criticism, a decent relation to society. They do help to envisage, in a phrase of Eliot's, the incredible public life and the intolerable private life of our time. They make a pattern of incongruity, incompatibility, and disrelation. The pattern was inevitable when, as was the case, the mind went through art for art's sake to find rhetoric and found rhetoric as a neutral, though troubled, methodology.

I do not know what sort of relation there is between these elements just laid down (and I am sure there are other elements not mentioned) and the "new criticism," but I am certain there is some sort of generic relation. When I think of these elements I seem to understand how the "new criticism" came about. We developed a prodigious conscious skill in the psychology of poetic language (that is, rhetoric, as modified by Coleridge) and entered thereby into the private worlds of the poets to find there private images of the great world not otherwise accessible to the reader and perhaps not otherwise creatable by the poet. So attractive as well as necessary were the techniques of this skill in language that they led to excess analysis, excess simplification, and excess application, which is the normal pathology of a skill become a method and a method become a methodology. What was required to be exemplary turned out to be omniverous daily practice—perhaps in the creation of poetry as well as its criticism; and the single practice was believed somehow to stand for all other pertinent practices. This is unity or wholeness by exclusion. The point is, that these conscious skills made an adequate, though never complete, criticism of certain poetry, some of it contemporary where the adequacy was high, some of it two centuries old where the adequacy was low; that these skills also illuminated corresponding aspects of all poetry without being an adequate criticism of it and without being a scholarship at all; and that, finally, the process of developing these skills educated into a special literacy a fairly large class of presumed readers. There was never a coherent critical position, certainly never a uniform practice; there was rather the development of habitual skills of the analysis of verbal texts made necessary by the cultural situation and some of the poetry written from it. These skills, along with certain claims that the poetry these skills analyzed was knowledge or experience, perhaps masqueraded as a position which relieved the mind of the need for any other mode of knowledge. The risk then is that the rote of response replaces the skill. Nobody ought to throw a skill away, but nobody seeing the excesses and degenerations of a skill ought to depend so much on it as when it was new and had élan.

The one thing the "new critics" shared was skill in analysis at a highly conscious level of the behavior of the words in poetry; that is, most of them have been engaged in making a rhetoric, but at the psychological rather than the grammatical level of language, and they have made their rhetorics dominate, or stand for, most other modes of the mind. What I would want is to keep the rhetoric but to get rid of its dominance and to put it into living and variable relation to other modes of the mind; I should like to add poetic and dialectic; I should like to build Aristotle on to Coleridge or develop Coleridge out of Aristotle; and I believe that by the pressure of a major force (I take the phrase from Dante, not from Hitler, not from the mechanists or Marxists) something of the sort is happening. Since I cannot say what this major force is, except that it has something to do with the reality that so presses upon us that we need all our modes of understanding, all our modes of mimesis and synergy to cope with it, let me illustrate.

John Crowe Ransom has these late years been extending the theory of his criticism beyond the rhetorical scope of tenor and vehicle and structure and texture into epistemology and ontology, that is to say into dialectic, and the last essay of his I have read was on Aristotle and moved into poetic. But the practice of his criticism is still under the rhetoric of tenor and vehicle and texture; the skill of his theory has not run down into the skill of his hands, and he has some scruples about permitting it to do so. His essay on Milton's *Lycidas* was called "A Poem Nearly Anonymous," and so far as he dealt with *Lycidas* as an exercise in his kind of rhetoric it was an excellent essay; but I do not believe it touched very much the matters in the poem which Milton's rhetoric dealt with and composed and which were not nearly so much dominated by it as Mr. Ransom's rhetoric would have you think: I mean the theology and politics and personal experience which are the intellectual and poetic subject of the poem: I mean precisely what Mr. Ransom's theoretic occupations now lead him to. There is a sense of the complementary just at hand and as if it had always been there but not noticed in the particular instance until too late.

Analogously, in the essays of Cleanth Brooks there is something not done crying out to be done, which is perhaps to be understood as somehow present in his best pieces, those on Yeats and Eliot. By and large, what Mr. Brooks has made is a rhetoric of Irony and Paradox, with sub-types of Ambiguity, Attitude, Tone, and Belief. How rhetorical his theory is may be seen in his objections to paraphrase: he will have nothing of any plain account of the material translated into the rhetoric of the poetry; but he nevertheless makes sensitive rhetorical paraphrases of various poems. The trouble is that his Rhetoric of Irony and Paradox when applied to Donne cannot deal with the intellectual experience which for Donne was the *other* part of the material of the poem. Where with Eliot and Yeats, men of middle age or better can take for granted the *other* part and get along tolerably well with Mr. Brooks's rhetoric, it is difficult to do so with Donne and impossible with Milton or Shakespeare. Not long ago Ronald Crane, the Chicago Aristotelian, took Mr. Brooks to task on these matters,[4] approaching the need for dialectic through the need for scholarship. The two objections I have to Mr. Crane are that he did not give enough credit to the positive illuminations, which need only their correctives and supplements, of Mr. Brooks, and that he did not himself push on to the poetics needed to correct and supplement both himself and Mr. Brooks.

If we look at the two volumes of William Empson and some of his recent essays, it turns out that he, too, has stuffed all his dialectic and most of his poetics into a Rhetoric of Ambiguity and Pastoral. While the results are exciting, they are one-sided and even deformed if taken, as Mr. Empson takes them, as a means of reading conformable to the poet's own intention or to the reading of readers differently trained. All the power of Mr. Empson's mind depends on the exclusiveness with which he transforms his rhetorical method into a total methodology. As Mr. Brooks had Mr. Crane, Mr. Empson has had a corrective applied by Miss Rosemond Tuve with regard to his interpretation of George Herbert's "The Sacrifice"; which is a very exciting poem in Mr. Empson's reading, but all on the level of the psychology of language, all on what the words do to the material and very nearly nothing on what the material does to the words through other than verbal modes of the mind. In Miss Tuve's meaning the specific and demonstrable mode of Christian allegory, both as a device of poetics and as a means of representing Christian thought aesthetically, is brought back into the poem, thus providing it with several levels of poetic experience of which Mr. Empson was ignorant. I rather suspect that Mr. Empson's answer to Miss Tuve would be that the modes of the mind she finds in Herbert no longer exist; if so he would be right, but only from the point of view of his methodology, which is what needs correction: precisely so that more of the poem might come into existence.

Mr. Ransom, Mr. Empson, and Mr. Brooks may object to being called rhetoricians; they have not conspicuously used the term of themselves; but Kenneth Burke must have found it his first cradle-word, and I think he would rather be called Rhetor, as honorific and as description, than anything else. I suspect that like Cicero in *De*

[4] R. S. Crane: "Cleanth Brooks; Or, the Bankruptcy of Critical Monism." *Modern Philology,* XLV, No. 4, May 1948, pp. 226-245.

Finibus[5] he regards poetry, philosophy, and religion as matters subordinate to rhetoric in the beginning and in the end to be transformed into rhetoric. His great work is interesting (I am still pursuing my analogy) in the titles of the three volumes. The first was called *A Grammar of Motives,* the second is called *The Rhetoric of Motives,* and for the third there is no certain title (as the book is not written) but he has twice referred to it as The Symbolic. If we remember that one of Mr. Burke's favorite key devices is contained in the remark that language is either *symbolic* action or symbolic *action,* I think we may hazard it that rhetoric will be doing the work in the symbolic. In Mr. Burke rhetoric always does all the work, and in order to do so it has to acquire two specific characters. It has to become very abstract—so abstract that Kant's categories become immediate sensations; and with its abstractness it also has to become neutral. The feeling of spate, of copiousness, you get in Burke is because of this abstract neutrality; he has no need to stop and there is nothing to arrest him: there are no obstacles he cannot transform into abstract or reduce to neutral terms in his rhetoric. He is a very superior example indeed of the mind in which the articulate organization has absorbed the material organized. The rhetoric is so good for any purpose that it very nearly engorges purpose. The methodology is a wonderful machine that creates its own image out of everything fed into it: nobody means what he says but only the contribution of what he says to the methodology.

Now I would suppose that Mr. Burke's rhetoric is a true rhetoric despite its abstractness and neutrality. I would suppose that his rhetoric is a heightened, elaborated, exemplary form of a stage every mind must pass through in taking up mutual relations with dialectic and poetic (or psychology and philosophy), but I am certain that this rhetoric is no place to stay. Nor will it help me to consider that this rhetoric is an act of unification and that the other modes of the

[5] This may be a little rough on Cicero. But in *De Finibus* (V, 3) Cicero says in praise of the Old Academy: "They have produced orators, generals and statesmen. To come to the less distinguished professions, this factory of experts in all the sciences has turned out mathematicians, poets, musicians, and physicians" (Loeb translation). I am indebted to Erich Auerbach for this quotation.

mind are to be found organized into it; indeed that is my objection, for, unified, bound toegther, the modes of the mind lose both their own distinction and the distinct aspects of things they were intended to handle; and furthermore, so closely organized, there is no room for the mind to contain anything besides itself. I would not have Mr. Burke other than he is; he is an exemplary monument; but I would use him, and I hope I do use him, quite other than he is.

Here, of course, I use him somewhat unfairly, as the last step in my effort to show the ultimately rhetorical character of the processes of the "new criticism." It is unfair because Mr. Burke is only a literary critic in unguarded moments, when rhetoric nods. As a regular thing Mr. Burke does not give an account of literature; he substitutes his account for the literature, with a general air that the account does well what the literature did badly and that the only sound use of literature is to furnish rhetoric with one of its incentives. I draw the inference that the characteristic risk of the "new criticism" is that its special skills of analysis may become an omnicompetent methodology and that the risk is underlined by the rhetorical nature of the skills. To put it another way, it is a natural sequence to move from art for art's sake to criticism for criticism's sake. But I do not wish to be misunderstood; I do not suppose there is one of the "new critics" who would not assent to these strictures, and I also suppose that these strictures may with point be applied to myself.

I only proceed from common ground, where "Behold, there was a swarm of bees and honey in the carcase of the lion"; and I hope we proceed toward that other common ground where we understand how from strength comes forth sweetness.

But that is rhetoric and is meant to be my apology for dealing with my colleagues of twenty years for a present purpose of my own, which has to do with the next twenty years. If, in summary, the "new criticism" was a high success in partial criticism, it would only improve the success if it were associated with a more nearly complete criticism. Parallel to this statement, it may be observed that in history criticism has been almost entirely of poetry and poetic drama. It would seem that until our own stage of culture was reached only poetry required criticism. Now all forms of literature require criticism and scholarship, each in its kind, and almost each in its example; it is part of the conditions of life. When I think of the criticism of poetry it sometimes seems to me that it is poetry's fault that we live in a rhetoric-sodden world. But there may then be an advantage in realizing that much of the old work of poetry is now done, and has been these three hundred and fifty years, in prose; all of which now requires criticism. It may be that this criticism will put rhetoric back into relation with dialectic and poetic, not losing any of the new skills of rhetoric but rather finding further skills in the other modes of the mind to go with them. We would then be back in the *Phaedrus,* or beyond that:

> Homer is my example and his unchristened heart.
> The lion and the honeycomb, what has Scripture said?

Among other things, Scripture says that in literature we are dealing with matters for which we do not have competent discursive techniques, although we habitually manipulate our responses to them by our existing discursive techniques. We do, however, have deep unconscious skills in literature which we may get at and learn initial aspects of by discursive means, though we may not apply them as absolute rules: e.g. metrics and the grammar of the rhetoricians may help us get at the deep skills of the lion and the honeycomb, of the little book which is sweet as honey in the mouth but bitter in the belly, just as the angel in Revelation said. Literature is one of our skills of notation of the incarnation of the real into the actual; and we have made many successive and sometimes recurrent agreements or conventions about the means of notation, but we have never been able to articulate very much of our deeper, far-reaching agreements about the skills themselves, much less about the sources of the skills. We "have eaten/Smooth creatures still living," as Eliot says. We have within us taste and skill. Part of the skill lies in what Coleridge calls the reality of words, and part lies in the plot which Aristotle calls the soul of the work or mimesis. These house the skills of the aesthetic sensibility. Taste, as we know, is variable and educable and transformable; it also seems to me a matter of faith, of faith testing life. Beyond skill and taste lie such matters as rhythm and play and gesture. And beyond that is our capacity to bring or to refuse to bring with us our good will, our own knowledge, our own creativity, our own empathetic power of imagination. That is why our final judgment—with all our scholarship and criticism—depends on the state of culture at a given time; just as what makes a work of art conformable to different cultures at different times is the unity of the reality under all cultures at all times.

Here is Aristotle on Coleridge: the form of forms creating in actual words some of the reality of the language under the words. I think this idea is represented by the development through fifteen years in two sentences of T. S. Eliot. The first said we can only tell whether a work is literature by literary means but can only tell whether it is great literature by extra-literary means. Here is the second: "To judge a work of art by artistic or by religious standards, to judge a religion by religious or artistic standards should come in the end to the same thing: though it is an end at which no individual can arrive."

What happens if you take this view is that the modes of the mind work together. The Coleridge demands the Aristotle and the Aristotle builds up and through the Coleridge. At this point the critic can get himself out of the way. He will know, with Montaigne, that "a beautiful matter will always be in place, wherever it is sown"; and by other skills he will know, in the language of the Chorus of Women of Canterbury, that he has "lain in the soil and criticized the worm." For it is at this point that the mind acknowledges that the force behind art exists outside art, but also that the work of art itself almost gets outside art to make a shape—a form of the forms—of our total recognition of the force that moves us.

[*This essay was originally presented as a MacGregor Room (now Peters Rushton) Seminar, University of Virginia, 3 March, 1950.*]

1950

12

A Burden for Critics

When George Santayana made his apology for writing a system of philosophy—one more after so many, one more after a lifetime of self-denial—he put his plea for forgiveness on the ground that he was an ignorant man, almost a poet. No doubt there was some reservation in Santayana's mind when he made that plea; no doubt there is some in mine when I adapt it to myself. This essay does not introduce a system of criticism; it is only a plea that criticism take up some of its possibilities that have been in abeyance, or in corruption, for some time; and it may be that like Santayana's philosophy it will look like an approach to a system. If so, it is the system of an ignorant man, and there is nothing in it that does not remind itself at every turn that it is the kind of ignorance which goes with being almost a poet. Poetry is one of the things we do to our ignorance; criticism makes us conscious of what we have done, and sometimes makes us conscious of what can be done next, or done again.

That consciousness is the way we feel the critic's burden. By a burden, I mean both a weight and a refrain, something we carry and something that carries us along, something we have in possession and something that reminds us what we are. It is the burden of our momentum. In relation to it we get work done. Out of relation to it we get nothing done, except so far as we are swept along; and of course we are mainly swept along. The critic's job is to put us into maximum relation to the burden of our momentum, which means he has to run the risk of a greater degree of consciousness than his mind is fit for. He risks substituting the formulas of relation for the things related. I take it the critic is a relativist; but his relativism does not need to be either deterministic or positivistic, as in our time it usually is; he may rather be the relativist of insight, apsiration, vision. He is concerned with choice, not prescription, with equity, not law; never with the dead hand, always with the vital purpose. He knows that the institution of literature, so far as it is alive, is made again at every instant. It is made afresh as part of the process of being known afresh; what is permanent is what is always fresh, and it can be fresh only in performance—that is, in reading and seeing and hearing what is actually in it at this place and this time. It is in performance that we find out relation to momentum. Or put another way, the critic brings to consciousness the means of performance.

Perform is a word of which we forget the singular beauty. Its meaning is: to furnish forth, to complete, to finish, in a sense which is influenced by the ideas clustered in the word *form;* so that *performance* is an enlightening name for one of our richest activities, rich with extra life. If it is the characteristic intent of the critic to see about the conditions of performance, it is his characteristic temptation to interfere with those conditions. He will find substitutes; he will make one condition do for every condition; he will make precedent do for balance, or rote for authority; and, worst of all, he will impose the excellence of something he understands upon something he does not understand. Then all the richness of actual performance is gone. It is worth taking precautions to prevent that loss, or at any rate to keep us aware of the risk.

The precautions of the past come down to us as mottoes; and for the critic of literature in our time I would suggest three mottoes—all Latin—as exemplary. *Omnis intellectus omniformis est:* every mind is omniform, every mind has latent in it all possible forms of the mind, even one's own mind. The temptation is to make some single form of the mind seem omnicompetent; omnicompetence becomes omniscience and asserts for itself closed authority based upon a final revelation. *Omnis intellectus omniformis est.* This is a motto of the Renaissance, and leads us directly to a motto of the high Middle Ages, which preceded, or initiated, rather than followed, an era of absolute authority: *Fides quaerens intellectus.* If the temptation of the Renaissance was to put one's own version of the mind in first place, the temptation of the Middle Ages was to identify God with either one's own knowledge of him or with one's particular form of faith. *Fides quaerens intellectus* is a motto meant to redeem that temptation; for it is faith alone that may question the intellect, as it is only the intellect that can curb faith. The very principle of balance, together with the radical precariousness of its nature, lies in the reversibility of this motto. Just so, the value of both these mottoes is heightened by putting them into relation with a third, which is classical in its time, and which has to do primarily neither with intellect nor faith but with the temptation of the moral sensibility. *Corruptio optima pessima:* in corruption the best is the worst. Here, in this motto, is that hard core of common sense—Cochrane's phrase—of which the Christian world has never got enough in its heritage from classical culture. It reminds the moral ego of its fatal temptation to forget that the ground it stands on is not its own, but other, various, and equal. Surely we have made the best in us the worst when we have either pushed an insight beyond its field or refused, when using one insight, to acknowledge the pressure of all those insights—those visions of value—with which it is in conflict. If we do not see this, we have lost the feeling of richness, the sense of relation, and the power of judgment; and without these we cannot, as conscious critics, bring our experience of literature to actual performance. We should know neither what to bring, nor what to look for.

All this is generality; it applies to literature chiefly in the sense that literature is one aspect among many of the general human enterprise. The horror, for critics, of most aspects of that enterprise, is that they are exigent in action and will by no means stand still for criticism until they are done for. The beauty of literature is that it is exigent in the mind and will not only stand still but indeed never comes fully into its life of symbolic action until criticism has taken up the burden of bringing it into performance and finding its relation to the momentum of the whole enterprise. Both what constitutes performance and the very nature of relation—that is to say, what must be done and what may be taken for granted—change from time to time. It seems likely that one reason there has been so little great literature is that at most times so little has been required of it: how often has a Vergil felt obligated to create the myth of imperial culture? It is even more likely that the ability to cope with the task was wanting when required: how often has a Dante turned up to put into actual order all that had been running into the disorder of the rigid intellect and the arbitrary will? Ordinarily, past times have required little of literature in the way either of creating or ordering a culture. The artist's task was principally to express the continuity of his culture and the turbulence that underlay it. That is perhaps why we find the history of criticism so much concerned with matters of decorum: that is to say, with conformity, elegance, rhetoric, or metrics: matters not now commonly found or considered in the reviews. In our own time—if I may be permitted the exaggerations of ignorance and of poetry—almost everything is required of the arts and particularly of literature. Almost the whole job of culture, as it has formerly been understood, has been dumped into the hands of the writer. Possibly a new form of culture, appropriate to a massive urban society, is emerging: at any rate there are writers who write with a new ignorance and a new collective illiteracy: I mean the Luce papers and Hollywood. But the old drives persist. Those who seem to be the chief writers of our time have found their subjects in attempting to dramatize at once both the culture and the turbulence it was meant to control, and in doing so they have had practically to create—as it happens, to re-crate—the terms, the very symbolic substance, of the culture as they went along.

I do not mean that this has happened by arrogation on the part of the writers; I mean they have been left alone with this subject as part of the actual experience of life in our time: which is always the subject which importunes every serious writer if he is honest and can keep himself free of the grosser hallucinations. The actual is always the medium through which the visitation of the Muse is felt. Perhaps a distinction will clarify what is meant. It is getting on toward a century since Matthew Arnold suggested that poetry could perhaps take over the expressive functions of religion. Possibly Arnold only meant the functions of the Church of England and the lesser dissenting sects. Whatever he meant, it did not happen, it could not and it cannot happen. All poetry can do is to dramatize, to express, what has actually happened to religion. This it has done. It has not replaced or in any way taken over the functions of religion; but it has been compelled to replace the operative force of religion as a resource with the discovery, or creation, of religion as an aesthetic experience. The poet has to put his religion itself into his poetry along with his experience of it. Think, together, of the religious poetry of George Herbert and of T. S. Eliot: of how little Herbert had to do before he got to his poetry, of how much Eliot is compelled to put into his poetry before he is free to write it. Consider too—and perhaps this is more emphatic of what has happened—the enormous mass of exegetical criticism it has seemed necessary and desirable to apply to Eliot's poetry and indeed to the whole school of Donne. This criticism neither compares, nor judges; it elucidates scripture.

Let us put the matter as a question. Why do we treat poetry, and gain by doing so, after much the same fashion as Augustine treated the scriptures in the fifth century? Why do we make of our criticism an essay in the understanding of words and bend upon that essay exclusively every tool of insight and analysis we possess? Why do we have to re-create so much of the poem in the simple reading which is only the preface to total performance? Do we, like Augustine, live in an interregnum, after a certainty, anticipating a synthesis? If so, unlike Augustine, we lack a special revelation: we take what we can find, and what we find is that art is, as Augustine sometimes thought, a human increment to creation. If this is so, how, then, has it come about?

We know very well how it has come about, and we come late enough in the sequence of our time so that we can summarize it in what looks like an orderly form—or at any rate a poetic form. It composes into something we can understand. We come late in a time when the burden of descriptive and historical knowledge is greater than any man or groups of men can encompass; when the labor by which our society gets along from day to day is not only divided but disparate and to the individual laborer fragmentary; and when, in an effort to cope with the burden of knowledge and the division of labor, we have resorted to the adulterative process called universal education.

As a natural effect of such a situation we have the disappearance or at least the submergence of tradition in the sense that it is no longer available at either an instinctive or a critical level but must be looked for, dug out, and largely re-created as if it were a new thing and not tradition at all. We have also a decay of the power of conviction or mastery; we permit ourselves everywhere to be overwhelmed by the accidents of our massive ignorance and by the apparent subjectivity of our individual purposes. Thus we have lost the field of common reference, we have dwindled in our ability to think symbolically, and as we look about us we see all our old unconscious skills at life disappearing without any apparent means of developing new unconscious skills.

We have seen rise instead a whole series of highly conscious, but deeply dubious and precarious skills which have been lodged in the sciences of psychology, anthropology, and sociology, together with the whole confusion of practices which go with urbanization. Consider how all these techniques have been developed along lines that discover trouble, undermine purpose, blight consciousness, and prevent decision; how they promote uncertainty, insecurity, anxiety, and incoherence; how above all they provide barriers between us and access to our common enterprise. Perhaps the unwieldy and unmanipulable fact of urbanization does more of the damage than the conscious techniques.

But this is not a diagnosis, it is a statement of sequence, a composition of things in relation. At the point where we arrest this sequence, and think in terms of what we can remember of our old culture, does it not seem plain to us what we have? Do we not have a society in which we see the attrition of law and rational wisdom and general craft? Do we not have an age anti-intellectual and violent, in which there is felt a kind of total responsibility to total disorder? Who looks ahead except to a panacea or a millennium which is interchangeable with an invoked anarchy, whether in the world or in the individual personality? Do we not above all each day wonderfully improve our chances of misunderstanding each other? These are the questions we ask of a living, not a dead, society.

They become more emphatic when we ask them about the schools of art and criticism which accompanied this shift in the structure of society. If we begin with Arnold's effort at the secularization of the old culture, it is easy to remind ourselves of the sequence which it began. Here it is, in very rough order. The hedonism in Pater, the naturalism of Zola, the impressionism of Anatole France, Art for Art as of the 'nineties, the naturalistic relativism of de Gourmont, the aestheticism of the psychologists, the rebirth of symbolism (as in Mallarmé and Yeats), the private mind, Imagism and Free verse, futurism, expressionism and expressive form, Dada and surrealism, dream literature, spontaneous or automatic form, anti-intellectual form, the school of Donne in English and American poetry, the stream of consciousness (that libel on Joyce), the revolution of the word, the new cult of the word. Some of these phrases will carry different meanings to different people; let us say that the general sequence runs toward some kind of autonomous and absolute creation and therefore toward total literalism.

That is on the positive side. On the negative side, every school on the list except Arnold's secularism, which was less a school than a plea for one, is an attack on disinterestedness of mind and imagination, though none of them meant to be so. And Arnold, who meant just the opposite, helped them at their business by seeing too much necessity in the offing. All of them either accepted or revolted violently against a predetermined necessity; none of them was able to choose necessity or to identify it with his will. None of them was apparently acquainted with the sense of our Latin mottoes. Their only causes were Lost Causes; their only individuals were atoms; they reflected their time, as schools must.

The world has about now caught up with these trains of ideas, these images, trends, habits, patterns, these tendencies toward either mass action or isolated action—equally violent whether in attraction or repulsion. It is a world of engineers and anarchs; rather like the Roman world when the impulse of Vergil and the Emperor Augustus had died out and the impulse of Benedict and Augustine had not yet altered the direction and aspect of the general momentum. It is a world alive and moving but which does not understand itself.

Of this world individual artists have given a much better account than the doctrines of their schools would suggest, and they have done so for two reasons. The arts cannot help reacting directly and conventionally to what is actual in their own time; nor can the arts help, whether consciously or not, working into their masterpieces what has survived of the full tradition—however they may contort or corrupt it. They deal with life or experience itself, both what is new and what is accumulated, inherited, still living. They cannot come *de novo*. They cannot help, therefore, creating at a disinterested level, despite themselves. That is why they constitute a resource of what is not new—the greater part of ourselves—and a means of focusing what is new, all that necessarily aggravates us and tears at our nerve ends in our friction with it. That is why Chartres Cathedral survives better than the schools of the Bishop of Chartres; though both were equally vital in their time.

Consider in this light what seem to be the masterpieces of our time. Consider the poetry of Eliot, Yeats, Valéry, Rilke; the novels of Joyce, Gide, Hemingway, Proust, Mann, Kafka; the plays of Shaw, Pirandello, O'Neill; the music of Stravinsky, Bloch, Bartok, Ravel, Satie, Schoenberg; the paintings of Matisse, Picasso, Rouault, Marin, Hartley; the sculpture of Maillol, Brancusi, Faggi, LaChaise, Zorach, Archipenko, Moore. Think also, but at another level, not easy to keep in strict parallel, of the architecture of Leviathan: the railway station at Philadelphia, the Pentagon, the skyscrapers, the gasoline stations, the highway systems, the East and West Side highways, apartment houses each a small city, and the interminable multiple dwellings. Think too of the beautiful bridges which connect or traverse eyesores: the Washington Bridge, the Pulaski Skyway. Lastly, for architecture, think of the National Parks, with their boulevards running at mountain peak.

What an expression of an intolerable, disintegrating, irrational world: a doomed world, nevertheless surviving, throwing up value after value with inexhaustible energy but without a principle in sight. And how difficult to understand the arts which throw up the values. Only Hemingway and Maillol in the roster above perhaps made works which seem readily accessible when seriously approached. Shaw is as difficult as Joyce, Mann as Kafka, if you really look into them. The difficulties arise, it seems to me, partly because of the conditions of society outlined above as they affect the audience and partly because of these same conditions as they affect the artist at his work. The two are not the same, though they are related. The audience is able to bring less to the work of art than under the conditions of the old culture, and the artist is required to bring more. What has changed its aspect is the way the institutions, the conceptions, the experience of culture gets into the arts. What has happened is what was said above: almost the whole job of culture has been dumped on the artist's hands.

It is at this point that we begin to get at the burden of criticism in our time. It is, to put it one way, to make bridges between the society and the arts: to prepare the audience for its art and to prepare the arts for their artists. The two kinds of preparation may sometimes be made in one structure; but there is more often a difference of emphasis required. Performance, the condition we are after, cannot mean the same thing to the audience and the artist. The audience needs instruction in the lost skill of symbolic thinking. The arts need rather to be shown how their old roles can be played in new conditions. To do either, both need to be allied to the intellectual habits of the time. Besides analysis, elucidation, and comparison, which Eliot once listed as the functions of criticism, criticism in our time must also come to judgment.

If we look at the dominant development in criticism in English during the last thirty years—all that Mr. Ransom means by the New Criticism—with its fineness of analysis, its expertness of elucidation, and its ramifying specialization of detail—we must see how natural, and at bottom how facile, a thing it has been. It has been the critics' way of being swept along, buoyed more by the rush than by the body of things. It is a criticism, that is, which has dealt almost exclusively either with the executive technique of poetry (and only with a part of that) or with the general verbal techniques of language. Most of its practitioners have been men gifted in penetrating the private symbolisms and elucidating the language of all that part of modern poetry we have come to call the school of Donne. With a different criticism possibly another part of modern poetry might have become dominant, say the apocalyptic school—though of course I cannot myself think so. In any case, it was a criticism created to cope with and develop the kind of poetry illustrated by Eliot's *Waste Land* and Yeats's *Tower,* two poems which made desperate attempts to reassert the tradition under modern conditions: Eliot by Christianity, Yeats by a private philosophy. Eminently suited for the *initial* stages of the criticism of this poetry, it has never been suited to the later stages of criticism; neither Eliot nor Yeats has been compared or judged because there has been no criticism able to take those burdens. For the rest, the "new criticism" has been suited for *some* older poetry, but less because of the nature of the poetry than because of the limitation of the modern reader. For most older poetry it is not suited for anything but sidelights, and has therefore made misjudgments when applied. It is useless for Dante, Chaucer, Goethe, or Racine. Applied to drama it is disfiguring, as it is to the late seventeenth- and all the eighteenth-century poetry. Yet it has had to be used and abused because there has seemed no other way of re-creating—in the absence of a positive culture outside poetry—a verbal sensibility capable of coping with the poetry at all. In a stable society with a shared culture capable of convictions, masteries, and vital dogmas, such a criticism might have needed only its parallel developments for the novel and the play and the older forms of all literature; such a society does not need much criticism. But in an unstable society like ours, precisely because the burden put upon the arts is so unfamiliar and so extensive (it is always the maximum burden in intensity) a multiple burden is put upon criticism to bring the art to full performance. We have to compare and judge as well as analyze and elucidate. We have to make plain not only what people are reading, but also—as Augustine and the other fathers had to do with the scriptures—what they are reading about.

Here I do not wish to be misunderstood. Critics are not fathers of a new church. I speak from a secular point of view confronting what I believe to be a secular world which is not well understood; and I suppose what I want criticism to do can as well as not be described as the development of aesthetic judgment—the judgment of the rational imagination—to conform with the vast increase of material which seems in our time capable only of aesthetic experience. This is not to define a revelation or create a society. It is to define and explore the representations in art of what is actually going on in existing society. I see no reason why all forms of the word *aesthetic* cannot be restored to good society among literary critics by remembering its origin in a Greek word meaning to perceive, and remembering also its gradual historical limitation to what is perceived or felt—that is, what is actually there—in the arts. I have here the company of Bergson who thought that the serious arts gave the aesthetic experience of the true nature of what the institutions of society are meant to control. And in another way, I have more support than I want in the philosophy of Whitehead, who found that the sciences in new growth, far from giving us knowledge with relation among its parts, give us instead abstractions good for practical manipulation but conformable only to a mystery. As a consequence, his philosophy of organism, with its attribution of feeling relations everywhere, is an aesthetic philosophy; in which knowledge comes to us as an aesthetic experience.

We do not need to go so far as Whitehead. The sort of thing that is wanted here to go on with seems to show clearly in James Joyce, whose *Ulysses* is the direct aesthetic experience of the breakdown of the whole Graeco-Christian world, not only in emotion but also in concept. Or again, Mann's *Magic Mountain* is the projected aesthetic experience of both that whole world and the sickness which is breaking it down. And again, Gide's *Counterfeiters* is a kind of gratuitous aesthetic experience—a free possibility—of what is happening along with the breakdown. Lastly, Eliot's religious poetry is a partly utopian and partly direct aesthetic experience of the actual Christian life today. That is what these works are about, and they cannot be judged aesthetically until full stock has been taken of what they are about. For us, they create their subjects; and indeed it is the most conspicuous thing about them that they do so. On each of these authors—even Eliot in his kind of reference—the whole substance of his subject is a necessary part of the aesthetic experience of it. It is for that reason that we have to judge the subject as well as what is done with it. To exaggerate only a little, in the world as it is, there is no way to get a mastery of the subject except in the aesthetic experience. How do we go about doing so?

That is, how does criticism enlarge its aesthetics to go with the enlargement of aesthetic experience? Here we must take again the risk of generalization, and we must begin with a generalization to get what the sciences have done with aesthetics out of the way. If we do not get rid of them by generalization we cannot get rid of them at all, for in detail their techniques are very tempting. Let us say then that psychology turns aesthetics into the mechanics of perception, that scientific logic turns it into semasiology, just as technical philosophers had already turned it into a branch of epistemology. All these studies are troublemakers and lead, like our social studies, to the proliferation of a sequence of insoluble and irrelevant problems so far as the critic of literature is concerned. Let us put it provisionally, that for the literary critic aesthetics comprises the study of superficial and mechanical executive techniques, partly in themselves, but also and mainly in relation to the ulterior techniques of conceptual form and of symbolic form. I do not say that one of these is deeper or more important than another, certainly not in isolation. But let us take them in the order given, and generalize a program of work.

By superficial and mechanical executive techniques I mean the whole rationale of management and manipulation through more or less arbitrary devices which can be learned, which can be made elegant, and which are to some extent the creatures of taste or fashion so far as particular choice is concerned. In some lucky cases they may be the sole preoccupation of the working artist, as in some unlucky cases they may be the one aspect of his work to which he seemingly pays least attention. In our own day they are troublesome to the extent that they are ignored in an abeyance from which they ought to be redeemed. It would seem to me, for example, that a considerable amount of potentially excellent verse fails to make its way because the uses of meter—in the sense that all verse has meter—are not well understood, though they are now beginning again to be played with: Mr. Eliot has just resorted to the metrics of Johnson and Milton. The critic who is capable of doing so ought to examine into the meters of his victims. Similarly, the full narrative mode is in little use by serious novelists, and the full dramatic mode is not in much more use; yet these are the basic modes of a man telling a story. If only because they are difficult, the critic ought to argue for them when he sees a weakness which might have been turned into a strength by their use. Again, and related to the two previous examples, there is a great deal of obscurity in modern writing which could be cleared up if writers could be forced (only by criticism) to develop a skill in making positive statement, whether generalized or particular, whether in verse or in prose. Statement may make art great and ought not to be subject to fashion.

And so on. The critic can have little authority as a pedagogue. The main study of executive techniques will always be, to repeat, in relation to the ulterior techniques of conceptual and symbolic form. By conceptual techniques I mean the rationale of what the artist does with his dominant convictions, or obsessions, or insights, or visions, and how they are translated into major stresses of human relations as they are actually experienced. Here we are concerned with the aesthetics of the idea in relation to the actual, of the rational in relation to what is rationalized. In Dostoevski, for example, we are interested in his conception of the Double only as we see what happens to it in the character of Versilov, or Raskolnikov, or Dmitri Karamazov. In Joyce's *Ulysses* it is not the Homeric pattern of father and son that counts, but what happens to the conception of intransigence in Stephen in concert and conflict with that transigent man Bloom. So in the later poems of Yeats, the concepts of the Phases of the Moon are interesting as they work or fail to work in the chaos and anarchy and order of actual lyric emotions. On a more generalized level, it is through concern with conceptual techniques that one notes that the European novels of greatest stature seem to follow, not the conceptual pattern of Greek tragedy but the pattern of Christian rebirth, conversion, or change of heart; which is why novels do not have tragic heroes. But examples are endless.

And all of them, as those just cited, would tend if pursued to lead us into the territory of symbolic techniques which underlies and transcends them. I am not satisfied with the term. By symbolic techniques I mean what happens in the arts—*what gets into the arts*—that makes them relatively inexhaustible so long as they are understood. I mean what happens in the arts by means of fresh annunciations of residual or traditional forces, whether in the language, culture, or institutions of the artist's society. I mean those forces that operate in the arts which are greater than ourselves and come from beyond or under ourselves. But I am not satisfied with the definitions any more than I am with the term. It may be I mean invokable forces, or raw forces, the force of reality, whatever reality may be, pressing into and transforming our actual experience. It is what bears us and what we cannot bear except through the intervention of one of the great modes of the mind, religion, philosophy, or art, which, giving us the illusion of distance and control, makes *them,* too, seem forces greater than ourselves. It is in the figure of Dante himself in the *Divine Comedy,* Faustus in *Faustus,* Hamlet and Lear in *Hamlet* and *Lear,* Emma Bovary in *Madame Bovary,* all the brothers in *The Brothers Karamazov*. It is in the conjunction of the gods of the river and of the sea with the Christian gods in Eliot's *Dry Salvages*. It is the force of reality pressing into the actuality of symbolic form. Its technique is the technique of so concentrating or combining the known techniques as to discover or release that force. It is for this purpose and in this way that the executive, conceptual, and symbolic techniques go rationally together: the logic, the rhetoric, and the poetic; they make together the rationale of that enterprise in the discovery of life which is art. But the arts are not life, though in the sense of this argument they may make a rationale for discovering life. Whether they do or not, and how far, is the act of judgment that is also the last act in bringing particular works of art to full performance. Because the arts are imperfect, they can be judged only imperfectly by aesthetic means. They must be judged, therefore, by the declaration and elucidation of identity in terms of the whole enterprise which they feed, and of which they are the play, the aesthetic experience. There is a confusion here that cannot be clarified for it is a confusion of real things, as words are confused in a line of verse, the better the line the more completely, so that we cannot tell which ones govern the others. The confusion is, that it is through the aesthetic experience of it that we discover, and discover again, what life is, and that at present, if our account of it is correct, we also discover what our culture is. It is therefore worthwhile considering the usefulness of a sequence of rational critical judgments upon the art of our time as an aid in determining the identity, the meaning in itself, of present society. Such a sequence of judgments might transform us who judge more than the art judged.

Here perhaps is a good point to sweep some bad rubbish into the bins. Critical judgment need not be arrogant in its ambitions, only in its failures. Nor is it concerned with ranks and hierarchies, except incidentally. What I mean by judgment is what Aristotle would have meant by the fullest possible declaratory proposition of identity. Again, the ideal of judgment—no more to be reached by critics than by other men—is theological: as a soul is judged finally, quite apart from its history, for what it really is at the moment of judgment. Our human approximation of such judgment will be reached if we keep the ideal of it in mind and with that aid make our fullest act of recognition. Judgment is the critic's best recognition.

Thus it is now clear that my purpose in proposing a heavy burden for criticism is, to say the least of it, evangelical. What I want to evangelize in the arts is rational intent, rational statement, and rational technique; and I want to do it through technical judgment, clarifying judgment, and the judgment of discovery, which together I call rational judgment. I do not know if I should have enough eloquence to persuade even myself to consider such a burden for criticism, did I not have, not this time as precautions but as mentors, my three Latin mottoes. *Omnis intellectus omniformis est. Fides quaerens intellectus. Corruptio optima pessima.* They point the risk, and make it worth taking.

1948

13

Notes on Four Categories in Criticism

Literature is the bearer (the vehicle, but implicated) of all the modes of understanding of which *words* are capable; and not only that: it also bears, sets in motion or life, certain modes which words merely initiate and symbolize. Cf. T. S. Eliot's notion that meaning persists after the words have stopped; or, again, the notion that words work upon each other to produce something apart from the words. Thus literature is not only the bearer, it is the agent of discovery in the whole field of its operation: that is, to repeat, in all the modes of understanding of which words *partake*.

There are many ways in which these modes can be separated for purposes of discussion (criticism) and of manipulation (technique or executive virtuosity); and there is an infinite number of ways in which these modes may be combined (or confounded) in the experience of literature. Experience suggests that to the degree that a given work is successful there is some point at which the elements subject to discussion and to manipulation reverse their roles. Are not the elements of Irish Nationalism in Yeats's "Easter 1916" a dominant part of the technique of the poem? Is not the Christian folk symbolism in "Clerk Saunders" in some sense *a technical* device to manipulate the poem? Is not the myth of authority in *Coriolanus* the *technical* innovation that moves, and it may be deforms, that tragedy? Is not the nominalism in Pirandello the *technical* agent in his plays and tales that keeps the wheels of action turning?—This is to ask, is not the subject of literature always specific and unique; never general and repeated? But the question may clarify itself the other way round. If the dominant ideas of a work may have a technical function, cannot we also ask, are not the technical resources and limits of literature sometimes the *object,* even the virtual truth, of the work—so far as the work is susceptible to discourse? Consider the form of the sonnet, not only the variations of the fourteen lined iambic pentameter but also the variations of syntactical structure, as: Then, Now, Thus; If, Then, So; Look, Look again, See, etc., where the octave, quatrain, and couplet are governed by syntactical expectations parading as logical analysis. Do not these technical devices often absorb and replace the so-called subject matter? Again, conceive what happens when a rigid form is employed on material commonly held inappropriate to it. The most familiar examples are in burlesque and parody, or in mock-heroics, perhaps in the whole hoax and horsing groups of literary works.

But more serious examples abound: e.g. Empson's application of the rigid "light" villanelle to "dark" purposes in his "Missing Dates." In such combinations it is hard to know in which respect a greater transformation takes place, in the discussable elements or the manipulatable elements. But it is certain that the subjects of the works in question have no positive locus in either element. Nor are the subjects assignable to any combination of the elements. Rather, does not the "subject" of the poem, which may or may not be the expression of the author's intention, appear as the product or discovery of the joint operation? Any other conclusion seems to me Pickwickian —where if you combine your information on metaphysics and China you understand Chinese metaphysics. At any rate the conclusion suggested—that literature is heuristic, or may be so, when its elements work upon each other—preserves as a principle our sense that literature is an actual experience of something fresh, or, as we say, a deepened or widened version of the familiar. Thus literature, working with highly abstract and generalized agents—nothing could be more highly abstract than words or the patterns large and small in which they can be arranged; nothing could be more generalized than the philosophies or attitudes or insights through which the author focuses his human stresses—thus literature discovers what is both unpredictable *and* specific: a new, because particular, in some sense direct, look at actual experience. The technique is how this is done.

In practice there may be in the making of literature a great deal of one or another kind of technique, whether apparently superficial and formalistic or apparently substantial or ideological, and this technique may be deliberate or habitual or traditional. On the other hand, there may be apparently very little technique. It is never possible, in the given case, to say even roughly how much or what kinds or combinations of kinds of technique were employed until after long intimacy and absorption of the work has, by vicarious mastery, made the question artificial; for then we *use* the work as we use other actual experience. Yet we should never achieve intimacy nor reach absorption if we did not along the way prepare ourselves by question and division, by some effort of *measuring* the modes through which we touched experience. We should not have exercised our minds enough to meet the stress. We should not know what we meant by saying that we cannot tell the dancer from the dance. We could only, unprepared, belittle our perception of literature in particular by our incapacity, *through failure in exemplary study,* to acknowledge literature in general. All this follows from the conviction that there is a general technique of the mind to which the special techniques of literature (the bearing or vehicular techniques) are only an operative addition: used for movement, relation, emphasis, limit, form. Yet this general technique, as it is engaged in literature, is changed in scope, role, and even in deportment, so that it gains a limited literary specificity. A major problem in criticism and in the teaching of literature as the content of the author's profession (i.e., creative writing) is the distinction, explication, and exemplification of these kinds of technique in their metamorphoses.

Let us for convenience (and taking for granted always the realm of actual experience or life pressing upon and establishing the convenience) set up a few categories in technique. Let there be four principal and as many subordinate and overlapping techniques as necessary. There is the category of superficial techniques, which may as in some insects have to do with the skeleton, with articulation and co-ordination of movement, and which may as in humans be the surface flesh, the flash and play of motion, through the modifications of which similarity and variation of gesture are perceived. Here we find all such matters as meter and plot, the whole collection of devices that *seem* to be meaningless except in the instance, but which most literature has used to carry the reader's attention and to unite it with the object of that attention. It is meter and stanza, rhyme and alliteration, that focus the reader's attention in "The Garden of Proserpine" so as to give the first effect of a much greater subject than turns out to be there. It is the plot and verse structure of *Lear* that carry the reader-audience into matters it would not otherwise have had the will to see. The superficial techniques may be defined as all those devices which are only primary. They ensure a kind of minimum existence to a given work but they do not validate it.

The second category is that of linguistic technique, and is concerned mostly with images and tropes: images are often a source of validation, and tropes are an evidence of relationship to other validations, whether intellectual, sensory, or emotional. An image in literature is a word or group of words grouped about a nucleus of insight, feeling, emotion, action, or state of being, where the nucleus itself is not verbal, not in the words, but transpires in them. Images are the small elements of the richness of what literature is about; they have to do with quality, and are hence radically inexplicable and ultimately inarticulable. To use an analogy from physics, images set up fields of attraction and repulsion which give reason and cause to the energy of superficial techniques: they are the symbols for that energy, and sometimes become symbols in their own right as well. Tropes, or figures of speech, when not merely ornamental, have as their commonest function to clarify the working of the images which are their chief elements: they combine the concrete image present in the field of the given work with some abstraction of another image from another work or some other field of the mind. When we say My Love is (like) a Lion, we mean my love is ravening, mighty, and magnificent; we would not say The Lion is (like) a man in love unless we meant that a Lion gorging his prey is like a man engaged in the brutalizing act of forced love: rape. The first figure illuminates the man; the second darkens the lion. Either the man or the lion has not been intellectually abstracted enough in the new context to take on the uniting function of the image which gives life to the metaphor. (Besides, the rule of the pathetic fallacy is at work here.) Of the man we know enough; but we should have to develop the lion to a similar state of concrete availability before we could apply to him an abstraction of man. A curious but fundamental limitation seems to be present here: though man in all of his habits can be compared to anything in nature (not man), comparisons that work the other way round are successful only by *tour de force*. Swift's Houyhnhnms are a case in point; either we take them as "really" men or we tend to reject them; but the Yahoos, for all their apparent degradation, we accept as second nature. A man may turn into an animal and preserve his man-quality, but an animal may not turn into a man without a more complete metamorphosis. The animals in Aesop and La Fontaine are men released or disguised. Swift's horses are not released at all, but condemned; it is they who are degraded rather than the Yahoos: or it is by their degradation that we measure the abasement of the Yahoos. Perhaps that is what Swift meant. "Go to the ant, thou sluggard," or "Busy as a bee" take a similar exegesis. (It is amusing to note that the more we know of the "civilizations" of ants and bees the more repulsively barbarous would a human culture be that modeled on them: we tend already to sink into like states.) What all this boils down to is that tropes best succeed in bringing a pair (or more) of images to life if the focal image is unreservedly human and concrete and if the enlightening image is abstract, typical, formularistic, intellectual. Tropes call on the intellectual and are fables in little. . . .

Along with images and tropes and in the same category of linguistic technique is the field of idiom, or turn of speech. It is the function of this technique to translate the special twist of a fresh perception into a fresh twist of language. Idiomatic language is the opposite of facile language: it is not the opposite but the enlivening part of formal language. Hume is as good idiom as Sterne. Idiom is perception in speech: speech breathing with perception. Thinking of written language it is speech supplied with the maximum possible quality of veracity to impulse and object which any well-spoken man does habitually give to his speech. Idiom is concerned also with representing the play of qualities, and with measuring them precisely, in the subject of discourse. Idiom is the accurate gauge of concrete perception, and, in writing, replaces it. . . . Here also, in this category, is the field of verbal play, language as high jinks, nonsense, pure ad libbing, play on meaning and sound for their own sakes, and also that more desperate play which is the search for meanings and sounds never found in the language before. . . . In short, it is in this category (image, trope, idiom, verbal play) that we deal with the medium of literature, the vehicle of actual perception. To discuss it is to say at length that literature *is* language, that language is in some sense spoken even when most written, and that it is one job of literature to preserve, purify, and enrich the language: in common speech, the heavenly ear.

The third category is the ulterior technique of the imagination: how the mind makes its discourse (or concourse) in images and idioms as meaningful as the original parallel experiences seemed when experienced in life. The field of this category is usually gotten at either through the inadequate approach of "technical" criticism or the mutilating approach of the criticism of "ideas" or intentions. Sometimes it is touched in what is called "Christian" in the study of Christian art; again it is found in criticizing the political or philosophical commitments of a writer; any deterministic approach aims at it: there is notably the Freudian approach, and once more the environmental approach. These approaches are not illegitimate; they are either inadequate or mutilating only when applied to successful writing; when applied to imperfect art they are inevitable. In the sense that all art is radically imperfect with regard to its ideals, its intentions, and its form they sanction the paths and purposes of historical criticism. It is impossible to do justice to any art of a time other than just previous to our own without the aid of historical criticism to fill in the gaps, not so much in our knowledge, as in the work of art itself. That it is often not possible to do this does not vitiate the injustice. That it is sometimes easy does not excuse the omission when it is hard. The art of the past that seems to us greatest—not in reputation but in experience—is in those works where either what is left out does not matter or where the interest of what was put in is both overwhelming and stable in all ages. Yet what is stable in most ages may disappear in our own, perhaps never to transpire. English and American literature to the present time, for example, has had a full piety for the sea and the land and the weather. With the concentration of culture in urban terms it seems likely that the meaning of the mere images as well as of the themes of rural or sea-going life will disappear because audiences (and artists) simply do not find them meaningful. The failure to distinguish between Hardy's rural poems and Markham's "Man with the Hoe" is an example. Urban peoples will soon find themselves in about the same relation to Millet or van Gogh as to the Italian Primitives or, worse, as to the falconry figures in Elizabethan drama. (I say nothing here of the difficulty that the democratization of the audience, if continued unchanged, will make the artist's true interests either intolerable, incomprehensible, or unavailably remote. Another form of genius may take care of this hardship: a new hero for a new villainy.) At any rate, some such considerations as these explain the various forms of historical, biographical, and scientific criticism which are bent on either explaining or getting rid of the substance of the arts, their relations to experience: these are the right things to do to imperfections and failures, explain and obviate. But they are right only, these approaches, if they also make room for what is not explained and not obviated, for what was not significantly an imperfection or a failure in the art with which they deal: that is to say, with the direct perception of actual experience which to be intelligibly represented had to call upon inadequate and failing means. The artist is concerned with all the world of actual experience to which human response is possible, and he has therefore the impossible double task both of finding means adequate to represent what experience he has had, and of finding, through the means he has, the experience he has not had. He can thus never tell whether his experience, his response, or his representation are complete at any given moment. Some artists in painting have devoted their lives to the human face, only adding, as it were, to the inexhaustibility of its interest; similarly, others have painted nudes without ever staling. Yet photographs of either must constantly be replaced; they *are* exhausted and *do* stale: they are much nearer to being entirely history and not at all response, though they contain superbly the materials for response. The difference is inexplicable, but the mode of the difference may be indicated: the response of the artist is not single but cumulative, or at any rate is made with the sense of many related responses pressing upon the freshly achieved direct perception. There is a wisdom necessary in perceiving a face or a backside which has nothing to do with the particular face or backside and everything to do with the stress or tension between the observer and the object: the wisdom of character and of sex in their visual versions; or if wisdom be too knowledgeable a word, it may be called rather a piety of the actual. Piety is the emotional form of the assent to the meaningful, and the arts which represent the experience of human life would be very poor things should they fail to find the experience of the actual meaningful. It is in the actual that all the "higher" or formulable meanings are lodged. And there is, too, an actual experience of the most remote ideas—the severest of intellections—to which alone full assent can be given and through which alone conviction or the sense of mastery can be mustered.

The arts do not supply assent or conviction, any more than they supply character or sex, but they show and illumine the actual experience of them. The arts exemplify the actual. They show the vision of God, the fear of God, the love of God, the absence of God, but not God. Yet the actual may be the avenue to the real; the real may become manifest in the actual: as we say that the eyes window the soul or that life is the warmth in the flesh, knowing the soul and life to be real, the eyes and warmth to be actual. The great drive is in the craving of the actual to become real: in which is the glory of the mind and its failure.

Perhaps the artist must be primarily indifferent to whether or not in his work the real shines through the actual. That is his appropriate humility: he must not put himself in first place and must struggle on all occasions which have the most interest for him to see that he does not inadvertently usurp first place. On lesser occasions —on structural or preparatory occasions—he may do as he likes, may assert divine or human or animal authority and ignore the actual altogether; but on important occasions, in his big scenes, his crises of vision and his climaxes of insight or action, he must limit himself to what he has actually experienced or to what he can actually project his experience into. It is his business to represent and thereby create; and it may be that he will reveal the real in what he creates—but he has not the authority to intend to do so.

Authority comes from past revelations, or from God who is reality by definition: the reality yet to be. When Eliot, thinking of Arnold, remarked that human kind cannot bear very much reality, he should have added that human kind cannot *know* very much reality and that what they do know they know only as it is embodied, shown forth, in the actual, and that the experience does not articulate itself, without loss and the need of actual renewal, in the formularies of authority. What the most of human kind does in its inability to bear reality is to rush heartlong into the arms of authority, if not the authority of some past revelation then the nearest spatch-cock authority to hand, when it is asserted as genuine and its own. Authority is ostrich.

It may be the ostrich is inevitable—you cannot put him out of the way; yet he is not necessary—there is a point of perception after which you can ignore him. Beatrice put the matter very well to Dante (Par. I. 88) *"Tu stesso ti fai grosso,"* she says, *"col falso imaginar, si che non vedi ciò che vedresti, se l'avessa scosso."*—you yourself make your self dense with false imagining, and so you don't see what you would see, if you had cast it off. Look at what is in front of you and never mind looking for what you thought you ought to see. It is this false imagining, that parades as authority, commanding us to see what we ought to see, which alone permits us to see anything. If we were not told to see we should never learn; and if we did not find that what we were told was largely false in the instance, and to our eyes, we should never see anything actual. This is not a paradox but a rule of thumb to represent our radical inability to know very much reality for ourselves.

It is *therefore* that we depend so much on authority, and the more so when we are in pursuit of the actual: we need, in practice, both the guidance, and the shock of contrast. This is easy to illustrate. Authority is expressed in conventions, in generalities, in statements. The actual is expressed in details which have been both freed of conventions and released by conventions, and it would be impossible to get the actual into the arts without both operative relations of authority—preparation by and delivery from *and* in. This is the process sometimes called refreshing conventions; it might better be called the supersession of conventions, or the actual experience of, above, and beyond them. Suppose we wish to represent the actuality of the contest between anarchy and authority within an individual—which is a favorite, even an obsessive theme with poets and novelists—it makes no difference which side of the contest the author weights, he will be equally bound to use the *idea* of law and the *idea* of lawlessness (the temptation of order and of anarchy) in order to set up the stress between them in terms of which the individual has his actual experience of the contest. Even the language of the author will fail of the required tension unless these ideas are present as given—as part of the *donnée;* without that tension there is nothing for the author to hang his images on. In the child's game the excitement depends on the cops *and* the robbers; in the fairy tale the meaning depends on the good *and* the bad fairy; in a detective story, there is need of the law to make the murder actual *and* of the murderer to make the law actual; in *Hamlet* the role of king is necessary to the role of marriage before the hero can achieve his own unformulable role. Without the authority of institutions and conventions and ideas, the author would have to tell all his story himself and so be incapable of form or finish and would never get his story done. The practice of total recall would ruin all the arts, as the possibility of it is the warrant of their existence: and works of art are under the necessity of putative existence.

More briefly, without authority the author could never get to the actuality. This rule applies in two relations: it permits the author to leave a great deal out, and it demands of the reader (the audience) what he must put in. A third consequence is that of effective objectification of the work from the author's point of view, which at the other end of the rod secures effective participation in the work by the reader. Thus the necessary scope of authority may be defined as the fundamental preliminary *and* serial agreements which enable both the author and the reader to get into a given work. The scope is variable with the work, and it seems likely that in every work of any complexity there will be both excess and defect, in different places, of the authority ideally required.

The presence of the actual and the tendency toward, or achievement of, the symbolic imagination—which is our fourth category—seems the only feasible test to apply; the result will unfortunately be variable with the community of author and reader; in any case, to make the test satisfactorily requires the fullest possible assent, discrimination, and judgment (in that order) on the part of the reader.

Examples may be adduced. In *Madame Bovary* the widowed doctor reaches the desire to marry Emma when he sees her tip her head back and insert her tongue into a cordial glass: she is given as nubile, ripe, romantic, and ready. In this image—this touch of the actual—are present, by authority, the institutions, conventions, and fictitional formulas that have to do with marriage. Flaubert knows how little he has to put in—the tongue in the glass—and how much he can leave out—all the human needs that are conveyed in marriage; he knows too, or the book knows (the institution of the novel knows), that the reader at all aware will put in everything else necessary out of his own experience and his own imagination to make the image represent the actual experience of the contest or configuration of the individuals *and* the institutions. Thus the conventions are renewed—refleshed; this is an actual example of how society works in the individual and how the individual responds to society; what happens between the individuals—the qualification of the institution and the modification of the individuals—though it cannot be said in the words is yet somehow represented, articulated in the image of Emma sticking her tongue into the little glass. Thus does the actual enact the craving to become real: by making, provisionally, and for once only, an image into a symbol.—Now it is plain that to the extent of the reader's awareness, he will in the reading respond to the whole passage as a unit and that his response will be unitary, too. Yet a complicated process may be disengaged beneath the simple prerequisite assent, a process determined by his intimacy and skill in the knowledge of language and of life: the process of discrimination and judgment. The assent is preliminary, to whatever it may be: the discrimination is of means and ends, that is to say, operative; and the judgment (which makes the terms of final assent, if any) is of the result of the operations of the means upon the ends and upon the nature of the end: the *quality,* in this case, of the image which Emma becomes. Judgment may come about at once or long after the first full impact. Judgment, in the sense that it is experience, is when authority stops being ostrich and becomes response and is thereby itself changed; that is to say, judgment is possible to the reader when a transformation of authority at the hands of the actual has taken place in him parallel and equivalent to that which took place in the book. Thus the difference between opinion and judgment is radical: the difference between formula and experience.

What writing drags into being and holds there while the writing lasts may be called the experience of the actual; what writing creates—what goes on after the writing has stopped—may sometimes be called symbol. It is symbol when it stands, not for what has been said or stated, but for what has not been said and could not be said, for what has been delivered by the writing into what seems an autonomous world of its own. Symbol is the most exact possible meaning, almost tautologically exact, for what stirred the words to move *and* what the moving words made. Symbol stands for nothing previously known, but for what is "here" made known and what is about to be made known. If symbol stands for anything else than itself continuing, it stands for that within me the reader which enables me to recognize it and to illuminate it with my own experience at the same moment that what it means illuminates further corridors in my sense of myself.—This is put down to obviate confusion between π which stands for the relations 3.14159 without change, and the symbol Caliban which stands for itself guiding what we bring. In *Madame Bovary* is it not Flaubert's *anticipation* of Emma's collapse exactly what leads to it and makes it inevitable? There was nothing in the situation that might not have been changed by a single different step; but then the satisfaction of the anticipation would have been lost and the book would have fallen apart. Is it not perhaps the actuality of that anticipation that craves reality? Flaubert—his book—and, so, his character—had all to look for, *to discover* the means and machinery of Emma's collapse; no recourse was too great, no resource too mean, for that purpose. Emma grows more lovely as her need grows more desperate: so, too, as her experience, and our experience of her, are based more and more upon the actual, the craving for the real becomes more intense: as she collapses she becomes a symbol satisfying Flaubert's anticipation and much more, articulating in her figure and in the configuration of the novel both the anticipation of the author and the actuality of her experience: she becomes, not a formula, but the unformulable whole of all that was meaningful in her: she becomes "Madame Bovary"—all we mean by the *title*. It is by these means that she becomes a symbol and takes on all the inexhaustible mode of being that goes with it.

1946

14

Dante's Ten Terms for the Treatment of the Treatise

It would seem likely that anything written on Dante as a critic could only echo, and echo imperfectly, what has been written before, and especially if written in English and from a point of view mainly concerned with the criticism of contemporary literature. These remarks, therefore, are meant to concern the Dante scholars only if the affliction seems so great in them of blunder and error that it must be corrected. It should be possible, though, to correct without destroying. There is a part of Dante which never came to life until our own time; which everyone knows is true of the poetry; but which does not seem generally recognized of the criticism—perhaps only because it is so rare to find any criticism surviving the generation or so after the time of its appearance. When criticism some six centuries old comes suddenly to life, and relevant life, in a new context, that new life cannot be destroyed even if it can be shown to be based on a misunderstanding of the life in the original text. We have a right—we literary critics with a little bent for poetry—to whatever life we can find.

There is a sentence in the letter to Can Grande which could hardly have been fresher the day it was written, though, for all I know, on the day it was written it may have represented only the dullest of commonplaces, true but over-recognized; mechanically apt but automatic in motion; relevant to actual creative technique but taken for granted; conceptually sound but reduced to hocus-pocus; in short, coinage debased by lip service. All this may be but does not seem likely; and even if true, our present purposes only need to remind themselves that only a life and a value originally honorable and genuine can be so debased. Besides, to repeat, the house of criticism is jerry-built—in constant need of reconstruction out of second-hand materials, wherever got and whatsoever kind, so long as sound. Nobody in his senses wants a critical structure to last even his own time; only the materials. Dante's sentence is obviously, once found, of lasting material. Here it is (*Epistolae* X, 9, *ad fin.*). Dante has been saying that the *form* of the comedy is twofold, the form of the treatise and the form of the treatment. After summarizing the form of the treatise he proceeds: "The form or method of treatment is poetic, fictive, descriptive, digressive, transumptive; and likewise proceeding by definition, division, proof, refutation, and setting forth of examples." To Dante it was evidently not desirable—perhaps Can Grande was the wrong correspondent—to develop or expound the feelings about poetry which arise when these terms are taken in their several relations; at any rate he says nothing about them and goes on at once to expound the title of his work at considerable length and with much discrimination. These remarks have therefore the liberty, under law, to develop as we please.

The law is the unwritten constitution of poetry itself; notoriously difficult to interpret and with very few standing decisions but by experience pretty much guaranteed to cover any cause which can be admitted to argument under it. Perhaps the reader may be reminded without offense to the excellence of his memory (since it so often snoozes under the comforter of tradition) of some of the case-law about poetry which Dante favored. He favored pretty much the use of the whole mind—all the way from its light-shot sanity to the steam of its most drunken night-bog—in the particular medium of poetry; just as, had he been writing theology he could no more have forgotten to bring poetry to bear than sin, or the intoxication of the irrational hope of death, or the pride of damnation; that he discriminated does not, in his case, mean that he denied the experience or its learning. To him the whole mind illustrated as near as possible the whole of human behavior and (a difficult mark to reach) was itself a part of behavior, and poetry could always focus an order for it though not always judiciously. If Cato got upset at the sweet music of Casella in the first part of *Purgatory,* it was perhaps because Cato had too much sharpened his sense of justice to a raw edge; certainly there is no complaint offered somewhat further on to the sweet new style of poetry Dante himself had invented. Dante loved music perhaps for secondary reasons; poetry he loved for its own sake and like any good lover found some form of everything else he loved somehow in the poetry. There was even as we know from the *Convivio* a hankering in him to find the actual lady he loved housing in her body of poetry both the lady of philosophy and the lady of theology; which is to say, really, and in his defense, that though the ladies differ in the embrace all love is the same.

However that may be, when the ladies were not an issue, this most rebelliously orderly of men could love language herself as if she were the lady of them all. Dante was of all poets the poet least *manqué;* and hence could afford not only the passion of the plunge but also the grasping passion of criticism. He understood (as in the dream of the siren from which he was *merely rescued*), and he was able to criticize, by the poetry of it, how it is that love colors its object so that it positively blushes to its own desire. That is why (poetry is why), as Mr. Tate observes, there is *also* the real woman, so long in desire never forgotten, in the eyes of Beatrice. If poetry can be that much Why, it can answer the child, can answer critically, and the brooking of the *anima semplicetta,* is thus, by criticism, the terrible freedom that it is.

One does not hope to clear such matters up; one merely mentions them; if they are mentioned they may help to stimulate a vital relation among the ten terms in the sentence from the letter to Can Grande without seeming excluded from the law; they stimulate by furnishing poetic examples of the treatment of the treatise in both forms at once. Another struggle—which has governed a large part of the poetry of Eliot—is the vast emptiness, so real, so constraining, of our embrace of shades, as when Statius embraces Vergil. Behavior is all, even when false.

Even when false! We must look harder than that, and Dante had a doctrine which encourages the hard look; the doctrine which to illusive hopes gives the whole show away and to genuine hopes saves it. A genuine hope, I take it, is the part of life which keeps us going. Poetry, said Dante, is a fiction, a thing made, something overlooked, but not prevented, in the Creation. Poetry, said he, is *fictio rhetorica in musica posita* (*De Vulgari Eloquentia,* II, 4, 20). Poetry is a rhetorical fiction (or composition) set to music. Music, one thinks, is expressive. Music is expressiveness. Music is what one creates under only arbitrary control. Music is the movement of syllables in sound, with the meaning only there in the beginning. It was thus that Dante found that poetry might yet (in *Convivio*) by its loveliness draw you through allegory to the inner truth and require you (later, in the letter to Can Grande) to apply the four-fold interpretation: literal, allegorical, moral, and anagogical to ascertain that truth. It is the movement from emphasis to emphasis in Dante's mind from the musical fiction to anagogical truth which leads to an understanding of the ten terms in the sentence addressed to Can Grande, and if we follow that movement we can see that he had no reason to expound them because by that time they had become the culminating statement of his aesthetic. Without ever having forgotten the loveliness of words he had bound it into the love of truth and God under the four-fold interpretation. What we must see in the ten terms is that this theory and this method of poetry was for Dante a mode of freedom not of slavery; like the terrible freedom of love, it took the greater part of his life and a great deal of equivocal thought to reach in fact.

It seems worth while insisting (even if in some instance it be false) that Dante generally never altered the order of importance to which he first assigned the four elements of poetry. What we call diction remained final in importance—*Gravitas sententiae* comes first, but only first; it is followed by *superba carmina,* succeeded by *constructionis elatio,* and all three are crowned by *excellentia verborum*. In other words, meaning (war, love, virtue), form as plot, style, and words themselves freed of all tricks constitute the order of poetic importance. In commenting on this order, Saintsbury thinks that Aristotle would have accepted this reversal of his own hierarchy of importance. It seems worth adding that the order Dante came on (he seems not have known the *Poetics*) reversed that of Aristotle because he was a poet not a philosopher; he understood what live words can and must do to meanings before they become poetry. When he gives merely prior importance to meaning it is rather like the prior importance of zero in the series of numbers; zero, over a gap, is the matrix from which all movement is drawn. I think it also bears some relation to what Eliot meant by his observation that morals are of only preliminary importance to the saint, only of secondary importance to the poet. The great importance to us in Dante's emphasis on words (however differently construed in his different works) is because Dante is above all the poet of meaning and form as well as style and diction. He knew that words are the medium of poetic knowledge and that only as we touch the medium do we touch the experience.

Who could have known this better than the man who wrote *De Vulgari Eloquentia?* There Dante succeeded in coming to terms with a new practice in rhetoric—a new way of looking at language for its own sake, and so prepared the first masterpiece in the Italian tongue which he justified and crystallized. Let us say he arranged the shift from the learned and secret language of Latin (which was a pretense at a universal language) to the common tongue into which the angels rather than antiquity had divided speech: a language where learning and secrecy lived *in* or *under* the words, and which made not a pretense but an ensampling of universal language. This was a shift from one level of rhetoric (the traditional variety) to another (what had survived the tradition and squirmed with idiom); from a language that made a noise which excluded the silence of perception to a language that carried the silence with it in its new noise. If we say that Dante carried the old rhetoric with him unimpaired it is with the wonderful difference that in the new language the rhetoric is re-united, made seriously congruous, with what had in Greek times been meant by poetics and dialectics. Not all this happened at once; nor does Dante take any spring from his theory to a problematic or boastful or apologetic account of poetry. Poetry remained a rhetoric and not until the composition of the *Comedy* does it become part of nature. No doubt it happened in the way that the burden of a dream reveals itself as memory cries out. Saintsbury thought part of Dante's critical accomplishment was his division of the three subjects of high poetry into *"Salus, Venus, Virtus*—Arms, Love, and religiously guided Philosophy." Saintsbury goes on that Dante knew better than the ancients in admitting Love to equality in principle. "Here also," he writes, "Dante knew better; here also he expressed consummately all the enormous gain of dream which the sleep of the Dark Ages poured into the heart and soul of the world."

Dante's trouble—or the trouble in him we can trace—came when he was no longer able to look with satisfaction on his own poems as lovely falsehoods and required rather to see in them allegories of truth progressing toward the moral and the anagogical. Thus in the *Convivio* he examined three of his odes to see what lay behind the letter, which, so to speak, may not have been in his mind at the time of composition—or at any rate not consciously in his mind—but which, under scholastic examination, is seen to have transpired there. What was passionate love in earthly flesh *transpires* now as contemplative love of Lady Philosophy; and it is of both that it may be said *La Donna mia porta negli occhi amore*. At any rate, so we say at best, and so Dante was later able to say of the eyes of Beatrice when he meets her in the Terrestrial Paradise at the end of the Purgatory. But when he was making his prose argument in the *Convivio,* Dante tended to insist—as if truth were a matter of equivocation rather than equivalence—on the allegorical phase of his poem as its only true content, and to insist that the odes had been addressed to Lady Philosophy exclusively in the first place. Thought finds it hard to assent to its own behavior.

The problem for us, with our psychology, is simpler. If we think biographically and in terms of known love poetry, we will reject the view of his odes which Dante struggled to express in the *Convivio*. But if we do that we shall be rather stuffy about the possibilities of the unity of apperception in the poetic imagination. Further we shall be arbitrary about two matters of the highest consequence in the theory of poetry: the constitution of poetic belief (spiritual) and the constitution of poetry itself (as near physical as words can come). Also, we shall be forgetting what happened to both these in the presence of the *habit* of allegorical interpretation.

Poetic Belief. Surely the attitude of poet and reader toward the conventions by which the poem operates has a great deal to do with what is or is not credible; as when we find a hard matter credible from the attitude of our own psychology whatever that is. The presence of Lady Philosophy in Dante's odes is no harder to take than the fabulous opening of *King Lear* or the whole structure of *The Tempest.* The matter becomes even simpler if we think of the imagery and the splendid freedom of our attitude toward that. In a sense (the sense related to the ultimate meaning before the words began *and* after they have stopped) both conventions and imagery are neutral, good for *any* congruous intention: whatever may turn out afterwards to fit in. Surely what is importantly intended has some right to be believed; and there is nothing impossible in finding that the true intent could only deliver itself later than the intention most viable at the time of composition; both intentions have their warrant, and each criticizes the other. What is the use of poetry if it cannot be used where the context of need may fall?

The Constitution of Poetry. This is the same thing, having regard for the actions and interactions of the words themselves. Surely it is a commonplace that poetry gradually reveals its substance, or its meaning, in terms of what we gradually learn to bring to it, or what we gradually learn to find in it: from the work its parts do on each other under the incentive of our attention. Dante's words were moved by two passions of love (each only theoretically present to us), by the eyes of two ladies, and perhaps at the same time. Though the words cannot change the one passion may well replace the other in dominance. But when he wrote the *Convivio* the passion of love which had become dominant was that of Lady Philosophy; by his commentaries he put the odes themselves under that dominance. We are at liberty to return to the first dominance, but enriched by the sense of the second; so we make a third thing, which is our own. The commentary is part of the poem, though not necessarily the same poem Dante named for us.

What made the commentary easy or natural for Dante in inception and laborious in practice was the presence of the *habit* of allegorical interpretation: the habit of believing and the means of discovering hidden meaning at a higher level than the literal. It is only a step from this habit to the belief that allegory is what we would call a creative habit (over the results of which we lack complete control) as well as an interpretive skill. Surely one's own words may contain allegory. As Auden says, How do I know what I mean till I see what I write? And surely at bottom there is only one theme, which is reality, and some traces of its higher forms ought to be present in even its most degraded representations; not only some traces but much more than you might think. St. Augustine, who helped invent this sort of interpretation, thought no poem entirely without the presence of God—perhaps if only in its silences.

In some such frame of mind, but in his psychology, not ours, it was a natural temptation for Dante to allegorize all his odes; but it was as natural that he should stop at three. Who can tell what may not reveal itself by this method? Dante himself gives us one instance. Ode XV, which is used as the text for the second treatise in the *Convivio,* is given to us with the lady allegorized as Philosophy line by line and word by word. But later we have the very pleasant adventure (*Paradiso* VIII, 34-37) of watching Dante recant his allegory and seeing the ode become a true love poem *di nuovo,* again or after all. One would say that it had been both all along. Dante gave us different meanings because he saw differently at different times what he had written. One would add that only the equivalence between the different visions was permanent. But the point for us here (leading up still to the ten terms in the letter to Can Grande) is that by the time Dante was working on the *Paradiso* he had acquired a riches in composition—a sense and skill of how much could be put together in viable and creative relation—where there was no loss or gain, poetic or otherwise, with reference to allegorical standards. That is, the ode would be allegorical in any case, since that was the way poetry was related to nature and God, but (and this was the riches—the product of the long dream) it might be allegorical in any one or any set of the many complementary modes of human understanding. Allegory had become an instrument of inclusive freedom rather than exclusive bondage.

That is the point. We are not concerned with the riches of the *Comedy,* only with the rich theory of poetry which it contained and which it exemplified. As we look at it, it is a theory which seems based partly on the old rhetoric, partly on the adaptation to poetry of the four-fold interpretation of scriptures, partly on a doctrine of inspiration which included the other two, and finally on belief in the power of words to work marvels on each other when set in the condition of music. In sum these amount to saying that Dante learned a great deal about poetry by trying to put everything into it and what he learned he could summarize—in our ten terms—without comment. We can only say that all four aspects of his theory as here put together depend on the active, conscious, deliberate presence of extremely highly developed skills in composition and understanding: a rich lore in the use of the mind available to Dante not only consciously but also to his very finger tips.

Not all finger tips resume the consciousness. Boccaccio, whose life overlapped Dante's, and who wrote his Life, did not have this skill or lore. Neither have the scholars had it, if my messengers tell me right. Only in the last twenty years or so has scholarship begun to recover understanding of the skill, and scholarship remains dubious, not of the skill, but of our knowledge of it. The disappearance of such skill is as hard to account for as the disappearance during the Dark Ages of the skill of making good bread. The guess may be hazarded that the secularization of literature destroyed the usefulness of the conceptual and imaginative aspects of the technique of scriptural interpretation and rhetorical executive techniques. What had been deeply useful in the understanding of life became a mere special competence and the competence became ornamental, and the ornamental became artificial with no longer any grasp on actuality. To get at a riddle is one thing, to solve a puzzle, though as laborious, another.

It is for us to recover the skill and resume the lore for our own purposes, if we can but find what they are. Dante, let us say, wrote at a happy time for poetry when the skills had become flexible and dramatic: they could imitate anything wanted out of human life, and without loss of authority over their materials but rather in balance with the new immediate aesthetic of common speech. What could demonstrate this better than the unglossed sentence in the letter to Can Grande? "The form or method of treatment is poetic, fictive, descriptive, digressive, transumptive; and likewise proceeding by definition, division, proof, refutation, and setting forth of examples." There it is; but if Dante did not need a gloss, we do; we forget too much.

The form or method of treatment is as follows:

1. Poetic: creative making, having regard to truth, formative, originating, and having neither fear nor desire for novelty. The notion of the poetic goes along with our notion of intuition, the seized perception in depth.

2. Fictive: imitative as feigned or inventive, using devices irrespective of truth. A convenient assumption by which to get over a disputed point or a field of ignorance.

3. Descriptive: expressive of quality, kind, or condition without necessary limitation (as: *red* rose), but also naming groups, classes, parts: what may be written out.

4. Digressive: that which goes apart, deviates, diverges or swerves from the main course of argument. What is digressive takes care of something not thought of, or of something the argument had not thought of. Another thing suddenly brought to attention. God knows why. What is digressive is flexible.

5. Transumptive: in rhetoric what is transumptive is what transfers terms (coming from *trans* plus *sumere,* to take across). To take one thing for another. To transubstantiate. That is to say, find a deep identification. Metaphor. All of these five terms represent major movements of the mind and are creative in tone.

The second quintet has to do with manipulation, logic, order, adjustment: that is to say, the guidance and topology of movement. Dante puts this batch second, saying that the form or method of treatment also proceeds by various ways.

6. Definition: limitation, setting of limits, with the idea of clarity, both in image and terms. This is an area where equivalence has to do with surfaces and outlines.

7. Division: separation as in widowing, severance by arbitrary act. In logic to make a distinction (the *abstract* kind of description) or in persuasion a contrast. It is how we turn the genus into species.

8. Proof: the effect of evidence which convinces the mind by its

urgency, that is, its adherence to recognized manipulative habits of thought: a test. (From *probare,* with over-notions of right and good and proper.)

9. Refutation: having to do with disproving, repelling, proving false or erroneous by argument or evidence (with a feeling in the process of violence, of beating).

10. The setting forth of Examples: Examples are taken out of larger quantities. Samples to show the quality of the set. Examples are to be followed or imitated. Also: illustrations of principle or rule.

Now, in order to get the beauty of these terms hot, alive and kicking, which is how we want them, it is only necessary to consider that the first five which have to do with qualities of movement are unlikely to appear in any poem except as attached to the second five which have to do with the management (not the force) of words. The first five belong to poetics (and rhetoric), the second to logic, and in the poetry we are here thinking of they will be joined in action both by the music of the language and the dialectic of the soul in the instance undistinguishable. A great many permutations and quite a large number of combinations would be possible among the two series, but it would seem quite suggestive enough for our purpose to take the five primary rearrangements of pairs from both sets. The poetic or the critical mind once put in motion is potentially seeded with all the rest. The pairing is of course made only provisionally and as a formal device to catch the attention of the mind which wants to seize on the great poetic art of flexibility, of ad libing, in the search for what, since it must always have been there in reality, must now transpire in the poetry, and must, once transpired, affect the shape, the conduct, and the content of the mind itself, so far as these may be congruous with the habits of words when sped in verse.

Let us begin with the order contained in Dante's own sentence, merely attaching number one to number six, and so on. This is how the series goes: Poetic Definition; Fictive Division; Descriptive Proof; Digressive Refutation; Transumptive Example. Miranda is poetic definition; *The Alchemist* is fictive division; Proust is descriptive proof; *Joseph in Egypt* is digressive refutation; *Lear* or *Hamlet* is transumptive example. Rather, more accurately, by a slight distortion and exaggerated emphasis, these examples may be fitted to the terms without prejudice to their enjoying the benefits of other pairs. But let us take the four remaining natural arrangements of the paired terms and let the order of the sentiments so induced shine as they should in their own light.

Poetic Division; Fictive Proof; Descriptive Refutation; Digressive Example; Transumptive Definition.

Poetic Proof; Fictive Refutation; Descriptive Example; Digressive Definition; Transumptive Division.

Poetic Refutation; Fictive Example; Descriptive Definition; Digressive Division; Transumptive Proof.

Poetic Example; Fictive Definition; Descriptive Division; Digressive Proof; Transumptive Refutation.

It seems to me that when Dante's ten terms are rehearsed after this fashion—and there is not, unless I am obsessed to fatuity, a dead pair among them—it seems to me that we come as close as a theoretic frame of words can come to seeing how the words of poetry, though drawing on and comprising every other mode of the mind, behave in their own way in their own medium, and so give every other mode the form of experience. It may be worth while to the dubious to give Dante a little backing in the words of an older poet from what is superficially another tradition. Lu Chi wrote in his *Wen Fu* (A.D. 302):

> As to the interaction of stimulus and response, the intermingling
> of the flow with the blocking of the flow:
> their coming cannot be prevented, their going cannot
> be stopped:
> underground things go like shadows vanishing, back
> to life they come like echoes awakening. . . .

And he goes on, remembering the need of the gift, what Dante implored of Memory and the Muses, and without which neither his poem nor the terms in which he described his form or method of treatment would have any life at all,—remembering his own version of all this Lu Chi goes on:

> Then comes the blocking of every kind of feeling, the will to create
> gone, the spirit held bound.

It is like being the stock of a sapless tree, being empty as a dried-up river.
Lay hold of the mutinous soul by sounding its secret depths,
pay homage to its vital fierceness as you search for the very self;
reason screened and obscured begins to creep forth, thought comes screaming, forced out from the womb.
These are the reasons why either there is much to repent when we write with our mood exhausted, or with our purpose in command we seldom err.

Let us say that if Dante had his purpose more often than not in command it was because he had the pretty constant presence in him of his ten terms. Here is an example, chosen because of its content in "poetics," after rehearsing which we may have done. In *Purgatorio* XXIV Dante comes on the poet Bonagiunta who asks him if he is not the one who invented the new rhymes—*trasse le nuove rime*—beginning, Ladies that have intelligence of love—*Donne ch'avette intelletto d'Amore*. "Ed io a lui: *'Io mi son un che, quando amor mi spira, noto, ed a quel modo che ditta dentro, vo significando.'* " ("I am one who when love breathes in me, take *note,* and by *that mode* he *dictates within* me go setting it forth.") " 'O brother,' said he, 'now I see the knot which kept back the Notary, and Guittone, and me, short of the sweet new style that I hear—*di qua dal dolce stil nuovo ch'i'odo.'* "

The specific reference is to the Odes and other Canzoni—but only the specific reference; the deep reference is to the whole of poetry as Dante understood it, certainly to the extraordinarily deliberate, complex, and almost infinitely varied poetry of the *Divine Comedy*. It is the language of a poet who is free to make full use of his inspiration, certain that *by one mode or another* he will be able to set it forth *to one degree or another*.

We may say that a new mode of love—a new mode of actualizing perception—a new mode of poetry—are here all shown in intimate relation. But such a relation, however deep and rich in itself, would be useless without a high skill in readiness to make the most of it. The modes must be ready for the perception, must be ready to set the perceptions in actual relation and so bring them to realization in language. This is the function of the ten terms. Who knows which created the other?

[NOTE: *The reader is referred for a different discussion of these ten terms to "Dante's Self-Exegesis" in E. R. Curtius,* European Literature and the Latin Middle Ages *(Pantheon Books, 1953), pp. 221-225.*]

1952

15

The Critical Prefaces of Henry James

The Prefaces of Henry James were composed at the height of his age as a kind of epitaph or series of inscriptions for the major monument of his life, the sumptuous, plum-colored, expensive New York edition of his works. The labor was a torment, a care, and a delight, as his letters and the Prefaces themselves amply show. The thinking and the writing were hard and full and critical to the point of exasperation; the purpose was high, the reference wide, and the terms of discourse had to be conceived and defined as successive need for them arose. He had to elucidate and to appropriate for the critical intellect the substance and principle of his career as an artist, and he had to do this—such was the idiosyncrasy of his mind—specifically, example following lucid example, and with a consistency of part with part that amounted almost to the consistency of a mathematical equation, so that, as in the *Poetics,* if his premises were accepted his conclusions must be taken as inevitable.

Criticism has never been more ambitious, nor more useful. There has never been a body of work so eminently suited to criticism as the fiction of Henry James, and there has certainly never been an author who saw the need and had the ability to criticize specifically and at length his own work. He was avid of his opportunity and both proud and modest as to what he did with it. "These notes," he wrote in the preface to *Roderick Hudson,* "represent, over a considerable course, the continuity of an artist's endeavour, the growth of his whole operative consciousness and, best of all, perhaps, their own tendency to multiply, with the implication, thereby, of a memory much enriched." Thus his strict modesty; he wrote to Grace Norton (5 March 1907) in a higher tone. "The prefaces, as I say, are difficult to do—but I have found them of a jolly interest; and though I am not going to let you read one of the fictions themselves over I shall expect you to read all the said Introductions." To W. D. Howells he wrote (17 August 1908) with very near his full pride. "They are, in general, a sort of plea for Criticism, for Discrimination, for Appreciation on other than infantile lines—as against the so almost universal Anglo-Saxon absence of these things; which tends so, in our general trade, it seems to me, to break the heart. . . . They ought, collected together, none the less, to form a sort of comprehensive manual or *vademecum* for aspirants in our arduous profession. Still, it will be long before I shall want to collect them together for that purpose and furnish *them* with a final Preface."

In short, James felt that his Prefaces represented or demonstrated an artist's consciousness and the character of his work in some detail, made an essay in general criticism which had an interest and a being aside from any connection with his own work, and that finally, they added up to a fairly exhaustive reference book on the technical aspects of the art of fiction. His judgment was correct and all a commentator can do is to indicate by example and a little analysis, by a kind of provisional reasoned index, how the contents of his essay may be made more available. We have, that is, to perform an act of criticism in the sense that James himself understood it. "To criticise," he wrote in the Preface to *What Maisie Knew,* "is to appreciate, to appropriate, to take intellectual possession, to establish in fine a relation with the criticised thing and make it one's own."

What we have here to appropriate is the most sustained and I think the most eloquent and original piece of literary criticism in existence. (The only comparable pieces, not in merit of course but in kind, are by the same author, "The Art of Fiction," written as a young man and printed in *Partial Portraits,* and "The Novel in 'The Ring and the Book,'" written in 1912 and published in *Notes on Novelists;* the first of which the reader should consult as an example of general criticism with a prevailing ironic tone, and the second as an example of what the same critical attitude as that responsible for the Prefaces could do on work not James's own.) Naturally, then, our own act of appropriation will have its difficulties, and we shall probably find as James found again and again, that the things most difficult to master will be the best. At the least we shall require the maximum of strained attention, and the faculty of retaining detail will be pushed to its limit. And these conditions will not apply from the difficulty of what James has to say—which is indeed lucid—but because of the convoluted compression of his style and because of the positive unfamiliarity of his terms as he uses them. No one else has written specifically on his subject.

Before proceeding to exhibition and analysis, however, it may be useful to point out what kind of thing, as a type by itself, a James Preface is, and what kind of exercise the reader may expect a sample to go through. The key fact is simple. A Preface is the story of a story, or in those volumes which collect a group of shorter tales the story of a group of stories cognate in theme or treatment. The Prefaces collocate, juxtapose, and separate the different kinds of stories. They also, by cross reference and development from one Preface to another, inform the whole series with a unity of being. By "the story of a story" James meant a narrative of the accessory facts and considerations which went with its writing; the how, the why, the what, when, and where which brought it to birth and which are not evident in the story itself, but which have a fascination and a meaning in themselves to enhance the reader's knowledge. "The private history of any sincere work," he felt, "looms large with its own completeness."

But the "story of a story" is not simple in the telling; it has many aspects that must be examined in turn, many developments that must be pursued, before its center in life is revealed as captured. "The art of representation bristles with questions the very terms of which are difficult to apply and appreciate." Only the main features can be named simply. There is the feature of autobiography, as a rule held to a minimum: an account of the Paris hotel, the Venetian palace, the English cottage, in which the tale in question was written. Aside from that, there is often a statement of the anecdote and the circumstances in which it was told, from which James drew the germ of his story. There is the feature of the germ in incubation, and the story of how it took root and grew, invariably developing into something quite different from its immediate promise. Then there is an account—frequently the most interesting feature—of how the author built up his theme as a consistent piece of dramatization. Usually there are two aspects to this feature, differently discussed in different Prefaces—the aspect of the theme in relation to itself as a balanced and consistent whole, the flesh upon the articulated plot; and the aspect of the theme in relation to society, which is the moral and evaluating aspect. Varying from Preface to Preface as the need commands, there is the further feature of technical exposition, in terms of which everything else is for the moment subsumed. That is, the things which a literary artist does in order to make of his material an organic whole—the devices he consciously uses to achieve a rounded form—are rendered available for discussion, and for understanding, by definition and exemplification.

These are the principal separate features which compose the face of a Preface. There are also certain emphases brought to bear throughout the Prefaces, which give them above all the savor of definite character. Again and again, for example, a novel or story will raise the problem of securing a compositional center, a presiding intelligence, or of applying the method of indirect approach. Again and again James emphasizes the necessity of being amusing, dramatic, interesting. And besides these, almost any notation, technical, thematic, or moral, brings James eloquently back to the expressive relation between art and life, raises him to an intense personal plea for the difficulty and delight of maintaining that relation, or wrings from him a declaration of the supreme labor of intelligence that art lays upon the artist. For James it is the pride of achievement, for the reader who absorbs that pride it is the enthusiasm of understanding and the proud possibility of emulation.

None of this, not the furthest eloquence nor the most detached precept, but flows from the specific observation and the particular example. When he speaks of abjuring the "platitude of statement," he is not making a phrase but summarizing, for the particular occasion, the argument which runs throughout the Prefaces, that in art what is merely stated is not presented, what is not presented is not vivid, what is not vivid is not represented, and what is not represented is not art. Or when, referring to the method by which a subject most completely expresses itself, he writes the following sentence, James is not indulging in self-flattery. "The careful ascertainment of how it shall do so, and the art of guiding it with consequent authority—since this sense of 'authority' is for the master-builder the treasure of treasures, or at least the joy of joys—renews in the modern alchemist something like the old dream of the secret of life." It is not indulgence of any description; it is the recognition in moral language of the artist's privileged experience in the use of his tools—in this instance his use of them in solving the technical problems of *The Spoils of Poynton.* James unfailingly, unflaggingly reveals for his most general precept its specific living source. He knew that only by constantly retaining the specific in the field of discussion could he ever establish or maintain the principles by which he wrote. That is his unique virtue as a critic, that the specific object is always in hand; as it was analogously his genius as a novelist that what he wrote about was always present in somebody's specific knowledge of it. In neither capacity did he ever succumb to the "platitude of statement."

It is this factor of material felt and rendered specifically that differentiates James from such writers as Joyce and Proust. All three have exerted great technical influence on succeeding writers, as masters ought. The difference is that writers who follow Joyce or Proust tend to absorb their subjects, their social attitudes, and their personal styles and accomplish competent derivative work in so doing, while the followers of James absorb something of a technical mastery good for any subject, any attitude, any style. It is the difference between absorbing the object of a sensibility and acquiring something comparable to the sensibility itself. The point may perhaps be enforced paradoxically: the mere imitators of the subject matter of Proust are readable as documents, but the mere imitators of James are not readable at all. It is not that James is more or less great than his compeers—the question is not before us—but that he consciously and articulately exhibited a greater technical mastery of the tools of his trade. It is a matter of sacrifice. Proust made no sacrifice but wrote always as loosely as possible and triumphed in spite of himself. Joyce made only such sacrifices as suited his private need—as readers of these Prefaces will amply observe—and triumphed by a series of extraordinary *tours de force.* James made consistently every sacrifice for intelligibility and form; and, when the fashions of interest have made their full period, it will be seen I think that his triumph is none the less for that.

There remains—once more before proceeding with the actual content of the Prefaces—a single observation that must be made, and it flows from the remarks above about the character of James's influence. James had in his style and perhaps in the life which it reflected an idiosyncrasy so powerful, so overweening, that to many it seemed a stultifying vice, or at least an inexcusable heresy. He is difficult to read in his later works—among which the Prefaces are included—and his subjects, or rather the way in which he develops them, are occasionally difficult to co-ordinate with the reader's own experience. He enjoyed an excess of intelligence and he suffered, both in life and art, from an excessive effort to communicate it, to represent it in all its fullness. His style grew elaborate in the degree that he rendered shades and refinements of meaning and feeling not usually rendered at all. Likewise the characters which he created to dramatize his feelings have sometimes a quality of intelligence which enables them to experience matters which are unknown and seem almost perverse to the average reader. James recognized his difficulty, at least as to his characters. He defended his "super-subtle fry" in one way or another a dozen times, on the ground that if they did not exist they ought to, because they represented, if only by an imaginative irony, what life was capable of at its finest. His intention and all his labor was to represent dramatically intelligence at its most difficult, its most lucid, its most beautiful point. This is the sum of his idiosyncrasy; and the reader had better make sure he knows what it is before he rejects it. The act of rejection will deprive him of all knowledge of it. And this precept applies even more firmly to the criticisms he made of his work—to the effort he made to reappropriate it intellectually—than to the direct apprehension of the work itself.

II

Now to resume the theme of this essay, to "remount," as James says of himself many times, "the stream of composition." What is that but to make an *ex post facto* dissection, not that we may embalm the itemized mortal remains, but that we may intellectually understand the movement of parts and the relation between them in the living body we appreciate. Such dissection is imaginative, an act of the eye and mind alone, and but articulates our knowledge without once scratching the flesh of its object. Only if the life itself was a mockery, a masquerade of pasted surfaces, will we come away with our knowledge dying; if the life was honest and our attention great enough, even if we do not find the heart itself at least we shall be deeply exhilarated, having heard its slightly irregular beat.

Let us first exhibit the principal objects which an imaginative examination is able to separate, attaching to each a summary of context and definition. Thus we shall have equipped ourselves with a kind of eclectic index or provisional glossary, and so be better able to find our way about, and be better prepared to seize for closer examination a selection of those parts of some single Preface which reveal themselves as deeply animating. And none of this effort will have any object except to make the substance of all eighteen Prefaces more easily available.

There is a natural division between major subjects which are discussed at length either in individual essays or from volume to volume, and minor notes which sometimes appear once and are done, and are sometimes recurrent, turning up again and again in slightly different form as the specific matter in hand requires. But it is not always easy to see under which heading an entry belongs. In the following scheme the disposition is approximate and occasionally dual, and in any case an immediate subject of the reader's revision.

To begin with, let us list those major themes which have no definite locus but inhabit all the Prefaces more or less without favor. This is the shortest and for the most part the most general of the divisions, and therefore the least easily susceptible of definition in summary form.

The Relation of Art and the Artist. The Relation of Art and Life. Art, Life, and the Ideal. Art and Morals. Art as Salvation for its Characters. These five connected subjects, one or more of them, are constantly arrived at, either parenthetically or as the definite terminus of the most diverse discussions. The sequence in which I have put them ought to indicate something of the attitude James brings to bear on them. Art was serious, he believed, and required of the artist every ounce of his care. The subject of art was life, or more particularly someone's apprehension of the experience of it, and in striving truly to represent it art removed the waste and muddlement and bewilderment in which it is lived and gave it a lucid, intelligible form. By insisting on intelligence and lucidity something like an ideal vision was secured; not an ideal in the air but an ideal in the informed imagination, an ideal, in fact, actually of life, limited only by the depth of the artist's sensibility of it. Thus art was the viable representation of moral value; in the degree that the report was intelligent and intense the morals were sound. This attitude naturally led him on either of two courses in his choice of central characters. He chose either someone with a spark of intelligence in him to make him worth saving from the damnation and waste of a disorderly life, or he chose to tell the story of some specially eminent person in whom the saving grace of full intelligence is assumed and exhibited. It is with the misfortunes and triumphs of such persons, in terms of the different kinds of experience of which he was master, that James's fiction almost exclusively deals.

It is this fact of an anterior interest that largely determines what he has to say about *The Finding of Subjects* and *The Growth of Subjects*. Subjects never came ready-made or complete, but always from hints, notes, the merest suggestion. Often a single fact reported at the dinner table was enough for James to seize on and plant in the warm bed of his imagination. If his interlocutor, knowing him to be a novelist, insisted on continuing, James closed his ears. He never wanted all the facts, which might stupefy him, but only enough to go on with, hardly enough to seem a fact at all. If out of politeness he had to listen, he paid no recording attention; what he then heard was only "clumsy Life at her stupid work" of waste and muddlement. Taking his single precious germ he meditated upon it, let it develop, scrutinized and encouraged, compressed and pared the developments until he had found the method by which he could dramatize it, give it a central intelligence whose fortune would be his theme, and shape it in a novel or a story as a consistent and self-sufficient organism. James either gives or regrets that he cannot give both the original *donnée* and an account of how it grew to be a dramatic subject for almost every item in the New York edition.

Art and Difficulty. Of a course, a man with such a view of his art and choosing so great a personal responsibility for his theme would push his rendering to the most difficult terms possible. So alone would he be able to represent the maximum value of his theme. Being a craftsman and delighting in his craft, he knew also both the sheer moral delight of solving a technical difficulty or securing a complicated effect, and the simple, amply attested fact that the difficulties of submitting one's material to a rigidly conceived form were often the only method of representing the material in the strength of its own light. The experience of these difficulties being constantly present to James as he went about his work, he constantly points specific instances for the readers of his Prefaces.

Looseness. Looseness of any description, whether of conception or of execution, he hated contemptuously. In both respects he found English fiction "a paradise of loose ends," but more especially in the respect of execution. His own themes, being complex in reference and development, could only reach the lucidity of the apprehensible, the intelligibility of the represented state, if they were closed in a tight form. Any looseness or laziness would defeat his purpose and let half his intention escape. A selection of the kinds of looseness against which he complains will be given among the minor notes.

The Plea for Attention and Appreciation. The one faculty James felt that the artist may require of his audience is that of close attention or deliberate appreciation; for it is by this faculty alone that the audience participates in the work of art. As he missed the signs of it so he bewailed the loss; upon its continuous exertion depended the very existence of what he wrote. One burden of the Prefaces was to prove how much the reader would see if only he paid attention and how much he missed by following the usual stupid routine of skipping and halting and letting slide. Without attention, without intense appreciation an art of the intelligent life was impossible and without intelligence, for James, art was nothing.

The Necessity for Amusement. James was willing to do his part to arouse attention, and he labored a good deal to find out exactly what that part was. One aspect of it was to be as amusing as possible, and this he insisted on at every opportunity. To be amusing, to be interesting; without that nothing of his subject could possibly transpire in the reader's mind. In some of his books half the use of certain characters was to amuse the reader. Henrietta Stackpole, for example, in *The Portrait of a Lady,* serves mainly to capture the reader's attention by amusing him as a "character." Thus what might otherwise have been an example of wasteful overtreatment actually serves the prime purpose of carrying the reader along, distracting and freshening him from time to time.

The Indirect Approach and *The Dramatic Scene.* These devices James used throughout his work as those most calculated to command, direct, and limit or frame the reader's attention; and they are employed in various combinations or admixtures the nature of which almost every Preface comments on. These devices are not, as their name might suggest, opposed; nor could their use in equal parts cancel each other. They are, in the novel, two ends of one stick, and no one can say where either end begins. The characterizing aspect of the Indirect Approach is this: the existence of a definite created sensibility interposed between the reader and the felt experience which is the subject of the fiction. James never put his reader in direct contact with his subjects; he believed it was impossible to do so, because his subject really was not what happened but what someone felt about what happened, and this could be directly known only through an intermediate intelligence. The Dramatic Scene was the principal device James used to objectify the Indirect Approach and give it self-limiting form. Depending on the degree of limitation necessary to make the material objective and visible all round, his use of the Scene resembled that in the stage-play. The complexities of possible choice are endless and some of them are handled below.

The Plea for a Fine Central Intelligence. But the novel was not a play however dramatic it might be, and among the distinction between the two forms was the possibility, which belonged to the novel alone, of setting up a fine central intelligence in terms of which everything in it might be unified and upon which everything might be made to depend. No other art could do this; no other art could dramatize the individual at his finest; and James worked this possibility for all it was worth. It was the very substance upon which the directed attention, the cultivated appreciation, might be concentrated. And this central intelligence served a dual purpose, with many modifications and exchanges among the branches. It made a compositional center for art such as life never saw. If it could be created at all, then it presided over everything else, and would compel the story to be nothing but the story of what that intelligence felt about what happened. This compositional strength, in its turn, only increased the value and meaning of the intelligence *as* intelligence, and vice versa. The plea for the use of such an intelligence both as an end and as a means is constant throughout the Prefaces—as the proudest end and as the most difficult means. Some of the specific problems which its use poses are discussed in the Prefaces to the novels where they apply. Here it is enough to repeat once more—and not for the last time—that the fine intelligence, either as agent or as the object of action or as both, is at the heart of James's work.

So much for the major themes which pervade and condition and unite the whole context of the Prefaces. It is the intention of this essay now to list some of the more important subjects discussed in their own right, indicating where they may be found and briefly what turn the discussions take. The Roman numerals immediately following the heading refer to the volume numbers in the New York edition.[1] The occasional small Roman numerals refer to pages within a preface.

The International Theme (XII, XIV, XVIII). The discussion of the International Theme in these three volumes has its greatest value in strict reference to James's own work; it was one of the three themes peculiarly his. It deals, however, with such specific questions as the opposition of manners as a motive in drama, the necessity of

[1] For possible convenience in reference I append the numbers and titles of those volumes which contain Prefaces. I Roderick Hudson; II The American; III The Portrait of a Lady; V The Princess Casamassima; VII The Tragic Muse; IX The Awkward Age; X The Spoils of Poynton; XI What Maisie Knew; XII The Aspern Papers; XIII The Reverberator; XIV Lady Barbarina; XV The Lesson of the Master; XVI The Author of Beltraffio; XVII The Altar of the Dead; XVIII Daisy Miller; XIX The Wings of the Dove; XXI The Ambassadors; XXIII The Golden Bowl.

opposing positive elements of character, and the use of naive or innocent characters as the subjects of drama; these are of perennial interest. There is also a discussion under this head of the difference between major and minor themes. In X (p. xix), speaking of "A London Life," there is a discussion of the use of this theme for secondary rather than primary purposes.

The Literary Life as a Theme (XV) and *The Artist as a Theme* (VII). The long sections of these two Prefaces dealing with these themes form a single essay. XV offers the artist enamored of perfection, his relation to his art, to his audience, and himself. VII presents the artist in relation to society and to himself. In both sections the possibilities and the actualities are worked out with specific reference to the characters in the novels and the tales. The discussion is of practical importance to any writer. Of particular interest is the demonstration in VII that the successful artist as such cannot be a hero in fiction, because he is immersed in his work, while the amateur or the failure remains a person and may have a heroic downfall. The thematic discussion in XVI properly belongs under this head, especially pp. vii-ix.

The Use of the Eminent or Great (VII, XII, XV, XVI) and *The Use of Historical Characters* (XII, XV). The separation of these two subjects is artificial, as for James they were two aspects of one problem. Being concerned with the tragedies of the high intelligence and the drama of the socially and intellectually great (much as the old tragedies dealt death to kings and heroes) he argues for using the *type* of the historical and contemporary great and against using the actual historical or contemporary figure. The *type* of the great gives the artist freedom; the *actual* examples condition him without advantage. If he used in one story or another Shelley, Coleridge, Browning, and (I think) Oscar Wilde, he took them only as types and so far transformed them that they appear as pure fictions. The real argument is this: the novelist is concerned with types and only with the eminent case among the types, and the great man is in a way only the most eminent case of the average type, and is certainly the type that the novelist can do most with. To the charge that his "great" people were such as could never exist, James responded that the world would be better if they did. In short, the novelist's most lucid representation may be only his most ironic gesture.

The Dead as a Theme (XVII). Five pages (v-ix) of this Preface present "the permanent appeal to the free intelligence of some image of the lost dead" and describe how this appeal may be worked out in fiction. "The sense of the state of the dead," James felt, "is but part of the sense of the state of living."

On Wonder, Ghosts, and the Supernatural (XII, XVII) and *How to Produce Evil* (XII). These again make two aspects of one theme and the rules for securing one pretty much resemble those for securing the other. They are shown best "by showing almost exclusively the way they are felt, by recognising as their main interest some impression strongly made by them and intensely received." That was why Psychical Research Society Ghosts were unreal; there was no one to apprehend them. The objectively rendered prodigy always ran thin. Thickness is in the human consciousness that records and amplifies. And there is also always necessary, for the reader to feel the ghost, the history of somebody's *normal* relation to it. Thus James felt that the climax of Poe's *Pym* was a failure because there the horrific was without connections. In both Prefaces the ghost story is put as the modern equivalent of the fairy story; and the one must be as economical of its means as the other. The problem of rendering evil in "The Turn of the Screw" (XII) was slightly different; it had to be represented, like the ghosts who performed it, in the consciousness of it by normal persons, but it could not be described. The particular act when rendered always fell short of being evil, so that the problem seemed rather to make the character *capable* of anything. "Only make the reader's general vision of evil intense enough, I said to myself—and that is already a charming job—and his own experience, his own sympathy (with the children) and horror (of their false friends) will supply him quite sufficiently with all the particulars. Make him *think* the evil, make him think it for himself, and you are released from weak specifications" (XII, xxi).

On the Use of Wonder to Animate a Theme (XI). This is the faculty of wonder on a normal plane and corresponds to freshness, intelligent innocence, and curiosity in the face of life; a faculty which when represented in a character almost of itself alone makes that character live. It is a faculty upon which every novelist depends, both in his books to make them vivid, and in his readers where it is the faculty that drives them to read. It is to be distinguished from the wonder discussed in the paragraph next above.

Romanticism and Reality (II). Seven pages in this Preface (xiv-xx) attempt to answer the question: Why is one picture of life called romantic and another real? After setting aside several answers as false or misleading, James gives his own. "The only *general* attribute of projected romance that I can see, the only one that fits all its cases, is the fact of the kind of experience with which it deals—experience liberated, so to speak; experience disengaged, disembodied, disencumbered, exempt from the conditions that we usually know to attach to it, and if we wish so to put the matter, drag upon it, and operating in a medium which relieves it, in a particular interest, of the inconvenience of a *related,* a measurable state, a state subject to all our vulgar communities." Then James applies his answer to his own novel (*The American*) "The experience here represented is the disconnected and uncontrolled experience—uncontrolled by our general sense of 'the way things happen'—which romance alone more or less successfully palms off on us." Since the reader knows "the way things happen," he must be tactfully drugged for the duration of the novel; and that is part of the art of fiction.

The Time Question (I, xii-xvi). Although the efforts dependent on the superior effect of an adequate lapse of time were consciously important to James, the lapse of time itself was only once discussed by him in the Prefaces, and there to explain or criticize the failure to secure it. Roderick Hudson, he said, falls to pieces too quickly. Even though he is special and eminent, still he must not live, change and disintegrate too rapidly; he loses verisimilitude by so doing. His great capacity for ruin is projected on too small a field. He should have had more adventures and digested more experience before we can properly believe that he has reached his end. But James was able to put the whole matter succinctly. "To give all the sense without all the substance or all the surface, and so to summarise or foreshorten, so to make values both rich and sharp, that the mere procession of items and profiles is not only, for the occasion, superseded, but is, for essential quality, almost 'compromised'—such a case of delicacy proposes itself at every turn to the painter of life who wishes both to treat his chosen subject and to confine his necessary picture." Composition and arrangement must give the *effect* of the lapse of time. For this purpose elimination was hardly a good enough device. The construction of a dramatic center, as a rule in someone's consciousness, was much better, for the reason that this device, being acted upon in time, gave in parallel the positive effect of action, and thus of lapsing time.

Geographical Representation (I, ix-xi). These three pages deal with the question: to what extent should a named place be rendered on its own account? In *Roderick Hudson* James named Northampton, Mass. This, he said, he ought not to have done, since all he required was a humane community which was yet incapable of providing for "art." For this purpose a mere indication would have been sufficient. His general answer to the question was that a place should be named if the novelist wanted to make it an effective part of the story, as Balzac did in his studies of the ville de province.

The Commanding Center as a Principle of Composition (I, II, VII, X, XI, XIX, XXI, XXIII). This is allied with the discussion of the use of a Central Intelligence above and with the three notes immediately below. It is a major consideration in each of the Prefaces numbered and is to be met with *passim* elsewhere. The whole question is bound up with James's exceeding conviction that the art of fiction is an organic form, and that it can neither be looked at all round nor will it be able to move on its own account unless it has a solidly posed center. Commanding centers are of various descriptions. In I it is in Rowland Mallet's consciousness of Roderick. In II it is in the image of Newman. In VII it is in the combination of relations between three characters. In X it is in a houseful of beautiful furniture. In XI it is the "ironic" center of a child's consciousness against or illuminated by which the situations gather meaning. In XIX it is in the title (*The Wings of the Dove*), that is, in the influence of Milly Theale, who is seen by various people from the outside. In XXI it is wholly in Strether's consciousness. In XXIII it is, so to speak, half in the Prince, half in the Princess, and half in the motion with which the act is performed.

The Proportion of Intelligence and Bewilderment (V). Upon the correct proportion depends the verisimilitude of a given character. Omniscience would be incredible; the novelist must not make his "characters too interpretative of the muddle of fate, or in other words too divinely, too priggishly clever." Without bewilderment, as without intelligence, there would be no story to tell. "Experience, as I see it, is our apprehension and our measure of what happens to us as social creatures—any intelligent report of which has to be based on that apprehension." Bewilderment is the subject and someone's intelligent feeling of it the story. The right mixture will depend on the *quality* of the bewilderment, whether it is the vague or the critical. The vague fool is necessary, but the *leading* interest is always in the intensifying, critical consciousness.

The Necessity of Fools (V, X, XI), and *The Use of Muddlement* (XI, XIX). These subjects are evidently related to that of Intelligence and Bewilderment. In themselves nothing, fools are the very agents of action. They represent the stupid force of life and are the cause of trouble to the intelligent consciousness. The general truth for the spectator of life was this: (X, xv)—"The fixed constituents of almost any reproducible action are the fools who minister, at a particular crisis, to the intensity of the free spirit engaged with them." Muddlement is the condition of life which fools promote. "The effort really to see and really to represent is no idle business in face of the *constant* force that makes for muddlement. The great thing is indeed that the muddled state too is one of the very sharpest of the realities, that it also has colour and form and character, has often in fact a broad and rich comicality, many of the signs and values of the appreciable" (XI, xiii).

Intelligence as a Receptive Lucidity (XI, XXI). The first of this pair of Prefaces almost wholly and the second largely deals with the methods of conditioning a sensibility so as to make a subject. In XI James shows how the sensibility of a child, intelligent as it may be, can influence and shape and make lucid people and situations outside as well as within its understanding. She, Maisie, is the presiding receptive intelligence, the sole sensibility, in the book, and is furthermore the sole agent, by her mere existence, determining and changing the moral worth of the other characters. In XXI Strether is outlined as the example of the adult sensibility fulfilling similar functions, with the additional grace of greatly extended understanding.

The Dramatic Scene (III, VII, IX, XI, XIX, XXI, and *passim*). We have already spoken under the same heading of James's general theory of the dramatic scene. It is too much of the whole substance of the technical discussion in many of the Prefaces to make more than a mere outline of its terms here possible. In III, xxii and XIX, xxiii, there is developed the figure of windows opening on a scene. The eye is the artist, the scene the subject, and the window the limiting form. From each selected window the scene is differently observed. In VII is discussed the theory of alternating scenes in terms of a center (p. xv). In IX which is the most purely scenic of all the books, the use of the alternating scene is developed still further. At the end of XI there is a bitter postscript declaring the scenic character of the form. In XXI there is intermittent discussion of how to use the single consciousness to promote scenes, and a comparison with the general scenic method in XIX. It is principally to IX that the reader must resort for a sustained specific discussion of the Scene in fiction and its relation to the Scene in drama, and to XIX, of which pp. xii-xxiii deal with the scenic structure of that book, where the distinction is made between Scenes and Pictures and it is shown how one partakes of the other, and where it is insisted on that the maximum value is obtained when both weights are felt. Subordinate to this there is, in the same reference, a description of the various reflectors (characters) used to illuminate the subject in terms of the scene.

On Revision (I, XXIII). The Notes on Revision in these Prefaces are mainly of interest with reference to what James actually did in revising his earlier works. He revised, as a rule, only in the sense that he re-envisaged the substance more accurately and more representatively. Revision was responsible re-seeing.

On Illustrations in Fiction (XXIII). This is perhaps the most amusing note in all the Prefaces, and it is impossible to make out whether James did or did not like the frontispieces with which his collected volumes were adorned. He was insistent that no illustration to a book of his should have any direct bearing upon it. The danger was real. "Anything that relieves responsible prose of the duty of being, while placed before us, good enough, interesting enough, and, if the question be of picture, pictorial enough, above all *in itself,* does it the worst services, and may well inspire in the lover of literature certain lively questions as to the future of that institution."

The Nouvelle as a Form (XV, XVI, XVIII). The nouvelle—the long-short story or the short novel—was perhaps James's favorite form, and the form least likely of appreciation in the Anglo-Saxon reading world, to which it seemed neither one thing nor the other. To James it was a small reflector capable of illuminating or mirroring a great deal of material. To the artist who practiced in it the difficulties of its economy were a constant seduction and an exalted delight.

On Rendering Material by its Appearances Alone (V). James had the problem of rendering a character whose whole life centered in the London underworld of socialism, anarchism, and conspiracy, matters of which he personally knew nothing. But, he decided, his wanted effect and value were "precisely those of our not knowing, of society's not knowing, but only guessing and suspecting and trying to ignore, what 'goes on' irreconcilably, subversively, beneath the vast smug surface." Hints and notes and observed appearances were always enough. The real wisdom was this:—that "if you haven't, for fiction, the root of the matter in you, haven't the sense of life and the penetrating imagination, you are a fool in the very presence of the revealed and the assured; but that if you *are* so armed you are not really helpless, not without your resource, even before mysteries abysmal."

And that is a good tone upon which to close our rehearsal of the major subjects James examines in his Prefaces. Other readers and other critics (the two need not be quite the same) might well have found other matters for emphasis; and so too they may reprehend the selection of Minor Notes which follow.

On Development and Continuity (I). Developments are the condition of interest, since the subject is always the related state of figures and things. Hence developments are ridden by the principle of continuity. Actually, relations never end, but the artist must make them appear to do so. Felicity of form and composition depend on knowing to what point a development is *indispensable.*

On Antithesis of Characters (I.) The illustration is the antithesis of Mary and Christina in this book. James observes that antitheses rarely come off and that it may pass for a triumph, if taking them together, one of them is strong (p. xix).

On the Emergence of Characters (X, xiii). James's view may be summarized in quotation. "A character is interesting as it comes out, and by the process and duration of that emergence; just as a procession is effective by the way it unrolls, turning to a mere mob if it all passes at once."

On Misplaced Middles (VII, XIX). Misplaced Middles are the result of excessive foresight. As the art of the drama is of preparations, that of the novel is only less so. The first half of a fiction is the stage or theater of the second half, so that too much may be expended on the first. Then the problem is consummately to mask the fault and "confer on the false quantity the brave appearance of the true." James indicates how the middles of VII and XIX were misplaced, and although he believed the fault great, thought that he had in both cases passed it off by craft and dissimulation.

On Improvisation (XII, xvi). Nothing was so easy as improvisation, and it usually ran away with the story, e.g., in *The Arabian Nights.* "The thing was to aim at absolute singleness, clearness and roundness, and yet to depend on an imagination working freely, working (call it) with extravagance; by which law it wouldn't be thinkable except as free and wouldn't be amusing except as controlled."

The Anecdote (XIII, vi). "The anecdote consists, ever, of something that has oddly happened to some one, and the first of its duties is to point directly to the person whom it so distinguishes."

The Anecdote and the Development (XV, ix, XVI, v). In the first of these references James observes that whereas the anecdote may come from any source, specifically complicated states must come from the author's own mind. In the second he says that *The Middle Years* is an example of imposed form (he had an order for a short story) and the struggle was to keep compression rich and accretions compressed; to keep the form that of the concise anecdote, whereas the subject would seem one comparatively demanding developments. James solved the problem by working from the outward edge in rather than from the center outward; and this was law for the small form. At the end of this Preface, there is a phrase about chemical reductions and compressions making the short story resemble a sonnet.

On Operative Irony (XV, ix). James defended his "super-subtle fry" on the ground that they were ironic, and he found the strength of applied irony "in the sincerities, the lucidities, the utilities that stand behind it." If these characters and these stories were not a campaign for something better than the world offered then they were worthless. "But this is exactly what we mean by operative irony. It implies and projects the possible other case, the case rich and edifying where the actuality is pretentious and vain."

On Foreshortening (VII, XV, XVII, XVIII). This is really a major subject, but the discussions James made of it were never extensive, seldom over two lines at a time. I append samples. In VII, xii, he speaks of foreshortening not by adding or omitting items but by figuring synthetically, by exquisite chemical adjustments. In XVII, xxv, the nouvelle *Julia Bride* is considered as a foreshortened novel to the extreme. In XVIII, xv, after defining once again the art of representation and insisting on the excision of the irrelevant, James names Foreshortening as a deep principle and an invaluable device. It conduced, he said, "to the only compactness that has a charm, to the only spareness that has a force, to the only simplicity that has a grace—those, in each order, that produce the *rich* effect."

On Narrative in the First Person (XXI, xvii-xix). James bore a little heavily against this most familiar of all narrative methods. Whether his general charge will hold is perhaps irrelevant; it holds perfectly with reference to the kinds of fiction he himself wrote, and the injury to unity and composition which he specifies may well be observed in Proust's long novel where every dodge is unavailingly resorted to in the attempt to get round the freedom of the method. The double privilege (in the first person), said James, of being at once subject and object sweeps away difficulties at the expense of discrimination. It prevents the possibility of a center and prevents real directness of contact. Its best effect, perhaps, is that which in another connection James called the mere "platitude of statement."

On Ficelles (XXI, xx). Taking the French theatrical term, James so labeled those characters who belong less to the subject than to the treatment of it. The invention and disposition of *ficelles* is one of the difficulties swept away by the first-person narrative.

On Characters as Disponibles (III, vii-viii). Here again James adapted a French word, taking it this time from Turgenev. *Disponibles* are the active or passive persons who solicit the author's imagination, appearing as subject to the chances and complications of existence and requiring of the author that he find for them their right relations and build their right fate.

The rule of space forbids extending even so scant a selection from so rich a possible index. But let me add a round dozen with page references alone. On Dialogue (IX, xiii); Against Dialect (XVIII, xvi); On Authority (XVIII, xviii); On Confusion of Forms (IX, xvii); On Overtreatment (III, xxi; IX, xxii); On Writing of the Essence and of the Form (III, xvii); On Making Compromises Conformities (XIX, xii); On the Coercive Charm of Form (IX, xvii); On Major Themes in Modern Drama (IX, xviii); On Sickness as a Theme (XIX, vi); On Reviving Characters (V, xviii); On Fiction Read Aloud (XXIII, xxiv); and so on.

The reader may possibly have observed that we have nowhere illustrated the relation which James again and again made eloquently plain between the value or morality of his art and the form in which it appears. It is not easy to select from a multiplicity of choice, and it is impossible, when the matter emerges in a style already so compact, to condense. I should like to quote four sentences from the middle and end of a paragraph in the Preface to *The Portrait of a Lady* (III, x-xi).

There is, I think, no more nutritive or suggestive truth in this connexion than that of the perfect dependence of the "moral" sense of a work of art on the amount of felt life concerned in producing it. The question comes back thus, obviously, to the kind and degree of the artist's prime sensibility, which is the soil out of which his subject springs. The quality and capacity of that soil, its capacity to "grow" with due freshness and straightness any vision of life, represents, strongly or weakly, the projected morality. . . . Here we get exactly the high price of the novel as a literary form—its power not only, while preserving that form with closeness, to range through all the differences of the individual relation to its general subject-matter, all the varieties of outlook on life, of disposition to reflect and project, created by conditions that are never the same from man to man (or, as far as that goes, from woman to woman), but positively to appear more true to its character in proportion as it strains, or tends to burst, with a latent extravagance, its mould.

These sentences represent, I think, the genius and intention of James the novelist, and ought to explain the serious and critical devotion with which he made of his Prefaces a *vademecum*—both for himself as the solace of achievement, and for others as a guide and exemplification. We have, by what is really no more than an arbitrary exertion of interest, exhibited a rough scheme of the principal contents; there remain the Prefaces themselves.

III

Although the Prefaces to *The Wings of the Dove* or *The Awkward Age* are more explicitly technical in reference, although that to *What Maisie Knew* more firmly develops the intricacies of a theme, and although that to *The Tragic Muse* is perhaps in every respect the most useful of all the Prefaces, I think it may be better to fasten our single attention on the Preface to *The Ambassadors*. This was the book of which James wrote most endearingly. It had in his opinion the finest and most intelligent of all his themes, and he thought it the most perfectly rendered of his books. Furthermore in its success it constituted a work thoroughly characteristic of its author and of no one else. There is a contagion and a beautiful desolation before a great triumph of the human mind—before any approach to perfection—which we had best face for what there is in them.

This preface divides itself about equally between the outline of the story as a story, how it grew in James's mind from the seed of a dropped word (pp. v-xiv), and a discussion of the form in which the book was executed with specific examination of the method of presentation through the single consciousness of its hero Lambert Strether (pp. xv-xxiii). If we can expose the substance of these two discussions we shall have been in the process as intimate as it is possible to be with the operation of an artist's mind. In imitating his thought, step by step and image by image, we shall in the end be able to appropriate in a single act of imagination all he has to say.

The situation involved in *The Ambassadors,* James tells us, "is gathered up betimes, that is in the second chapter of Book Fifth. . . . planted or 'sunk,' stiffly or saliently, in the centre of the current." Never had he written a story where the seed had grown into so large a plant and yet remained as an independent particle, that is in a single quotable passage. Its intention had been firm throughout.

This independent seed is found in Strether's outburst in Gloriani's Paris garden to little Bilham. "The idea of the tale resides indeed in the very fact that an hour of such unprecedented ease should have been felt by him *as* a crisis." Strether feels that he has missed his life, that he made in his youth a grave mistake about the possibilities of life, and he exhorts Bilham not to repeat his mistake. "Live all you can. Live, live!" And he has the terrible question within him: "*Would* there yet perhaps be time for reparation?" At any rate he sees what he had missed and knows the injury done his character. The story is the demonstration of that vision as it came about, of the vision in process.

The original germ had been the repetition by a friend of words addressed him by a man of distinction similar in burden to those addressed by Strether to little Bilham. This struck James as a theme of great possibilities. Although any theme or subject is absolute once the novelist has accepted it, there are degrees of merit among which he may first choose. "Even among the supremely good—since with such alone is it one's theory of one's honour to be concerned—there is an ideal *beauty* of goodness the invoked action of which is to raise the artistic faith to a maximum. Then, truly, one's theme may be said to shine."

And the theme of *The Ambassadors* shone so for James that it resembled "a monotony of fine weather," in this respect differing much from *The Wings of the Dove,* which gave him continual trouble. "I rejoiced," James said, "in the promise of a hero so mature, who would give me thereby the more to bite into—since it's only into thickened motive and accumulated character, I think, that the painter of life bites more than a little." By maturity James meant character and imagination. But imagination must not be the *predominant* quality in him; for the theme in hand, the *comparatively* imaginative man would do. The predominant imagination could wait for another book, until James should be willing to pay for the privilege of presenting it. (See also on this point the discussion of Intelligence and Bewilderment above.)

There was no question, nevertheless, that *The Ambassadors* had a major theme. There was the "supplement of situation logically involved" in Strether's delivering himself to Bilham. And James proceeds to describe the novelist's thrill in finding the situation involved by a conceived character. Once the situations are rightly found the story "assumes the authenticity of concrete existence"; the labor is to find them.

"Art deals with what we see, it must first contribute full-handed that ingredient; it plucks its material, otherwise expressed, in the garden of life—which material elsewhere grown is stale and uneatable." The subject once found, complete with its situations, must then be submitted to a process. There is the subject, which is the story of one's hero, and there is the story of the story itself which is the story of the process of telling.

Still dealing with the story of his hero, James describes how he accounted for Strether, how he found what led up to his outburst in the garden. Where has he come from and why? What is he doing in Paris? To answer these questions was to possess Strether. But the answers must follow the principle of probability. Obviously, by his outburst, he was a man in a false position. What false position? The most probable would be the right one. Granting that he was American, he would probably come from New England. If that were the case, James immediately knew a great deal about him, and had to sift and sort. He would, presumably, have come to Paris with a definite view of life which Paris at once assaulted; and the situation would arise in the interplay or conflict resulting. . . . There was also the energy of the story itself, which once under way, was irresistible, to help its author along. In the end the story seems to know of itself what it's about; and its impudence is always there—"there, so to speak, for grace, and effect, and *allure*."

These steps taken in finding his story gave it a functional assurance. "*The* false position, for our belated man of the world—belated because he had endeavoured so long to escape being one, and now at last had really to face his doom—the false position for him, I say, was obviously to have presented himself at the gate of that boundless menagerie primed with a moral scheme which was yet framed to break down on any approach to vivid facts; that is to any at all liberal appreciation of them." His note was to be of discrimination and his drama was to "become, under stress, the drama of discrimination."

There follows the question, apparently the only one that troubled James in the whole composition of this book, of whether he should have used Paris as the scene of Strether's outburst and subsequent conversion. Paris had a trivial and vulgar association as the obvious place to be tempted in. The revolution performed by Strether was to have nothing to do with that *bêtise*. He was to be thrown forward rather "upon his lifelong trick of intense reflexion," with Paris a minor matter symbolizing the world other than the town of Woolet, Mass., from which he came. Paris was merely the *likely* place for such a drama, and thus saved James much labor of preparation.

Now turning from the story of his hero to the story of his story, James begins by referring to the fact that it appeared in twelve installments in the *North American Review,* and describes the pleasure he took in making the recurrent breaks and resumptions of serial publication a small compositional law in itself. The book as we have it is in twelve parts. He passes immediately to the considerations which led him to employ only one center and to keep it entirely in Strether's consciousness. It was Strether's adventure and the only way to make it rigorously his was to have it seen only through his eyes. There were other characters with situations of their own and bearing on Strether. "But Strether's sense of these things, and Strether's only, should avail me for showing them; I should know them only through his more or less groping knowledge of them, since his very gropings would figure among his most interesting motions." This rigor of representation would give him both unity and intensity. The difficulties, too, which the rigor imposed, made the best, because the hardest, determinants of effects. Once he adopted his method he had to be consistent; hence arose his difficulties. For example, there was the problem of making Mrs. Newsome (whose son Strether had come to Paris to save), actually in Woolet, Mass., "no less intensely than circuitously present"; that is, to make her influence press on Strether whenever there was need for it. The advantage of presenting her through Strether was that only Strether's feeling of her counted for the story. Any other method would not only have failed but would have led to positive irrelevance. Hence, "One's work should have composition, because composition alone is positive beauty."

Next James considers what would have happened to his story had he endowed Strether with the privilege of the first person. "Variety, and many other queer matters as well, might have been smuggled in by the back door." But these could not have been intensely represented as Strether's experience, but would have been his only on his own say-so. "Strether, on the other hand, encaged and provided for as *The Ambassadors* encages and provides, has to keep in view proprieties much stiffer and more salutary than our straight and credulous gape are likely to bring home to him, has exhibitional conditions to meet, in a word, that forbid the terrible *fluidity* of self-revelation."

Nevertheless, in order to represent Strether James had to resort to confidants for him, namely Maria Gostrey and Waymarsh, *ficelles* to aid the treatment. It is thanks to the use of these *ficelles* that James was able to construct the book in a series of alternating scenes and thus give it an objective air. Indispensable facts, both of the present and of the past, are presented dramatically—so the reader can *see* them—only through their use. But it is necessary, for the *ficelles* to succeed in their function, that their character should be artfully dissimulated. For example, Maria Gostrey's connection with the subject is made to carry itself as a real one.

Analogous to the use of *ficelles,* James refers to the final scene in the book as an "artful expedient for mere consistency of form." It gives or adds nothing on its own account but only expresses "as vividly as possible certain things quite other than itself and that are of the already fixed and appointed measure."

Although the general structure of the book is scenic and the specific center is in Strether's consciousness of the scenes, James was delighted to note that he had dissimulated throughout the book many exquisite treacheries to those principles. He gives as examples Strether's first encounter with Chad Newsome, and Mamie Pocock's hour of suspense in the hotel salon. These are insisted on as instances of the representational which, "for the charm of opposition and renewal," are other than scenic. In short, James mixed his effects without injuring the consistency of his form. "From the equal play of such oppositions the book gathers an intensity that fairly adds to the dramatic." James was willing to argue that this was so "for the sake of the moral involved; which is not that the particular production before us exhausts the interesting questions that it raises, but that the Novel remains still, under the right persuasion, the most independent, most elastic, most prodigious of literary forms."

It is this last sentiment that our analysis of this Preface is meant to exemplify; and it is—such is the sustained ability of James's mind to rehearse the specific in the light of the general—an exemplification which might be repeated in terms of almost any one of these Prefaces.

IV

There is, in any day of agonized doubt and exaggerated certainty as to the relation of the artist to society, an unusual attractive force in the image of a man whose doubts are conscientious and whose certainties are all serene. Henry James scrupled relentlessly as to the minor aspects of his art but of its major purpose and essential character his knowledge was calm, full, and ordered. One answer to almost every relevant question will be found, given always in specific terms and flowing from illustrative example, somewhere among his Prefaces; and if the answer he gives is not the only one, nor to some minds necessarily the right one, it has yet the paramount merit that it results from a thoroughly consistent, informed mind operating at its greatest stretch. Since what he gives is always specifically rendered he will even help you disagree with him by clarifying the subject of argument.

He wanted the truth about the important aspects of life as it was experienced, and he wanted to represent that truth with the greatest possible lucidity, beauty, and fineness, not abstractly or in mere statement, but vividly, imposing on it the form of the imagination, the acutest relevant sensibility, which felt it. Life itself—the subject of art—was formless and likely to be a waste, with its situations leading to endless bewilderment; while art, the imaginative representation of life, selected, formed, made lucid and intelligent, gave value and meaning to, the contrasts and oppositions and processions of the society that confronted the artist. The emphases were on intelligence —James was avowedly the novelist of the free spirit, the liberated intelligence—on feeling, and on form.

The subject might be what it would and the feeling of it what it could. When it was once found and known, it should be worked for all it was worth. If it was felt intensely and intelligently enough it would reach, almost of itself, toward adequate form, a prescribed shape and size and density. Then everything must be sacrificed to the exigence of that form, it must never be loose or overflowing but always tight and contained. There was the "coercive charm" of Form, so conceived, which would achieve, dramatize or enact, the moral intent of the theme by making it finely intelligible, better than anything else.

So it is that thinking of the difficulty of representing Isabelle Archer in *The Portrait of a Lady* as a "mere young thing" who was yet increasingly intelligent, James was able to write these sentences. "Now to see deep difficulty braved is at any time, for the really addicted artist, to feel almost even as a pang, the beautiful incentive, and to feel it verily in such sort as to wish the danger intensified. The difficulty most worth tackling can only be for him, in these conditions, the greatest the case permits of." It is because such sentiments rose out of him like prayers that for James art was enough.

1934

16

The Loose and Baggy Monsters of Henry James

NOTES ON THE UNDERLYING CLASSIC FORM IN THE NOVEL

All that I have to say here springs from the conviction that in the novel, as elsewhere in the literary arts, what is called technical or executive form has as its final purpose to bring into being—to bring into performance, for the writer and for the reader—an instance of the feeling of what life is about. Technical form is our means of getting at, of finding, and then making something of, what we feel the form of life itself is: the tensions, the stresses, the deep relations and the terrible disrelations that inhabit them as they are made to come together in a particular struggle between manners and behavior, between the ideal insight and the actual momentum in which the form of life is found. This is the form that underlies the forms we merely practice, and it is always different—like any shot in the dark—from the technical preconception of it: what you expected when you applied your technical skills in order to find it. It is also different—as anything revealed in a body of its own always is—from what your moral and intellectual preoccupations expected: for morals in action are never the same as morals prescribed; and indeed, this form, when found, refreshes and recharges your morals, remodels and revivifies your intellect. Thus there is a mutual interaction. There is a wooing both ways; what is found is in some respect affected by the tools used, technical, moral, and intellectual; and it is also true that what is found affects, for the instance, the medium in which it emerges, technical, moral, and intellectual. Out of all these in mutual relationship is created what Croce means by theoretic form for feeling, intuition, insight, what I mean by the theoretic form of life itself. This form, whatever you call it, because it persists for new emphasis, because it endures through phase after phase and through different kinds of attention after attention, I call classic: the underlying classic form in which things are held together in a living way, with the sense of life going on.

The classic, let us say, is the life that underlies the life we know: it is the source of our behavior, it informs our behavior, it is what we cope with when we cope with our behavior. A little reflection tells us that the most interesting questions we can raise about the underlying classic form in the novel will be those which enquire into the relations between it and the various forms of the mind with which it is always associated in fact, and which indeed are the only handles by which we take hold of it. This is especially so in a period like our own when works tend to be composed, and are largely read, as if the only conscious labor were the labor of technical form: the labor of the game of the mind, the play of its conventions and the play of its words. That is, we have to enquire what technical mastery has been made to stand for. If we do not ask such questions we are likely to be left with the notion that all that is necessary to heroism, in art or life, is technical skill and have no notion at all what it was—in morals, in intellect, and in what underlay both—that animated into action the art we heroize.

Something like this is the situation into which a good deal of Henry James criticism has lately fallen. To say this is not to make a discovery but a commonplace in the bad sense; it has been said all along, and to little point. My point is that the technical or executive forms of Henry James, when turned into fetishes if not rules, have been largely misunderstood both with regard to themselves and with regard to their mutual relations with other forms. Both the ideal and the substantial origin of classic form has been ignored, on the one hand; and on the other hand, by critics concerned immediately with morals or what is called the liberal imagination, the poetic—the creative—aspects of James's language and the conventions of his forms have been minimized and cheapened to perception. I am not concerned to repair these damages but to meditate on them along several paths of meditation. The paths are well known and our feet fit them, if not our thoughts; we have only to fit our thoughts to the uneven ground.

One path is the parallel path of verse. In verse, we know that the meter does something to the words, even though the meter be the most rigidly prescribed arrangement of syllables. We know also that the rhythm does something to the meter and to the words, something not the same thing but related. Beyond that we know that the meter and rhythm and words do something to both the intellectual structure and the moral perception of the poem. We understand all this because we appreciate the strains separately as well as feel them together: we know that by their joint operation something has been brought into the poem, which is vital to it, and which would otherwise not be there. What we ought to know is that something comparable to this is true of the novel and we should suspect that we need training in appreciation to recognize it: training so that we may see not only what the author consciously intended but also where he struck on something over and above, or other than, what he intended. We must understand that the poetic mind is as much at work in prose as in verse, and we must understand that nobody—not even Dante, not even James Joyce—can be conscious of, or deliberately take care of, all the skills he uses in the moment of composition. The nine muses may be conscious, but they are too many to hear at once. The poor poet—the poor novelist—must be contented to hear what he can, yet must act with the pressure and power of the others in his writing fingers—the pressure and the power he can feel conscious of only as a haunt that has just left him.

No wonder then, if such is his case, he will confuse what he does know and can hear with what he does not know and cannot hear: a confusion sometimes made with great effect. Half the English poets of the seventeenth century thought that if technical mastery of the heroic couplet could be had, then the English epic might be written, when the fact was that the deep form—the underlying classic form—of *Paradise Lost,* not written in couplets at all, heroic or homely, had solved the problem of the epic for Milton: had solved the problem of what new phase of being the epic of Homer, Vergil,

Dante had reached in Protestant, Christian, seventeenth-century England. Other powers, other skills of mind and sensibility had entered into thc struggle than the poets knew; yet for all we know the argument over metrical form was the efficient agent for the birth of the new deep form. That there have been no Miltons since, counts nothing; there have been no Dantes since Dante; nor should we want any. It is only the path we want to follow.

If the argument about the heroic couplet helped produce Milton, and if the argument about the "very language of men" helped produce Wordsworth, and if the argument about the "heightened form of the best conversation of the time" helped produce Eliot and Yeats—all these along with a good many confusions and ignorances as to what else helped—then I think we might strike it rich for the field of the modern novel if we look at one of the most confused, most arrogant, and most fertile statements ever made—among so many—by Henry James. The statement is often quoted, and it comes in the Preface he wrote to the revised version of *The Tragic Muse.* I suggest that it is there precisely because at the moment of writing James was prodded—his writing fingers were twisted—by the very muses of deep form that he was only hauntedly aware of. Since he was criticizing, not creating, his response was irritated.

The Tragic Muse, I may say, seems to me a failure as a Henry James novel precisely because its form is so nearly only executive form, and not, as James partly allowed, because he did not give the executive form warrant enough to remake the characters. I take this as the unconscious source of James's irritation in the following remarks.

A picture without composition slights its most precious chance for beauty, and is moreover not composed at all unless the painter knows *how* that principle of health and safety, working as an absolutely premeditated art, has prevailed. There may in its absence be life, incontestably, as "The Newcomes" has life, as "Les Trois Mousquetaires," as Tolstoi's "Peace and War," have it; but what do such large loose baggy monsters, with their queer elements of the accidental and the arbitrary, artistically *mean?* We have heard it maintained, we will remember, that such things are "superior to art"; but we understand least of all what *that* may mean, and we look in vain for the artist, the divine explanatory genius, who will come to our aid and tell us. There is life and life, and as waste is only life sacrificed and thereby prevented from "counting," I delight in a deep-breathing economy of an organic form.

It is curious that James should have reversed the order of words in Tolstoy's *War and Peace,* and if we had time when we got done asking what the whole passage stands for we might ask what that reversal stood for. In brief I think it stood for not having read the book, if at all, with good will—for having read it with a kind of rudderless attention. The important thing is that *War and Peace* does have every quality James here prescribes: composition, premeditation, deep-breathing economy and organic form, but has them in a different relation to executive form than any James would accept. Indeed, put beside *War and Peace, The Ambassadors, The Wings of the Dove,* and *The Golden Bowl* are themselves "large loose baggy monsters" precisely because an excess use was made of James's particular development of executive form, and precisely because, too, of the consequent presence of James's own brand of the accidental and the arbitrary, and because these together make access difficult to James's own "deep-breathing economy and organic form." It is these last, however, that hold us to James as they hold us to Tolstoy, and it is in them that we must find the "principle of health and safety"—or of deep ill and final danger—which James found in consciously practiced executive form; just as we would have to show in Tolstoy that his practice was virtually tantamount to an admirable executive form, and must indeed have been so used by Tolstoy. In James we have to deepen the level of our interest in the creative process; in Tolstoy we have to show that the deep things of the mind and the sensibility must after all, when they become literature, be exercised as a game, in the delight of the mind's play, like waterlights, upon its experience. It is true that Tolstoy, in a worse case than Chaucer, denied any worth to his novels compared to life; and it is true that James insisted that literature stood for everything worth living in a free life: he was himself he said that obstinate finality, the artist. But we can afford the excesses of the great—though we must counter with our own smaller excesses of enquiry to which the great were not committed. The "divine explanatory genius" will never appear to tell us why Tolstoy—let alone Dumas and Thackeray—is "superior to art," but it seems to me possible for a talent not divine at all to suggest why both Tolstoy and James made superior forms of art. Here our business is with James; and all we have to keep in mind of Tolstoy—of Cervantes, of Dostoevski, of Balzac and Flaubert, of Fielding, Smollett, and Scott—is that on the evidence of endurance and recurrence of interest, on the evidence of the always available and availing feeling of stature, such work must have in every significant sense at least its necessary share of "deep-breathing economy" and "organic form." We must assume that if we asked we might find out indications of how that principle worked and we can be certain that we could find in such work what James meant by the principle of composition—which is what is here meant by executive form. The novel has changed, since Cervantes, and has taken on different aspects of the general burden of literature according to the phase of culture and the bent of the writer, but I doubt that since, with Cervantes, it first undertook a major expressive task, it has reached any greater degree of mastery or perfection or possible scope. It is only the criticism of the novel, not formerly needed, that has yet to reach mastery—a lack here sorely felt; and a lack you will feel for yourselves if you will think of the relatively much greater maturity of the criticism of poetry. To go on with the present job requires the assumption of a critical maturity we do not have in fact and which we do in fact need if we are to make full response to the novel.

This is not to say that James needed in fact or in any other way to ask our critical questions or any others than he chose to ask. For a man concerned with consciousness and conscience, and perhaps because of the supremacy of that concern, James had singularly little need of consciousness outside his chosen perspective of vision, and almost no need at all of conscience—in the sense of knowing things together, with or without remorse—in regard to anything but the conventional and technical aspects of his work. But even if he had been as conscious as an oyster of his pearl, or had he had the conscience of a saint over his last sin, he had as an artist only the need to ask those questions of which he needed the answers in order to look workmanlike at his work. If those answers came then the questions must have stood for everything that counted.

It is different with us; we are not at work, we are using work done; and we have a right curiosity to understand what his questions stood for in the dark as well as what they asked for in the open of daily practice. We know, in a way that no individual novelist thinking of his own work can know, that the novel is all of a piece, and that if examples have not the same end in view, they have likely the same source, analogous means, and a common fate. Thus we have to ask at once how it is that the three novels *The Ambassadors, The Wings of the Dove,* and *The Golden Bowl* should be at the same time modeled on the well-made social play, exercises in the indirect perception of human character and action, direct to the point of the intolerable expressions of the general human predicament, and, finally, symbolic patterns—themselves in their own action—of the permanent struggle between the human condition and human aspirations; how it is, in short, that the most conventional, the most abstract, approach possible should yet exemplify one of the closest scrutinies—the closest forms—ever made of life itself. We have the shudder of beauty—of the many reduced to one, as Pythagoras says; we have the shudder of beauty—the condition of more than usual emotion and more than usual order—as Coleridge says; we have the shudder of beauty—in a unity of response felt as achieved without any feeling that the substance unified has been cheated in the theoretic form in which the unity is expressed. This is the praise of the late novels of Henry James. It may be we cannot say how it happened; if we can possibly say merely *what* happened we shall have made the judgment to go with the praise.

You will remember the well-made play-like structure of these novels—one of the ways in which they differ from all other novels of similar stature. In *The Ambassadors* the hero, Lambert Strether, is sent to Paris by a widow with whom he has 'prospects,' to rescue her son from an immoral life. Once in Paris, Strether has a classic recognition: Europe is not immoral, it is life itself, and the widow's morality is blatant and empty. Then follows a reversal of roles, equally classic with the recognition: the young man insists on giving up his mistress, who is a great lady, and returning, a cad for riches and a glutton for money, to his mother's America, while, on the contrary, Strether, having discovered life at last in Paris in middle age insists on remaining at the cost of his 'prospects' with the widow, and at the worse cost of all security in life. As he has made his recognition and achieved his reversal too late in life the denouement is that he has to renounce all that has come his way in the person of Maria Gostrey, the American expatriate who picked him up at the moment of landing. Thus Strether turns out to have been less an ambassador than a pilgrim: the goods he has achieved are spiritual, to be signified best by the badge of a new face, even a new look in the shoulders seen from behind.

In *The Wings of the Dove,* an American millionairess, Milly Theale, doomed to early death, makes her pilgrimage to Europe to see and live the most she can before she dies. She falls in with an engaged couple who cannot marry for lack of money; they—particularly the girl, Kate Croy—conceive the idea of marrying the young man to Milly Theale so that after inheriting her money at her death they can marry into power and ease. Milly's pilgrimage is broken by her recognition, which is forced upon her, of the plot to get her money in the disguise of love. She dismisses the young man, dies, but leaves him her money nevertheless. The young man, recognizing what he has done in terms of Milly Theale, suffers if not a reversal a deep change of role and finds himself compelled, like Strether, to renounce the worldly goods he has gained. He is left seeing things with new eyes forever.

In *The Golden Bowl* there is a similar but more complex predicament. Adam Verver, a multi-millionaire, and his daughter Maggie make their pilgrimage to Europe innocent as lambs in their riches and their love of each other. Maggie marries Prince Amerigo who requires money and power to preserve himself. Her father marries the Prince's 'true love,' the American expatriate Charlotte Stant, who requires to preserve herself money and—not power—but further relations with the prince. In due time—in the second act—Maggie discovers that her husband and her step-mother have been improving and expanding their relations. After her recognition scene, in what might be called the third act, she too reverses her role; out of her changed goodness and innocence—no less good and no less changed—she draws the power to make something tragically good and ultimately innocent of the two marriages. The sacrifice that she makes is that she renounces the old ground of her beseeching—the aspiration of her innocence, candor, and energy, the innocence of her money—and stands on the new and terrible ground of the conditions of life itself.

It is interesting to observe—and I think it can equally be observed of most great European novels—that the Aristotelian terms recognition and reversal of roles apply sharply to the major motions of the plot and that complication or intrigue applies firmly to the minor motions. But instead of the journey of *hubris* or overweening pride, we have the journey of the pilgrim, the searcher, the finder. And instead of katharsis—the purging in pity and terror—we follow rather the Christian pattern of re-birth, the fresh start, the change of life or heart—arising from the pity and terror of human conditions met and seen—with the end not in death but in the living analogue of death, sacrifice, and renunciation. So it is in James; and so it is in Tolstoy with the difference that sacrifice may take the form of death as with Anna in *Anna Karenina,* subsidence into the run of things as with Levin in that book or with Pierre in *War and Peace,* or disappearance into the heroic unknown as with Vronsky in *Anna Karenina.* In James the end is always a heightened awareness amounting to an exemplary conscience for life itself, accomplished by the expense, the sacrifice, the renunciation of life as lived in the very conditions on which the consciousness and the conscience are meant to prevail. James's novels leave us with the terrible exemplars of conscience seen coping with the worst excruciations of which their consciousnesses are capable. The order in the three late novels is interesting, and it is the order of composition if not of publication. Strether, in *The Ambassadors,* is the exemplar of the life of senses. Kate Croy, in *The Wings of the Dove,* is our lady of philosophy or practical wisdom shown as the exemplar of all that is torn and dismayed, but still persistent in that role. Maggie Verver, in *The Golden Bowl,* is perhaps as near the exemplar as James could come to our lady of theology or divine wisdom; she is James's creation nearest to Dante's Beatrice, stern and full of charity, the rock itself but all compassion, in the end knowing all but absorbing all she knows into her predetermined self, not exactly lovable but herself love. Not that James would have admitted any of these conceptions except the first.

For in the first, which is Strether as the life of senses, that is exactly what James's own language shows: Strether's consciousness and his conscience are applied to render an indirect view of the beauty and the excruciation of the life of the senses: he assents to it, he knows it, but he is only an exemplar of knowledge and assent: he himself is not finally up to that life. This James clearly must have meant. But what he meant by Kate Croy in *The Wings of the Dove* must remain uncertain and I think ought to remain uncertain. Kate as construed from the notes James left behind, notes which may be read in Matthiessen and Murdock's book, was meant originally to be the villainness in a standard social melodrama, and she never entirely loses that role—which explains both her resoluteness and her strange, occasional overriding blind commitment to action. But it explains neither her beauty—she is physically the most beautiful of all James's women by a surpassing margin—nor her instructed humanity, her sense of what is what, and the necessity, in the given conditions, of her fall from that beauty and that humanity. Somehow Kate the beauty, the girl on the make who will be nothing if she makes nothing of what other people are, somehow Kate is the destructive persistent element of practical philosophy which criticizes, and places, and makes intelligible, and disposes of the overweening image of moral beauty which is Milly Theale, princess in her own American right and heiress of the ages. Kate is criticism which does not destroy but modulates: under her impact we see the nominal heroine of the novel, Milly Theale, for what she is, an aspiration impossible of realization; she is that temptation seen on the high places which is the worst temptation, once seen the most corrupting, appealing with the best impossible appeal to the worst in our natures. That is not what a man wants to do with his image of moral beauty, but it is what the imaginative man, when he sees his image in terms of the actual conditions of life, sometimes must in honesty do. The wings of the dove are still clean and silvery, but the sheepfold is fouler than ever; for the dove has created its dirt.

Maggie Verver as Beatrice—the Queen or at least the Princess of all forms of knowledge walking in human flesh—is perhaps a more tremendous image than James could quite create. It is hard to turn a lamb into a sovereign even among the lions—even, that is, among those predatory creatures of necessity who are best equipped to know that the lamb of innocence exists. That is why, no doubt, James gives Maggie and her father the added strength of their limitless millions: making the godly surrogates of Caesar. The possibility is haunting, and breathless, that such a combination might be effective; but it is not enough, for on some other level of belief—the level Dante and Shakespeare had—the conviction of unity is lacking. Maggie has the kind of imperiousness that goes with the deepest waywardness, the waywardness that is the movement of life itself; but she has no capacity for exerting the imperium itself except in aspiration. There is too much fear in her: she feels too much of her new knowledge as chill; she is too much there to be preyed on; she is too much an ideal ever to take on full power. But she does a great deal just the same; if by her goodness and innocence she cannot make other people good, she can yet by that goodness breed their wrong. By her goodness she is able to put her husband and his mistress (who is also her step-mother) between Scylla and Charybdis: between "the danger of doing too much and the danger of not having any longer the confidence or the nerve . . . to do enough." And that, she says, "that's how I make them do what I like." When her confidante Mrs. Assingham tells her, after hearing this, that she is amazing, that she is terrible, Maggie makes her great answer. No, she says; she can bear anything for love, not for love of her father, not for love of her husband, just for love. What we see is Maggie learning in the abyss of a London stage drawing room two of the lessons Dostoevski found in the enormous abyss of *The Brothers Karamazov:* that most men find beauty in Sodom and that love in action is a harsh and terrible thing. But Maggie can accept neither the beauty of Sodom nor the action in love. Thus Mrs. Assingham is right when she tells her husband "we shall have to lie for her till we're black in the face." Her goodness and her love is all of a piece; the broken golden bowl which she can barely hold together with all her force is herself; it is flawless only to those who would protect her and defraud her, who would at once plunder and deceive her, all in the name of love and admiration of her goodness.

Maggie is all of a piece in another sense as well. When early in the book Mrs. Assingham tells the Prince—that image of Old Europe, the Italy of life and crime—that he has all the senses that make a man good, he answers her, answers Maggie, answers the reader whoever he may be; answers in an image which is a major strain in the underlying moving form of the book. No, he says, the moral sense I have not got. "I mean always as you others consider it. I've of course something that in our poor dear backward old Rome sufficiently passes for it. But it's no more like yours than the tortuous stone staircase—half-ruined into the bargain!—in some castle of our quattrocento is like the 'lightning elevator' in one of Mr. Verver's fifteen-storey buildings. Your moral sense works by steam—it sends you up like a rocket. Ours is slow and steep and unlighted, with so many of the steps missing that—well, that it's as short in almost any case to turn round and come down again." Maggie and Milly, and Strether too, work by the terrible amazing steam of their own innocence and candor and courage. They go up like rockets and somehow work great havoc on those who are led, or forced, to go up with them.

In the havoc as it moves and shapes and heaves is the underlying form of the book: the form in which is apprehended the conditions of life. The strongest shape and the sharpest motion—the deepest heaving qualm—James is able to create out of that havoc is the shaping in heaving motion of a conscience out of consciousness. The structure and the gradual emergence of that conscience seem to me the overt and visible acknowledgment of the underlying form. Conscience is the bite of things known together, in remorse and in incentive; conscience is that unification of the sense of things which is moral beauty; conscience comes at many moments but especially, in James, in those deeply arrested moments when the will is united with the imagination in withdrawal.

It is on such moments that each of our three novels ends. In *The Golden Bowl* the Prince tells Maggie "I see nothing but you." That means he is united with his conscience. "And the truth of it had with this force after a moment so strangely lifted his eyes that as for pity and dread of them she buried her own in his breast." The moment was gone. At the end of *The Wings of the Dove* our lady of philosophy Kate Croy and her lover Merton Densher feel stretch over them the dove's wings of the dead Milly Theale. "She turned to the door, and her headshake was now the end. 'We shall never again be as we were.'" Beauty and a shade had passed between.

So it was too with Strether in *The Ambassadors* and there are thoughts in his mind toward the end of that book, applied to the wonderful mistress of the caddish young man he had come to Paris to rescue, but fitting exactly the situation in other books as well. "It was actually moreover as if he didn't think of her at all, as if he could think of nothing but the passion, mature, abysmal, pitiful, she represented, and the possibilities she betrayed." These were the powers the image of moral beauty—of conscience—had attempted to transform. It is the perennial job of uprooted imagination, of conscience, choosing from beauty and knowledge, to raise such an image; but it may not transgress actuality without destruction; the images must not be mistaken for reality though the heart craves it. As Dante says (*Purg.* XXI-133-36):

Or puoi la quantitate
comprender dell'amar ch'a te mi scalda,
quando dismento nostra vanitate,
trattando l'ombre come cosa salda

Now may you comprehend the measure of the love that warms me toward you, when I forget our nothingness, and treat images as solid things.

The poor shade of the poet Statius had tried to embrace Vergil, and these were Vergil's words in answer. There the shadow was the only actual. It is interesting to use an insight from Dante here, because in his construction of conscience and moral beauty, James is himself making a late gesture in the aesthetic-moral tradition of the Christian world which Dante did so much to bring into poetry. With both men, it was only a hair's breadth, a mere change of phase, between the spiritual and the sensual, the ideal and the actual; and this is because there was in them both the overwhelming presence of felt, of aesthetic, reality as it fastened like a grapple upon individual souls and bodies.

Also to think of Dante here may remind us again of the great intellectual spiritual form in which James worked: the form of conversion, rebirth, the new life. That is the experience of Strether seen against the actual world, and in that world—"in the strict human order." Not a tragedy in the old sense—that is in its end—its tragedy lies in its center: in the conditions of life which no conversion, no rebirth, no turning, ever leaves behind—not even in saints till they have gone to heaven. The tragic tension lies partly between what is re-born and what is left over, and partly between the extremes toward which conversion always runs and the reality which contains the extremes.

The extremes with which Henry James was obsessed had largely to do with the personal human relations and almost nothing at all to do with public relations except as they conditioned, marred, or made private relations. It may be said that James wooed into being—by seeing what was there and then going on to create what might be there in consciousness and conscience—a whole territory of human relations hitherto untouched or unarticulated. I do not say not experienced, only unarticulated. So excessive is this reach into relation, there is no escape possible for the creatures caught in it except by a deepening or thickening of that relation until, since it cannot be kept up, it must be sacrificed. That is to say, its ideal force becomes so great that its mere actual shade becomes intolerable. So it was with Strether; he denied Marie de Vionnet and Maria Gostrey wholly in order to be 'right' with the ideal which the actual experience of them had elicited in his mind. But the denial was a gesture of this ideal, and it could have been otherwise, could in another soul have been the gesture of assent; for the beauty and the knowledge were still there, and the reality, which contains both the ideal and the actual, and so much more, stands, in its immensity, behind.

Behind is a good place. If we think of what is behind, and feel what we think, which is what James did, we will understand all the better the desperation out of which Strether created his image of moral beauty, the virtuous connection, and how it stood up, no matter what, as conscience. Otherwise, like Strether at his low point, we "mightn't see anyone any more at all." As it is we see with Maria Gostrey: "It isn't so much your *being* 'right'—it's your horrible sharp eye for what makes you so."

We have gotten, as we meant to, rather far away from the mere executive form—gotten into what that form merely articulates and joints and manipulates and takes into itself, itself being charged and modified thereby; but it has been there all along, that form, and we can now look at at least one facet of it with double vision: to see what it is and to see at the same time what happens to it—like what happens to a meter—in use. There are many possibilities—all those executive habits of the artist James names in his Prefaces, some of them never named before; and all those other devices, rhetorical and imagistic which James uses without naming—but for my purpose, which is to show how a technical device criticizes the substance it puts in motion and how the substance modifies the device, there is none so handy or so apt as James's use of the conventional figure of the confidante, a figure common to European drama, but developed to the highest degree of conventionality in the French theater James knew best.

Each of the three novels has examples, and in each the uses to which they are put are somewhat different. In the theater the confidante is used to let the audience know what it otherwise would not; she blurts out secrets; carries messages; cites facts; acts like a chorus; and is otherwise generally employed for comic relief or to represent the passage of time. Generally speaking, the confidante is stupid, or has the kind of brightness that goes with gossip, cunning, and malice. In these three novels the case is different: each confidante has a kind of bottom or residual human stupidity and each is everlastingly given to gossip; but the gossip has a creative purpose—to add substance to the story—and the stupidity is there to give slowness and weight and alternative forms to the perceptions and responses which they create. This is the gossiping stupidity for which there is no name in any living language, but which the Sanskrit calls *Moha,* the vital, fundamental stupidity of the human race by which it represents, to the human view, the cow, or as we would say the sheep. It is what the man has been caught in when he gives you a sheepish look; he was caught a little short of the possibility he was trying to cope with. It is this role—so much more fundamental than the conventional original—that James's confidante is given to play; and saying so much it should be evident that she will qualify as well as report action, she will give it substance, and gain substance by it, as well as precipitate it.

The simplest form of confidante in our three novels is that taken by Susan Stringham in *The Wings of the Dove.* Susie is Milly Theale's paid companion; it is she who makes out of Milly a Princess and overdeclares her value, volubly and credibly, until there is a general conspiracy to accept as operative truth the ideal she puts up: she gives human and fabulous names—a fairy-godmother sort of name—to the attributes in Milly which James could not at first directly present; but she is not otherwise a part of the story. In *The Golden Bowl* Fanny Assingham and her husband Colonel Bob have nothing at all of the fairy god-parent about them, but have rather just the opposite function: to make the most intolerable, grasping, greedy, predatory behavior socially and humanly acceptable at the same time that they make out between them that the behavior *is* predatory and *is* intolerable. They fulfill in short the old role of truth-telling, lie-making clowns at the drawing-room level. They are the comic relief, but it is a curiously ugly, unredeemable sort of penetrating, revelatory comedy that they practice. Fanny with a refinement of perception—wrong or right—past belief and with an only barely credible polish of diction, and Colonel Bob with the good-hearted cynicism appropriate to the best clubs, dig into the tenderest perfidy and the most charitable frauds they can find, and when they cannot find they create. These are the people, wonderfully rendered in voice and gesture and texture of situation, who stand for all the intrigue that passes for human motive before human motive is created. Colonel Bob assumes that any such substitute will pass muster if let alone; by such as him, the world would get by. Fanny makes a very different but congruous assumption: that no motive inspected—and inspect them she must—could ever get by unless inspected, protected, edited, rearranged, and covered up. Her great sign of the truth is that it shall be worth lying for; and her great warrant for lying is that a lie may create a truth. To her, a mistake only proves her policy right, and a real blunder only asks for redoubled effort. It is people like the Assinghams that ensure the service of the gods of this world; they are that rhetoric of manners that masquerades as decency to cover the plea of guilty or inadequate action. They create the scandal they would excuse. What they make in the world is hopelessness, futility, emptiness; but they make these tolerable by making them a game, yet without them nobody could get along, least of all the Ververs, Charlotte, and the Prince, the truly innocent and the truly wicked, for without the Assinghams they would have no meeting ground.

Maria Gostrey, in *The Ambassadors,* shares the gossip and the creativeness of the Assinghams, but with the difference that she is the go-between who has something in common with both things she goes between, and that her creativeness is not a substitute and seldom a mistake, for she is, rather, when she pushes herself, clairvoyant. That she pushes herself often makes her a part of the story and part of the emotion that holds the story together. The gift of clairvoyance, the gift of seeing so into the center of things as to become a part of them, and of doing so merely by nature and the skill of a lifetime, gives her powers quite opposite to those of the Assinghams. Instead of hopelessness she creates hope, instead of futility possible use, instead of emptiness fullness; and she never makes tolerable that which ought to remain intolerable. That is why she becomes, in the deep sense, a part of the story, and why the story lifts her from a means to a substance. If it were not that a device ought not to be called so, I would say that this instance of the conventional device of the confidante was also an instance of classic form.

There remains the middle ground of what is nowadays called the mind or the intellect to enquire into: the conceptual, dogmatic, tendentious part of the whole mind: the part inhabited and made frantic by one's ideology. Although there has been a good deal of talk to the effect that James was defective in this quarter, I think all that talk will vaporize on the instant if the question underlying the talk is differently put. Not what ideas did James have, but with what ideas—abroad then and now—is James's imaginative response to life related? It will be these ideas that will illuminate and partake of his underlying form. In short we want to get at the ideas in James's mind that were related to his whole work; and in James these occupy a precarious but precious place. He is not a Dante or a

Thomas Mann; his humanism is under cover, part of his way of seeing, part of his "deep-breathing economy of organic form."

But it had got twisted by his time and by the superstitions of his time; for although he was 'against' his time he had necessarily to collaborate with it—from the very honesty of his inward eye for the actual, no one more so. I do not know that the nature of this collaboration can be made plain, but a few generalizations may be risked. They have to do with the tendency toward expressionism in art and social thinking, which stem from what is meant by art for art's sake, and they have to do with the emergence of a new concept of the individual as isolated and detached from society in everything but responsiveness, which is a concept that springs, I think, from those changes in society that are related to the facts of population growth and the mass-form of society.

There is a sense in which art for art's sake as we have had it since the *Parnassiens* is itself a reflection of the shift in the bases and the growth in size of any given modern society. As the bourgeois base turns into the industrial base—as the great population engulfs the 'great society'—we get on the one hand something called pure poetry with a set of feelings in the poets who write it which has something to do with the impulse to escape (to deny, to cut away) and the conviction of isolation (the condition of the incommunicable, the purely expressive, the fatally private—the sense of operating at a self-created parallel to the new society). At the same time, on the other hand, we get a belief in that monster the pure individual, whose impulse is to take life as a game, and whose ambition is to make the individual *feeling* of life the supreme heroism; so that the tropes of one's own mind become the only real parallel to life. In both cases—in pure art and in the pure individual—we pretend that it was like this in the past just behind our past.

No doubt this is so of some past, but not where it is looked for, in the Great Europe. It is more likely so in some of the over-populated periods in Egyptian or Byzantine history, or in the Rome of the second century: each of which ended in the culture of the fellaheen, where the individual was purified to extinction, from which only Rome has so far recovered. What we overlook in our pretense to a tradition is the difference between a population-burst accompanied by the disappearance of knowledge and the shrinking of the means of subsistence, which is what the past shows us (Egypt, China, India, Rome) and a great continuing population growth accompanied by the division of culture and the specialization of knowledge, along with the tremendous multiplication of the means of subsistence and of war—all of which has been our experience. What we see is the disappearance of the old establishment of culture—culture safe from the ravages of economy—and we do not know whether another culture is emerging from the massive dark, or, if it is, whether we like it. Whatever has disappeared or is emerging is doing so without loss of vitality except in the cultural establishment (now everywhere a prey to the economy) and with otherwise what seems a gain in vitality. What has above all survived in our new mass society is the sense of the pure individual—by himself, or herself, heir to all the ages. Because of the loss of the cultural establishment we have put a tremendous burden on the pure individual consciousness. It seems to us that in order to hang on to the pure individual we must burden his consciousness beyond any previous known measure. We make him in our art, especially the art of literature, assume the weight of the whole cultural establishment—above all that part of it which has to do with behavior, manners, human relations: with insight, with conformity and rebellion, and with the creation or ability to create absorbing human motives. For all this the artist has to find, by instinct since his culture does not sufficiently help him, what I called to begin with the underlying classic form in which things are held together in a living way, with the sense of life going on.

Sometimes this burden of consciousness seems to obscure, if not to replace, the individuals we create, whether in ourselves or in our arts. At any rate, this burden of consciousness is what has happened to our culture. There is no longer any establishment, no longer any formula, and we like to say only vestigial forms, to call on outside ourselves. There is only the succession of created consciousnesses—each of which is an attempt to incorporate, to give body to, to incarnate so much as it is possible to experience, to feel it, the life of the times, including the culture no matter what has happened to it—

and including also of course all those other things which never were in any culture, but which press on us just the same.

These generalizations seem to me one of the useful backgrounds against which to look at the novels of Henry James. As background it reflects light on the extremes to which he pushed the limits of his created individual consciousnesses, so much less varied than those of Gide, Proust, Mann, Kafka, and Joyce, but no less intense, no less desperately grasping after life, and the form of life, for and in the name of the individual. In that light we can but understand what Strether, in *The Ambassadors,* is up to when he says *Live all you can!* We can understand also how Mme. de Vionnet, the young man's splendid mistress, is up to the same thing under what are fundamentally the same conditions. We understand how much there is to see—to see unaided by ourselves—how much there is to intensify into form—in the simplest relation between human beings.

James at fifty-eight, when he wrote *The Ambassadors,* had experienced and therefore could dramatize the disestablishment of culture and the shift in the bases of society, and he could do so all the better because he did not, and probably could not, have understood them intellectually or historically. He was concerned with the actuality he found and with the forms under the actuality. He was himself an example of disestablishment and a forerunner of what we may expect to find a prevalent form of disinherited sensibility, the new 'intellectual proletariat,' and he had therefore only to write out of himself against the society which 'intellectually' or by common assumption he thought still existed, in order to create an extreme type of transitional image of the future time. Not unnaturally his original audience—barring the young who were ahead of themselves—thought he had created sterile fantasies; the richer his subjects grew and the deeper he got into them, the more his sales fell off. His own experience of 'America' and of 'Europe,' where America had apparently moved faster than Europe toward the mass society, toward the disinheritance but not the disappearance of the individual, had moved him ahead of his contemporaries; had moved him to the 1930's when he began to be read seriously, and the '40's when he got to be the rage, and now to the '50's when he seems, so to speak, an exaggerated and highly sensitized form of the commonplace of our experience: the sensitized deep form.

If Strether is our example of 1902 looking ahead, what Strether would feel now would seem like the music of Adrian Leverkühn in Mann's *Doctor Faustus:* a heightening but not a disintegration of his feelings of 1902; and it would be a heightening, as in Mann's novel, by parody and critique, because like Leverkühn he would have had so much more of the same thing behind him, and so much more of the same burden put upon him, than he had in the earlier time. Our theoretic new Strether would have found out how much more had to be re-established in a form greater than its own than he had then felt; how much more, by necessity and by choice, must be reborn into actuality out of its hidden form. But the difference between the two Strethers would be by bulk and by kind, not by quality, by scope and not by reach. The reach is into the dark places where the Muses are, and all the rest is the work we do to bring into the performance of our own language the underlying classic form in which they speak.

1951

17

Between the Numen and the Moha

NOTES TOWARD A THEORY OF LITERATURE

The following remarks are meant to suggest one way of seeing how it is that morals get into literature and what happens to them when they get there. Morals is what we think about in our quarrel with behavior, and I should say at once I mean to deal with how behavior gets into literature and what it does to morals when it gets there. Behavior is what upsets morals, both disrupting and resuming their task. This is easy to see in Tolstoy and Flaubert. What Anna Karenina's behavior does to the morals of her husband and of her lover; what the panic at Moscow (panic is a great monster of behavior) and the subsequent retreat of Napoleon's armies do to Pierre's morality in *War and Peace;* what the general, characteristic behavior of the French village (another monster of behavior) does to the morality of Emma Bovary; and what all these do to the morality of the reader: this seems to me of the highest interest.

These novels, and I think all others of magnitude, illustrate both what Henry James must have meant when he said that the morality of a work of art depended on the amount of felt life in it, and also what one of the Goncourts meant when he said (in Ezra Pound's translation) that the novel is ethics in action. Feeling and action. What is felt and what is in action—a little under our will, a little apart from our intent—are exactly our behavior. At least it is behavior before it becomes anything else, before it becomes a theory of life, and so before it modifies (for that is its strength, to modify) other theories, especially the theory we call morals, that may be present in the writer's or the reader's mind.

This is because the novel, and every other form of literature, is a confrontation of behavior. To confront is to make the brief abstract of the time; to hold the mirror up to nature is to confront. So is to imitate the actions of men. We confront behavior. Our great fear is that our behavior may overwhelm us; our great delight is when we have transformed our aspirations into behavior; our fate is that we shall be mainly incarnations of our behavior. *Macbeth* is our fear; *The Tempest* is our delight; *Antony and Cleopatra* our fate. When we are passionately involved with other people we minutely scrutinize, or refuse to recognize, their behavior. The arts and especially the arts of literature give theoretic form to these passionate preoccupations. This is why, I think, Coleridge argued that, ideally, poetry should exhibit a state of more than usual emotion and more than usual order; for it is under these conditions—perhaps never found in life—that we can give our richest theoretic forms to behavior. A theoretic form is a way of seeing: no more.

No more. It will be interesting to exemplify in some detail from certain novels, how much of the force of life is contained in that "no more." To find a way of seeing what has happened to us sometimes seems our highest legitimate aspiration. It is what criticism taken as appreciation, as interpretation, as recognition, as the avenue to the use of literature, has been up to all along. But we had better wait for our examples until we can make a provisional formula, at a reflective level, which will explain, without justifying, how criticism goes about its perennial task of bringing the work of art to the condition of performance. The problem to keep in mind is contained in my first sentence: how morals get into literature and what happens to them when they get there. We want not a philosophy of criticism (except as one wants a philosophy of billiards or of courtship) but a means of noting how criticism relates to philosophy and particularly moral philosophy. We can move rather fast. We do not need to begin with Genesis or with Plato. We can begin, right up to the minute, at the threshold of our own consciousness, the point where what we do first declares itself, which is also the point where what we have thought mires itself in action. This is the point where dreams indeed become responsibility and thought a nightmare.

It is the point where criticism begins and to which it must be occasionally forced back. I take it criticism is a skill which as it deepens and grows habitual becomes to some degree a routine of second nature and which, when irritated in argument, sometimes pleads for itself as second sight. It becomes, as we say, unconscious, so crowded it is with intuition, and cries in the dark, crowding its darkness into the blaze of noon. Then it becomes pure criticism of pure literature: pure heroism in a world without heroes, pure expression without reflection. Here, as I see it, is the point where moral philosophy has business with literature, and where, if you like, religion has business with both. Philosophy has the business of bringing back across the threshold of consciousness, back into the story of the whole mind, the reflective power which had thickened into habit. It will come back thick with new life. Philosophy reminds criticism that it is critical, that (like the artist with his behavior, like Coleridge with his ideal poetry) criticism must confront a state of unusual emotion with a state of unusual order. The emotion will be the same, the order different. The critic must confront the immediate with what survives of what he has inherited, or has studied out, and if he cannot do that he will have lost both his second nature and the rational content of the skill upon which it depended.

That is what philosophy reminds criticism of, its reflective and ordering power: the meaning of the tradition which had become its skill. But philosophy gives criticism no power over the substance (the felt life, the behavior) which it reflects and orders. Religion reminds both moral philosophy and criticism that their task is to reflect upon and give order to the relation of human behavior to the underlying or overweening force which is the momentum of things and of life. Religion reminds moral philosophy and criticism of their subject matter. In saying this I am of course expressing my belief that literature—that all the arts—somehow exhibit our actual experience of the relation between human behavior and the force which moves it. It was Henry James who said (in "The Lesson of the Master") that the artist finds his material in the enormous lap of the actual; and the artist presents the actual relation. Literature renders this relation as it gets into behavior, and all the trouble our morals have with that. To this Macbeth amply testifies in what would otherwise be his set speeches; so do Francesca and Brunetto in the different mode of the *Divine Comedy;* and so does Ivan's poem "The Grand Inquisitor" in *The Brothers Karamazov* (based upon a belief in God and a denial of his created world): which should be ample testimony, at least for the moment. Behavior is the medium in which our lives take place. Literature and religion, with their different authorities and different revelations, give us—to repeat the refrain I have stolen and modified from Croce—theoretic forms of our lives seen as behavior. Literature and religion give us, too, between them, with ferocity of observation and charity of apprehension, almost the only secure knowledge we have of what happens to our mind and our spirit when we behave as the wind behaves.

Think of *Madame Bovary* as a close ordering—a theoretic form—of a vision of the wind's behavior. We see the terrible cost of beauty out of place, and we hear Emma's words, addressed in supplication of spirit to her faithless lover, words which if they only made the bears dance were yet spoken with a mighty longing to move the stars. The wind ruffles the flesh, and in the end Charles Bovary says it was the fault of fatality. As Santayana says, "Spirit chills the flesh and is itself on fire." But it is reason, the whole rational mind, that when it contemplates Emma Bovary and Macbeth can acknowledge the fire of memory in the flesh and is itself the chill shock of recognition. Perhaps it is by that acknowledgment and by that recognition, when they are present and never when they are absent, that tragedy becomes a rational art: in perspective *and* in immediacy, in behavior and in form, in that fire and in that chill. Tragedy is the form we give out of the piety of long knowledge to what has happened to us again, and again. This only reason knows, and what it learns is this tragic certainty. The downfall of morals, when confronted by behavior, cannot be justified, with whatever charity it may be explained. Morals must always be remade, always on the old grounds. No wonder we associate tragedy both with the idea of goats and the idea of katharsis.

II

These are large words around a theme which I hope will have begun to emerge: precisely the theme of rational art. And here we come, not again on my first sentence about how morals get into art, but upon my title. Rational art and morals too, stand within the terms of my title. *Between the Numen and the Moha.* These are both simple and I think fundamental terms: plain names for the predicament of our common adventure and our permanent effort. Both are very old words for ever-present things. But to make them worth while we must take them up afresh.

The *Numen* or *numinosus* is that power within us, greater than and other than ourselves, that moves us, sometimes carrying us away, in the end moving us forward unless we drop out, always overwhelming us. So far as it may be felt in literature it resembles the force of the sublime described by Longinus—the blow that transports us. It is a force sometimes cultivated as magic, as superstition, as mystery: it is related to the rhythm which gives meaning to action. Religion has always cultivated this force with the piety of excruciated sense, and religion has always taken it as the spring of absolute, or rational, action—not the action but its spring, as the Incarnation or the Crucifixion. Thus the *Numen* enters, though it is not itself, behavior. It is the reality that presses into behavior but never reaches whole incarnation there.

For unfortunately, when the *Numen* gets into behavior it gets transformed, or gets deflected, or degraded, into that privation of humanity for which the best name I know is *Moha:* the uncontrollable behavior which tends to absorb and defile both the chill and the fire of spirit. I suppose some people would call the *Moha* the devil; but it is much more human and ornery than that; nor is it the mere *miseria* of the spirit. *Moha* is a Sanskrit word I got from a physicist (one time a poet), who in turn got it while studying that language for relief at Los Alamos during the war. I suppose the atomic bomb was a labor of the *Moha.* At the juncture when I got the term it was given as an attribute of the faculties of high institutions of learning—bodies of men and women by nature subject to incalculable, capricious explosions of behavior. The attribution was correct. *Moha,* then, is a term for the basic, irremediable, irreplaceable, characteristic, and contemptuous stupidity of man confronted with choice or purpose: the stupidity because of which he goes wrong, without which he could not survive. *Moha* refers to what is sottish, oafish, and drunken, to what is slothful but active in man's nature. But *Moha* also refers to the stubborn tenacity of will—of blind, necessary action—by which man puts up with what is intolerable in his life. We admire it as valiance, reject it as the rushing crime of fools, and often observe it as the damned spot that will not out. It is the remains of aspiration.

For *Moha* has something to do with the basic lies we tell; which may be noble and the very limit of aspiration, or which may be as absolutely without dignity as behavior itself. All Dostoevski's great novels form a drama of the two extremes in conflict, and again the fable or poem of "The Grand Inquisitor" is an example to move us like Longinus' blow.

But perhaps the central meaning of the term is reflected in its history. *Moha* is from a language which grew in a land where cattle are both sacred and obstacles to rational action; much as our pastoral terms come from a land of sheep and goats. *Moha* means cow: the cow that fattens off the land and has right of way in any traffic. Thus by analogy the word contains all we mean by "sheepish" in look or gesture, but it means it in action and fundamental nature. It is Pasiphaë become a cow, the cow that is in all of us, as Dante observes in his Purgatory. It is what our behavior, unenlightened and unimpeded, would leave us at. It is what we are like when we deprive ourselves of the three things reason requires of beauty: *consonantia, integritas, claritas:* harmony, wholeness, radiance.

Reason's requirements are never met. But it is this beautiful reason which stands between the *Numen* and the *Moha*—either as art or as the reflective faculty—acknowledging, ministering to, and representing both, in the names of memory and hope. Reason is in this sense the whole mind, the residual form of all we have been, and the conceiving matrix of all that we may become. Reason is a servant, the housekeeper who keeps things going by criticism, by philosophy, by art. To change one of T. S. Eliot's lines: the worm criticizes the soil that it eats and so puts all the modes of intelligence into that relation where they criticize by absorbing each other and reinaugurate the reason itself. It is Ophelia, crying after Hamlet's most whirling words, who sums it up: "T'have seen what I have seen, see what I see!"

The worm of reason criticizes the soil that it eats. This formula for relating philosophy to criticism is seductive but untrustworthy, and it cannot be used alone. But it has a kind of twin in a simpler and more naked formula. Let us put together the notions of the *Numen* and of *myth,* and at the same time think of literature. To expand this formula to its furthest confines would be to adventure in a land only darkly known, no doubt full of familiar nightmares and disconsolate chimeras, for we should be tampering with the powers of our own natures. Let us here merely sense the possibility of expansion. This is how thought becomes emotion, emotion thought.

It is the other half of Ophelia's cry. Let us think that the emotion which variously fills us and deserts us is single, though unknown in its shifting character: as if emotion were one substance: what we mean when we say of a man that he was filled with emotion; or again, that every trace of emotion left him; in each case without specification. Let us think of that emotion as our sense of the raw or underlying force which in reality—whatever *that* may be—moves us. This is how literature often thinks. This is how Tolstoy's *War and Peace* and *Anna Karenina* regard emotion: as the shaping blows of raw force: the emotion we crave *and* shun.

In making these thoughts we are only reflecting our common actual experience. In such thoughts we credit, we certify, what happens to us that does not arise from, but springs in, ourselves. What do we do then? We move on either of two paths which are much the same in history (as they are much the same in Tolstoy's character Pierre) but which in our present general frame of mind seem incongruous. Either we cultivate that emotion and beseech that force in religion under the immediate form of mystery, or we cultivate them under the mediated form of myth. In religion there is the direct recognition, the immediate blow—the shock of light. In myth the perception is mediated or enacted through behavior. There is the substance of faith and the story of Christ. Who shall say one is not a phase of the other? Both can be creative, both destructive. Both, as we discourse on them (though not in the original experience), are theoretic forms requiring reason to persist or to be recognized afresh. "T'have seen what I have seen, see what I see!"

Surely if we think along these lines we have a means of seeing how philosophy—moral philosophy—is not only possible but necessary, in the criticism of literature. Literature, if you take a decent span of it, uses all modes of perception indifferently. Moral philosophy is the mode of mind which estimates and adjusts the relative values of the whole structure. On the other hand, literature—the skills of poetry—is full of the *Lore,* things picked up almost by instinct and preserved by practice, literature is full of the *Lore* of all modes. But only reason can tell the uninitiate the meaning of the *Lore*.

The prospects I see for this formula or train of thought are entrancing, but I distrust it taken either alone or as a mere twin to the *Numen* and the *Moha.* I want to combine them, to make them compose, in the interests of beautiful reason. The mind which makes that happen will do so by a series of jumps. I know what it feels like to jump, but to say so here would be to make a poem: for the *process* of every jump is in the dark, it represents the behavior of the mind. It seems more propitious to our present purpose to imagine a kind of diagram to remind us of the complexity of possible jumps and of the flexibility of the muscles used in jumping, and above all to suggest the breadth and depth of the gaps jumped. It is the diagram of the atom that reminds us of the gaps in the knowledge we use.

Let us suppose our diagram rather large, ungainly and approximately square in outline. At the center is the twinned pair, the one above the other, the *Numen* and the *Moha,* with the *Numen* somehow astride the *Moha* out of sheer human prejudice. Then let us put, more or less at the corners, sets of notions which seem to go together as congruous or cognate modes of mind. At one corner there might stand Philosophy (who ought also to be called our lady of *Filosofia* to represent the kind of work philosophy does in the poetry of Dante, Lucretius, and Goethe). Under philosophy we should find Scientia, the common sense of the perpetual pagan world—the absolute knowledge of the tribe—hardened and illuminated by principle and purpose. Next, at a second corner, we should find Lore, the chief lady of our daily devotions, all our skills and knowledge of being we never knew we learned. Under *Lore* (where we are not so much devoted as committed unawares) would naturally appear the haunt of Jung's *Collective Unconscious* and the theoretic *Pre-conscious* of Freud: to represent how the modern consciousness has worked out techniques to recover *Lore* which has been lost. Then, under or neighboring these, the grim goddess *Fortuna* (so often denied, so invariably supplicated) would certainly find a place, for she is that goddess of chance and womanhood by whose aid we confront the incalculable with arbitrary and reckless confidence—and else with a lottery of despair.

So much for half our ungainly square. At a third corner surely *Myth* would appear, shimmering almost into flesh, shuddering almost into vapor. For myth is not only what we ordinarily mean by it, a significant and powerfully symbolic myth of the mind. Myth is also what it meant to Aristotle, namely plot, the soul of the action, the creative arrangement or energetic ordinance of the story of behavior. Here also we should find *Historia,* for *Historia* claims right to interpret and theorize the story as it seems to her fitting, that is, as it happened within the scope of her interest. *Historia,* one would suppose, looks across the way askance at *Fortuna.* At the fourth and last corner there can only be *Poetry. Poetry* is not here a row of books and she needs in her corner no companion but the grand heaving figure of the unconscious with which she works and which she transforms into conscience. Poetry is the *nous poetikos,* that deep habit of mind, deeper than any sea of hope, calmer in its long swell than any mirror of despair, which imitates in forms and images dear to herself the life she has lived, the life she dreads to live, and the life she aspires to live. She looks everywhere about her, for she contains in her own way everything she sees. "T'have seen what I have seen, see what I see!"

So much for our diagram of diagnosis. It indicates samples of the modes of the mind, furnished with a little rhetoric. If the diagram is right all these modes are attracted by each other, and are also repelled, as they are attracted and repelled and related by the *Numen* and the *Moha* in the center. The lines of force are clear in possibility, and the series of possible relations are very numerous. If we apply the simple rule of permutation we come out with a hundred and twenty series, which are enough for even a very ambitious and intelligent mind to encompass. Indeed that is how the mind works actually: it is only the languages we use which must abbreviate and truncate our full discourse: which is why we find ourselves making first one emphasis, then another, and why therefore our arguments grow heated. But the important thing here is not the number of possible relations we grasp and cannot bring wholly into a given language. The important thing is that the *shape,* and therefore our understanding, of the *Numen* and the *Moha* are affected by the modes of the mind predominant in any given relation that we do express. That is, each relation is theoretic, a way of seeing, and hence none is complete, though each may be as near living, as near the thing seen, as any creation of the mind can be. This is the life that moves in the rhythm of our words. This is the situation that philosophy, itself deeply affected, must take account of, and it does so by criticism. "T'have seen what I have seen, see what I see!"

I am indeed embarrassed, if not lost, among all these riches: but they are the real riches of the human mind, our ancient resource, and have been about for a long time as can be seen by the languages from which the terms are drawn: from Aristotle to Jung and Freud. My embarrassment springs from the suspicion that my own response to them smacks of heresy, tykishness, and over-seriousness: as if I chose a kind of wilted primrose path to the everlasting bonfire. There is no redemption in saying my formula is itself a mode of thought, just as it would only compound damnation to insist, which is true, that the formula is a kind of critical poem imitating the behavior of the mind.

Luckily I have stout defenses taken from the words of other men, all in good analogy to my formula of the *Numen* and the *Moha,* whether twinned and diagrammed or not. Here are three sets of words to help my case. One is words heard not long ago in the fascination of living speech (though they are now in print) from a philosopher himself almost a poet. One is from a poet who was never a philosopher, but whose words are part of the standard baggage of the history of criticism. The third set is from a philosopher who ought to have written criticism of literature as well as of life, but who, except for a fragment or so, never did. My authorities are Maritain, Ronsard, and Montaigne. That all three are French is accidental. They have little enough in common, aside from race, and might be expected to stop short at that point in intimacy where understanding forced each to repudiate the others in the great family quarrel of the mind. But if you think of them in a permutation of relationship like those in my imaginary diagram—my mandala—of the *Numen* and the *Moha,* then it will appear that they not only get along well together, but do, together better than separately, support the cause of beautiful reason. Maritain is a neo-Thomist who loves poetry. Ronsard loved a lady in poetry. Montaigne descended all the stairs of doubt (an action which is one of the great poems of the mind) because he loved life herself so much. Reason, thinking of things together, finds not identity, but unity and all its ache. Unity, as we should know (for Henry Adams says it in one of the last great strokes of his *Education*), "Unity is vision; it must have been part of the act of learning to see." Unity is vision in reason. "T'have seen what I have seen, see what I see!" Unity is either one of the great creations of the mind, approaching reality, or it is the chimera looming in the rancorous fog of wanhope; and sometimes it is both. But here are my citations which I shall twist to the defense of my formula.

Let us take M. Maritain first because he is alive and I shall have to twist him very little: he goes along with what I have been saying. Art, said he, with that smile the mind makes when it abandons itself to reality, "Art bitten by poetry longs to be freed from reason." All we need to remind ourselves of here is that "poetry" is *nous poetikos,* the mind that makes something by miming the actions and behavior of men. Christianity added behavior to action. Perhaps we should also remember that "reason" is here (and everywhere for Maritain) the residual, trained, conceptual power of the mind to keep sight of things in their unity. Here poetry is self-expressionism, where the poet succumbs masterfully to the wonderful temptation to combine the arbitrary and the spontaneous in his own language, even when the language is private. Here reason is the great reminder of the constant and the grave: what sees the unity, the disparity, the permanent behavior of things. Great art, then, is twice bitten.

Here is Ronsard. He is looking, I think, for some formula to give both freedom and authority to his work, a formula to bind the trio together. It begins like Aristotle. "As the end of the orator is to persuade, so that of the poet is to imitate, invent, and represent the things that are, that can be, *or that the ancients regarded as true.*" To imitate is to mime, to re-enact; to invent is to make a structure that will hold together, to compose. To represent is to transform what has been imitated and invented into a way of seeing. It is what we mean when we say a man made certain representations of his cause. A representation is a generalization with the particulars kept in. So far, Ronsard is on even ground. What interests me—what fortifies my position—is the final clause of his sentence: *"or that the ancients regarded as true."* The ancients are those who were before us, those who were nearer the gods and nearer chaos than we are. I mean chaos in the old sense, as Ovid used the word at the beginning of the *Metamorphoses*—those great representations of experience in theoretic form: *chaos, rudis indigestaque:* the dark mass within and without and in back of us which men call chaos, *quem dixere chaos:* the chaos of the stars which may yet be seen moving in order. So poetry is the astronomy of the psyche as she labors out of her dark. Over this labor Ronsard's ancients preside. The ancients saw both the gods and behavior—the *Numen* and the *Moha*—in something like a single experience and in their poetry made myths which were plots of the relations between the two. Something of the same sort seems to have taken place in the work of Dostoevski, Joyce, and T. S. Eliot—the Eliot of the *Four Quartets,* not of the *Cocktail Party*. What Ronsard found in his ancients was a rational defense for importing human behavior, particularly the behavior of men and women in love (commonplace with us, it was in Ronsard's day a subject only lately reborn) into poetry. On the side of theory the renaissance aesthetic (as later the reformation and counter-reformation aesthetic) had grown hard and narrow and severely moralistic when it did not become merely technical. Yet in practice the arts had their own strength. Ronsard wanted authority for the overwhelming interest in conduct, and the authority of the gospel parables (if he thought of it) was not enough. For him his remark—"or what the ancients believed to be true"—authenticates interest in all that lay outside the mere moral imperative which had, so it thought (as if art could be bitten by reason alone), freed itself from response to actual behavior by asserting authority over it. His ancients gave him the freedom and justification he needed.

But it will not do as much for us; it only points the way, and is at most only a preliminary consolation. Ronsard touched gingerly on what Montaigne, with the engine of what is called his skepticism but had better be called reason based on direct perception, both his own and that of the ancients, took hold of with both hands. Montaigne was a skeptic, not a Pyhrronist. He doubted in order to bring his mind, not to obloquy or disuse, but to responsive action: which is why his writing is today so fresh. There is never enough response to go round, though like the turkey on the table there is always more than enough for one. But here is my Montaigne, which I take in Zeitlin's translation, from Book I, chapter XXXVII.

> Here is a wonder: we have far more poets than judges and interpreters of poetry; it is easier to write it than to understand it. At a certain level one may judge it by rules and by art. But the true, supreme, and divine poesy is above all rules and reasons. Whoever discerns the beauty of it with assured and steady sight, he does not see it any more than the splendor of a flash of lightning. It does not seduce our judgment; it ravishes and overwhelms it.

My meat is of course in the last three sentences. There it strikes us at once that the language is that of another Longinus, whom it appears Montaigne never read, but whose *Lore* he had by heart. But the earlier part of the passage—on the scarcity of decent critics and the difficulty of understanding poetry except as it conforms to a system of versification—points up all that is sound in the dogmas which are supposed to be asserted in the so-called New Criticism. Let us keep in our own domain and observe merely that when he says "it is easier to write [poetry] than to understand it," Montaigne means that the poet suffers from the temptation in Maritain's sentence: "Art bitten by poetry longs to be freed from reason." To Montaigne, in that suffering may be his power; for the poet's words, so released in temptation, approach nearer and nearer to the condition of pure behavior and pure inspiration: nearer, that is, to the twinned image of the *Numen* and the *Moha.*

It is never certain how much may be found in another man's words, but let us stop playing with the beginning of Montaigne's paragraph and chew the meat of its last three sentences. There not a word fails to count and some mime the very thing they speak of. One wonders only whether the words are legitimate in themselves or whether they make a law of their own. Montaigne's words free poetry both from its own rules and from the rules of reason and give it a role superior to both: to ravish and overwhelm judgment. One wishes one knew better what poetry he had in mind; the touchstone lines about Cato the Younger (which is the title of this essay) are not very helpful to a modern taste. One does not like in Montaigne any more than in Shelley or Arnold, Poe or Mallarmé or I. A. Richards, the assertion of untenable claims for poetry. With this reservation, let us say we see in this passage a claim not only tenable but necessary, a claim which asserts only what actually happens in certain reaches of great poetry where the words take fire from each other. We see the pride of imagination, which is confronted with reality, in the act of breaking down the pride of reason, which manipulates reality in a merely administrative rather than an understanding sense. Montaigne had the heart of poetry in him but his heart beat for the sake of his philosophy, which he wishes always to reinvigorate. Thus we see him reconstitute the bases of reason in the last sentence. Poetry "does not seduce our judgment; it ravishes and overwhelms it." The two verbs "ravishes" and "overwhelms" are the actions of poetry on judgment. It is as if we said: it is by the plunder and rape of judgment—by a kind of violent charity, by a predatory compassion—that we reawaken reason to its perennial vital task to see things together, to be the subject not the agent of refreshment, to be the adjudicator not the master of the permanent but changing turbulence of the union of the *Numen* and the *Moha.* We see how it is that for Montaigne reason is our common sense of the intractableness of both behavior and reality. It is art, by ravishing reason's judgment, that reminds reason of its role. Art keeps reason on its toes, makes it jump and shift its ground, and jump again; for both have the same arena of action, between the *Numen* and the *Moha.*

In the practice of criticism it is almost the other way round. In criticism it is reason (particularly the phase of reason called moral philosophy) that tells us what jumping is like. By the rehearsal of memory and expectation, of perspective and aspiration, reason teaches us to recognize the jumps, the shifts of ground, and whence each springs. Without the presence of reason, all the force in us would seem merely arbitrary, and all our behavior merely spontaneous. The relation of reason to the criticism of literature (for literature is only one of the domains of criticism) seems obvious if you remember and agree that literature is a theoretic form for our experience of life: of the drama in the unsteady union of the *Numen* and the *Moha.* Literature is the "other" form of moral philosophy: the old truepenny fellow in the cellarage who never stops walking up and down. Criticism keeps the sound of his footsteps live in our reading, so that we understand both the fury in the words and the words themselves.

The echoes from Shakespeare in these notes are not accidental but represent our customary modes of perception. In another time, perhaps soon to come, other customs of the mind may predominate. But for our time, the skills of the mind I have been discussing must be our steady preoccupations, the itches (often mistaken for motives) disturbing the lifetime in every moment. Yet for all that these are our deepest skills we never quite know what to do with them, and as we acknowledge them they transform us. Our reason feeds on the element, as Marianne Moore's poem calls it, of beautiful unreason underneath; and as Eliot's poem says, we know and partly know. We move because we are moved. We know there is something ineluctable about literature—it is too deep in behavior; and we know there is something transitory about criticism because we feel our own attitudes are precarious and provisional. Yet we are devoted to literature and committed to criticism. Our reason, pressed by our skills, is flexible like muscles; and it only reflects the profoundly divisive state of our culture if the flexibility is that kind which goes better with a sense of danger than with the sense of conviction, of necessity than purpose, of chances won than choices made. That is what it seems to be like in our version of the arena between the *Numen* and the *Moha.* "T'have seen what I have seen, see what I see!"

III

Once when I was in hospital there was in my ward a patient suffering from an inoperable intercranial lesion. His days were short and what we call his mind was already partly gone. He read his newspapers upside down and spent a good deal of time washing himself behind his drawn curtain, usually spilling his basin and dropping his soap. Preoccupation was his state, both hidden and overt. Yet he was not without hope and had effective means of expression. Many times during the day but always at the juncture when he had either dropped his reading or just emerged from his curtains after washing, he would make a guttural, explosive cry of the single word twice or thrice repeated: Hallelujah, hallelujah, hallelujah! This cry was addressed to no one, certainly not to himself, but was pure representation: an individual, hoarsely protestant ejaculation: with the "j" sound pronounced and the accent heavy. It was the word of praise turned pure behavior, for behavior was all this man had left. One day there was a new patient brought from the operating room and installed in a neighboring bed. The new man had long tapered and curling mustaches, grown with a lifetime's care. His eyes were very bright, like a man wakened from a vision that still moved him. Indeed so it had been. He had been taken to the hospital near dead because he couldn't breathe: his throat had throttled itself out of some deep self-caused disorder of the body struck by some bite or some food with the protein of another and alien body. Now, after tracheotomy, he could breathe and he was about to be brought a little ice cream. It was a new life. Just as the nurse arrived with the tray our first friend dropped his paper and made again his triple ejaculation: Hallelujah, hallelujah, hallelujah! This not so much startled the man with new life as raised him into appropriate and answering song. He sat up a little higher on his elbows, looked all round in sheer delight, and sang a long syllabic Alleluia—All—e-lu-i-a-a-a-a! Then he added, his mustaches still trembling, in a voice echoing the praise of his song: "We all be dead pretty soon, hey!" Here was behavior drawn out of inspiration in pure praise: not what this man had left but what he had suddenly come on. To be between the two was to be between the *Moha* and the *Numen.*

IV

Now by the roundabout route of discursive reason and direct anecdote we are returned to where we began, to the two sentences about (one) how morals get into literature and what happens to them when they get there, and about (two) how behavior gets into literature and and what it does to morals when it gets there. Morals get there through all our life of reason and once they are there the force of behavior refreshes them, makes them urgent and problematic and necessitous. In literature morals are compelled to respond to the turbulence of actual life. Indeed in that response is the source of social structures and of morals themselves; for that response is the rational insistence of the individual on his right to survive no matter what the obstacles. Literature is our account of such survivals and failures to survive. Literature is our theoretic struggle with behavior; but we feed on what we fight and move in the form of our struggle. For behavior gets into literature as the outward and sensible form of our momentum, the forces which carry us on, some our own, and some alien to us: some the breathing of our dearest selves, some the air that suffocates us. Behavior, in literature, criticizes and undermines both our aspirations and our institutional or dogmatic morality. What else is *King Lear* or *Le Rouge et le Noir?* Our behavior has always known how to estimate Rousseau's vision on the dusty noontime road: that the evil in our lives comes from our institutions, so soon as they harden. Not that behavior is necessarily anarchic; it may merely want a different sort of order. So does refreshed reason. So do the arts, and especially literature. What else is the drive of the *Antigone* or of *Don Quixote?* The arts want the sort of order which is responsive to every movement of behavior and every pulse of inspiration: an order which gives room to fresh disorder whenever it occurs. (I suppose this is what people mean when they speak of organic order or form in the arts.) Thus we see in literature the constant effort to create new forms of order, new theoretic forms for the conflict, or the fusion, of the reality which is revelation or epiphany, never wholly known, and that other reality which compels behavior and is never completely manifest. This is our effort to find theoretic forms for the struggle in us between the alleluia and the hallelujah, between the *Numen* and the *Moha.*

I do not suppose that there is a great novel of which this cannot be said, for it is the novel since at least the eighteenth century which has had the charge of organizing all our disorders into theoretic forms of life. To think about the novel in this way leads to the discovery of the elements of its underlying form. Not the conceptual form, which is the management of intent; not the executive or technical form, which is the management of convention and detail; not the symbolic form, which is what is created and gives lasting power to literature; but the underlying form—those movements of the soul which is the form of forms—the underlying form in which we see what it is the novel is really about: the everlasting struggle, the concert of conflict, between the two realities of aspiration and behavior. "T'have seen what I have seen, see what I see!"

Sometimes this underlying form is conspicuous and reaches for an almost rational structure: as in *The Magic Mountain* or *Doctor Faustus,* and indeed if there is a destructive criticism of Mann's novels it is that his conceptual structure is sometimes so schematic that in invades and destroys his substance. But this is perhaps the sickness of our times, which have invented the term "ideology" and have puerilized the term "dialectic." This is one of the ways the struggle between the *Numen* and the *Moha* actually takes place. One could say as much, thinking of another century, of *Candide* or *Gulliver's Travels.* There too the schemata of things damage by enforcing the substance; in Swift and Voltaire the madness of reason hung between the *Numen* and the *Moha.* In Stendhal's *Rouge et le Noir* and *Chartreuse* we have the condition of love in Shakespeare's sonnet: we have the expense of spirit in a waste of shame and find what was past reason hunted past reason hated, and so, with a heavy emphasis on conventional form, we get an overwhelming burlesque—almost a travesty—of the underlying struggle. Thus we have one of the more tolerable and more seductive theoretic forms of the contest between behavior and inspiration. Of Marcel

Proust we should have something very different to say. Thirty years ago Ramon Fernandez accused Proust of a lack of moral progress (*progrès moral*). Precisely. Proust's long novel adds to our permanent stock of sensibility by providing a theoretic form which criticizes morality in its very springs of inspiration and behavior. So do the novels of Jane Austen, George Eliot, and Henry James. What else do they do but criticize and refresh morality in terms of the deep contest of the adverse wills of individual men and women? But I do not mean to differentiate so much as to join.

At the end of Joyce's *Ulysses* we find in Molly's monologue what is surely a fusion of the *Numen* and the *Moha.* The whole book is a theoretic form for the struggle for that fusion. It is also the central struggle within each hero. Leopold Bloom flowers upwards into the *Numen,* as in his humility the good man can. Stephen Dedalus, full of pride and a kind of gluttony for making epiphanies, insists on reaching downwards into the darkness shining in the light which the light does not comprehend: the very darkness of the *Moha.* Everything in the book both fortifies that struggle and is forfeit to it. It is hallelujah, and alleluia; and these are joined in Molly's last cry: "Yes I will. Yes."

So it is in Dostoevski's *Brothers Karamazov,* but in another way; for it is the glory of the novel, among the institutions of life, that it has always another way. Where Joyce, even more than Thomas Mann, has provided close and dovetailed structures for his books out of all the baggage of culture (which is out of past ways of looking), Dostoevski is happiest in his energy when he can merely confront human forces with human forces. Thus in his four great novels he wrote narratives of murder and lust. We should remind ourselves that under murder and beyond lust lie pleas for another order of things; perhaps impossible, certainly vital. Dostoevski dovetails the forces which are the substances we order.

Here it is in the *Brothers.* We have a family characterized by absolute baseness and sensuality of behavior—the Karamazov baseness, theirs by birth. Father and brothers are joined by their relations to drunkenness, debauchery, crime, random action, and a profound rebelliousness of spirit. Each of the three brothers (though not the fourth illegitimate brother) has an overwhelming belief in the reality of God. Two brothers, Dimitri and Ivan, have an overwhelming inability to believe in or accept the created world. It is the effort of Alyosha, the third brother (Dostoevski's "True hero" whose end was never written) to fuse in great anguish of flesh and spirit, the belief and disbelief, the inspiration and the behavior. He knows how harsh and dreadful a thing love in action is. That is why Alyosha, that paradigm of a saint, is called more a realist than any or them. But he is not alone; it is their father, who is murdered, who is always with them. Old Karamazov, their father and their source, whom they slay through the debased agency of their bastard brother, is raw behavior issuing in buffoonery and caprice, and obstinate in every issue. He is the man from underground come out in the open air, which is stifling. I cannot see but that again we come very near the *Numen* and the *Moha.*

But we are nearer still at the end of this great work. It is the funeral of a little boy who ought not to have died, but who did die, not in spite of himself, but in spite of everybody else: all those who would suddenly keep him alive, but who cannot, and who, as they cannot, instead cry aloud: Hurrah for Karamazov! It is no doubt the condition of life—here where the children cry at the burial of a child: Hurrah for Karamazov—where all are guilty and none are guilty. It is no doubt a gesture. But it is in such great gestures of the spirit—chilling the flesh and itself on fire—that the *Numen* penetrates the *Moha,* the *Moha* envelops the *Numen,* and hallelujah becomes alleluia. The youthful figure of Alyosha, neither monk nor man, but more realist than any of them, pierces us like an impossible but necessary hope. It is only a theoretic form, but it embodies a hope: that behavior might for once, through the moment of a lifetime, wholly incarnate its inspiration. Almost, so much of the force of life does this mere theoretic form of it contain, almost we believe it. It is only our moral philosophy, chastened and strengthened by the vision and the sound of the boys crying to Alyosha, that denies without discrediting it.

But who cares for theories of theories? Even Voltaire knew that one must cultivate one's own garden. Yet the better the garden the better the conversation: for among the flowers of spirit even one's own words have the chill of heaven. Was it not the old peasant, in *War and Peace,* who cured Pierre by his nightly proverbial prayer in the garden of their prison: Let me lie down, oh God, like a stone, and wake like fresh bread? That is, between the *Numen* and the *Moha.*

1954